Gender Commodity

Also Published by Bloomsbury

The Bloomsbury Handbook of 21st-Century Feminist Theory (2019)
edited by Robin Truth Goodman
Understanding Adorno, Understanding Modernism (2020)
edited by Robin Truth Goodman
Feminism as World Literature (forthcoming 2022)
edited by Robin Truth Goodman

Gender Commodity

Marketing Feminist Identities and the Promise of Security

Robin Truth Goodman

BLOOMSBURY ACADEMIC
NEW YORK • LONDON • OXFORD • NEW DELHI • SYDNEY

BLOOMSBURY ACADEMIC
Bloomsbury Publishing Inc
1385 Broadway, New York, NY 10018, USA
50 Bedford Square, London, WC1B 3DP, UK
29 Earlsfort Terrace, Dublin 2, Ireland

BLOOMSBURY, BLOOMSBURY ACADEMIC and the Diana logo are trademarks
of Bloomsbury Publishing Plc

First published in the United States of America 2022
This paperback edition published 2023

For legal purposes the Acknowledgments on p. 171 constitute an extension of this copyright page.

Cover design by Eleanor Rose
Cover photograph: Man dressing a mannequin in lingerie, April 1958, by Angelo Rizzuto (1906–1967).
Anthony Angel Collection, Library of Congress Prints and Photographs Division, Washington,
D.C. 20540 USA

Library of Congress Cataloguing-in-Publication Data
Names: Goodman, Robin Truth, 1966- author.
Title: Gender commodity: marketing feminist identities and the promise of security /
Robin Truth Goodman.
Description: New York: Bloomsbury Academic, 2022. | Includes bibliographical references
and index. | Summary: "An interdisciplinary study that brings together gender studies,
media studies, Marxist thought, and literary theory to explore contemporary issues
of precarity and the symbolic production of gender as a commodity"– Provided by publisher.
Identifiers: LCCN 2021041001 (print) | LCCN 2021041002 (ebook) |
ISBN 9781501388026 (hardback) | ISBN 9781501388064 (paperback) |
ISBN 9781501388033 (epub) | ISBN 9781501388040 (pdf) | ISBN 9781501388057 (ebook other)
Subjects: LCSH: Feminism. | Women–Identity. | Sex role. | Feminist theory. |
Sex role in literature. | Sex role in mass media.
Classification: LCC HQ1155 .G664 2022 (print) | LCC HQ1155 (ebook) |
DDC 305.42–dc23/eng/20211021
LC record available at https://lccn.loc.gov/2021041001
LC ebook record available at https://lccn.loc.gov/2021041002

ISBN: HB: 978-1-5013-8802-6
PB: 978-1-5013-8806-4
ePDF: 978-1-5013-8804-0
eBook: 978-1-5013-8803-3

Typeset by Deanta Global Publishing Services, Chennai, India

To find out more about our authors and books visit www.bloomsbury.com and sign
up for our newsletters.

Contents

Introduction

Gender Commodity

I: Gender Alienation and the Loss of Community

Gender has become a *commodity*. Gender can be bought and sold, *produced* as an *object*, and demands constant work. Commodifying gender turns subjects into objects: made, circulated, exchangeable, and up for sale. Gender commodity confronts us as *something alien*. Gender commodity promises security in a world made insecure through the commodification of our bodies, identities, contextual lifeworlds, and subjectivities.

In the *Economic and Philosophical Manuscripts of 1844*, Marx writes of the commodity, "[T]he object which labour produces—labour's product—confronts it as *something alien*, as a *power independent* of the producer" (71). This is his definition of "the *objectification* of labour," which appears as "*loss of reality* for the workers" or as "*alienation*" (71–2). Though Marx is concerned with industrialization, the making of objects, and the loss of "the human," today's economy trades in symbols and narratives as much as in objects. Gender is just such a commodity. I am using the designation "gender" to introduce a broad range of contemporary situations: gender as a symbolic structure and cultural configuration; gender as a social relation to bodies, symbols, and systems; gender as a life narrative, kinship term, or reproductive role (as in "women,"[1] life stages, kinship, and family (e.g., identities of "daughter," "wife," and "mother")); gender as a term for the division of labor (including reproductive labor, both inside and outside the home); and gender as a political identity that makes demands on the state (as in equality, safety,

---

[1] Masculinity and "men's roles" are also being commodified in various ways, but it is not within the scope of this book to analyze that tendency.

welfare, and rights). Also, I am using the designation "gender" as integral to feminism, not only as a target of feminist thinking and practice but also as an incitement to practice feminism and often as a visible code for recognizing the feminist. My sense of gender is that it does not have to be binary, but that the binary forms of gender, because of their outmodedness, are insistent, even dogmatic; their insistence is, ultimately, a reaction to the overwhelming social and cultural forces that are challenging, unraveling, and dismantling their dominance.

Marx illustrates in *The Manuscripts of 1844* that the commodity is the life of the worker that is stolen from him. Years later in *Capital*, Marx returns to the theme of the commodity, famously identifying it as a fetish, that is, "a very queer thing, abounding in metaphysical subtleties and theological niceties" (319). What makes the commodity object appear mysterious is that it takes the form of the worker's social relations—his subjectivity—that are stamped into the object and taken away from him. In other words, the commodity character of the object seems to have a life of its own and confronts the worker as *something alien* and lost because it makes his social relations seem as something distant, disassociated from him, and unalterable. *Gender Commodity* argues that gender is a social relation made into just such an alienated object, especially now.

Alongside Marx, with his conceptualization of the commodity as a fetish into which the worker pours his life, the definition of the commodity applied here is that it is a defensiveness against the dissolution of certain seemingly stable social meanings that are no longer durable or relevant and may already be extinguished. That is, the commodity is an admission of social "outmodedness"—a disavowal of a social organization that is out of fashion or past its prime. This view of the commodity can be attributed to two sources: to Walter Benjamin's definition of the commodity as the "recently outmoded" and to Friedrich Engels' conclusions that the monogamous nuclear family is no longer necessary or viable as it has lost its usefulness. Writing about surrealist writer André Bréton, Benjamin notes:

> he can boast of an extraordinary discovery: he was the first to perceive the revolutionary energies that appear in the 'outmoded'—in the first iron constructions, the first factory buildings, the earliest photos, objects

that have begun to be extinct, grand pianos, the dresses of five years ago, fashionable restaurants when the vogue has begun to ebb from them. (*Selected Writings 2*, 210)

Meanwhile Engels writes:

Sex-love in the relationship with a woman becomes, and can only become, the real rule among the oppressed classes, which means today among the proletariat—whether this relation is officially sanctioned or not. But here all the foundations of typical monogamy are cleared away. Here there is no property, for the preservation and inheritance of which monogamy and male supremacy were established; hence there is no incentive to make this male supremacy effective. What is more, there are no means of making it so... And now that large-scale industry has taken the wife out of the home onto the labor market and into the factory, and made her often the bread-winner of the family, no basis for any kind of male supremacy is left in the proletarian household—except, perhaps, for something of the brutality towards women that has spread since the introduction of monogamy. (38)

For Engels here, the gendered social order existed only for the maintenance of property and inheritance, but since working people had no property to keep or inheritance to hand down, the gender system was outmoded, and its only function was the perpetuation of useless violence that would be dissolved with the state and with capitalism itself.

The reasons for the commodification of gender becoming obvious and relevant now may not be that property and inheritance are on the verge of dissolving. Yet fundamental bedrock political ideologies about gender are not adequately legitimizing distributions of wealth, income, and rights, and this makes the solidity of traditional gender identifications appear "outmoded." There are many signs of this tendency: gender assignment, for example, is being increasingly treated as changeable through surgery, cosmetics, medication, and conduct that can be learned and managed through self-help and therapies; "feminine" traits like sympathy, caringness, and "teamwork" capacity are being marketed as beneficial to employment in service and management, as well as growing sectors of the labor market, and are being mass-produced through training workshops, self-help, and the like; natural reproduction can be manipulated through surrogacies and medical interventions,[2] while social reproduction like childcare, upbringing, and gender assignment is increasingly commercialized, medicalized, and outsourced, not only through new corporate educational technologies and corporate insurance bureaucracies but also through international markets in pharmaceuticals and domestic service, which guide women (for the most part) into adopting the sought-after characteristics of submission, obedience, flexibility, and demureness.[3] In the name of solicitude, or a generalized sense that the line of objects cares for you by becoming identical to you and absorbing you into its system of signs, consumption organizes social experience into life pathways for more consumption. *Consumption gives you the body "you dream of" as "your own"* (Baudrillard, *Consumer Society*, 194; my emphasis).

My argument is that positive gender identities stand in the place of the social and political institutions through which citizens in a democracy traditionally expect a type of redress that has been diminished under the onslaught of a neoliberal turn toward markets and commodities to resolve problems and disputes. That is, "Woman" as commodity is the ideological form taken by democracy's apparent "outmodedness," expressing the social insecurities that the demise of democracy would incur. She is recognition and disavowal of a social lack and therefore of democracy's ultimate necessity, the recognition of its timeliness. This "Woman" is celebrated for promising the happiness, care, and support that the commodity ensures at this time when happiness, care, and support have become increasingly insecure because of the commodity's replacement of democratic vitality, and individuals instead are increasingly compelled to take responsibility for tackling vital social problems on their own and resiliently. In the face of this expectation, "Woman" would need to

---

[2] Sophie Lewis illuminates, "[I]t's been but a series of logical steps from that hegemonic notions of reproductive meritocracy to the beginnings of the pregnancy 'gig economy' we can glimpse today. In unprecedentedly literal ways, people make babies for others in exchange for . . . money" (5–6).

[3] As Aihwa Ong demonstrates about the response to Singapore's technology surge in the Philippines and Malaysia, "The government advertises in global news magazines, claiming that 'Filipino workers . . . were born with a natural ability to adapt to many cultures." Labor recruiters for overseas markets stress the flexibility and docility of female Filipino workers. . . . There is thus a process of feminization of migrant labor" ("Bio-Cartography," 162).

be protected as the symbolic and fetishistic presence of the qualities she used to represent but are no longer believable. As Horkheimer and Adorno say, she "endlessly cheats [her] consumers out of what [she] endlessly promises" (111). In today's situation of radical insecurity, people are reaching out and identifying with objects—including symbolic ones — that promise quite falsely that they grant stability, duration, and fulfillment, and gender has been made into one of those.

Thus, "Woman" is a symbolic identity that would have had to be invented for the neoliberal age even if her neoliberal existence sits on top of generations, eras, and regions where her social functions, roles, and positions may have been different or similar. "Woman" is a perfect ideological infrastructure for neoliberalism because neoliberalism can be said to be the result of a crisis in reproduction, where capital has found means of profit that do not involve investments in reproducing the next day of labor or the next generation of labor, as in housing, public spaces, education, health care, food security, and pro-family supports. As Susan Watkins details, "The World Bank's 'feminist turn' was argued on purely neoliberal grounds: 'women's empowerment' would boost economic growth and could help reduce fertility rates" (41). She continues, "From the early 1990s, the Bank issued a series of policy guidelines instructing its functionaries that national programmes should aim to identify 'gender-related barriers to growth' and encourage women's participation in the labor force, to overcome the 'rigidities,' 'inefficiencies' and 'lowered output' created by the existing division of labor" (41). Seemingly at odds with growth systems, "Woman" in neoliberalism is seen as a barrier because of her associations with domesticity and reproduction, and her "success" appears through her greater inclusion in productive cycles and the expansion of debt. Watkins argues that such World Bank "empowerment" projects were part of a post–Cold War Washington-consensus agenda to advance privatization by making women responsible for alleviating poverty through microcredit, girls' education, and other post-development redistribution schemes.

Neoliberalism can be distinguished as a stage of capitalism, mostly dated from the 1970s and ongoing, where capital disassociates from its productive and reproductive landscapes by disinvesting in workers, welfare, citizens, localities, and environments. These disinvestments take the form not only of austerity measures or cuts to welfare and social safety nets, including health care and education, but also of the reorganization of land, business ownership, taxes, and credit. As Wendy Brown puts it, "Neoliberalism is most commonly associated with a bundle of policies privatizing public ownership and services, radically reducing the social state, leashing labor, deregulating capital, and producing a tax-and-tariff-friendly climate to direct foreign investors" (17–18). It is, she goes on, "a *global* project" (18) that was "*designed* to quash working-class expectations in both the developed world and developing postcolonial regions" (19). Whereas Catherine Rottenberg maintains that the overlap between neoliberalism—which is about "the state shedding its obligations towards its citizenry" (180)—and feminism—which is about "a progressive stance that makes claims on the state" (180)—seems contradictory, Nancy Fraser, on the other hand, attests that powerful forces acting in the name of neoliberalism appropriated feminism's "critique of androcentric state-organized capitalism" (2009: 99). Feminism, says Fraser, was skeptical about the state's role in balancing the economy in that it upheld white men as workers and treated inequality as a technical, bureaucratic problem targeted at passive recipients of state largesse—patients, customers, wards, or clients. Clearly, as Fraser observes, capitalism is adept at stitching together pieces of available culture and belief to build its social vision, and feminism has supplied some raw material to its ideological bedrock, even if inadvertently.

Michaele Ferguson has faulted a trend in feminist thinking on neoliberalism. Much of the criticism, she notes, assumes political ideologies as unchangeable through action and analysis. Such scholarship, she says (using Nancy Fraser as an example), "leaves neoliberalism relatively undertheorized and undefined, and yet attributes to it extraordinary powers" (224) by ascribing it overwhelming agency. "We are mistaken to say," she goes on, "that neoliberalism has co-opted feminist ideas for its own purposes: neoliberalism can no more co-opt another ideology than it can have purposes" (224). In contrast, Ferguson outlines three features that she sees as defining neoliberal feminist ideology attributable from "observable phenomenon" (230) in actual practice and belief: "*individualization of persistent gender inequality . . . privatization of political responses . . .* [and] *liberation through capitalism*" where "[t]he feminist is the entrepreneur" (230)—not very far from Fraser's own assessment, though Fraser also focuses on redistribution and anti-statism, not just on identity formation. An important difference between Fraser and Ferguson that Ferguson does not mention is that Fraser is interested in hegemony, not ideology. Hegemony is a struggle between different sectors that takes place in ideas and in class formations together. Though in many instances like this one, "hegemony" and "ideology" overlap, an important distinction is that, whereas ideologies are a set of ideas or ideals set in place through social structures that precede subjects, hegemonies additionally depend on "historical blocs," or groups of people with class interests and power who are able to set the main agendas and determine what is just and right at a certain historical moment. Ferguson says that ideologies claim power through "a lack of political imagination on the part of those persons who would wish to resist" (228), showing that she thinks of "neoliberal feminism" as only a set of ideas in a marketplace of ideas where each idea is equal to others in its chances of winning the game; contingently, she thinks of feminists themselves as blamable for their "lack of imagination." Ferguson does not consider how those in power can enforce their interest and even their ideas by controlling the use of force and the dominant media. In hegemonic terms, neoliberalism as dominant—contra to Ferguson's claims— is, indeed, able to coopt less dominant cultural trends like feminism; in Fraser's terms, this would not be a "lack of imagination" or a denial of the possibilities of feminist agency as other class interests would contribute other feminist ideas to a counter-hegemonic bloc that would rise up through the crisis of the social and of legitimization that neoliberalism now faces. Because neoliberalism furthers a crisis in reproductive economies, "Woman"—mother, for example, femininity, and, I would argue, feminism as well—has become a field of hegemonic contestation over care and security: At a time when the public sector fails to give the support and refuge against capital's vicissitudes that the liberal contract was meant to provide, she is expected to fill in the gap with maternal solicitude.

"Woman" can therefore be said to be the form taken by gender commodification in a neoliberal age. In the world of commodified gender with its imperative to discard the old and the durable of outmoded social relations, the subject is fragile and impermanent, but also impermanent are the lifeforms in which the subject comes to be and live as a subject. Often, the social context of failing social institutions of care and security is transformed, within the gender commodity's legitimation narratives, into dangers and threats lurking on the horizon in the form of criminal, monster, or other horror-film caricatures from which the feminist subject as hero needs to separate for protection. Gender is a constantly transitioning symbolic to be grasped at in a quest for elusive security in an age of precarity.

Identifying with this commodity promises safety in the face of a world made unsafe and insecure through mass commodification's assault on public investment called "neoliberalism." For Zygmunt Bauman, today's commodity transforms a society of producers—based in solid, durable, reliable, and secure forms of human togetherness—to a society of consumers, based in accelerating in-built obsolescence and precarity, disposable and destructible pleasures necessary to "*discard* and *replace*" (36), and insatiable needs, leading to "inconsistency and lack of cohesion" (32) and deepening "the sentiment of insecurity" (46). The response, says Bauman, has been what he calls "*subjectivity fetishism*" (14), or the "*transformation of consumers into commodities*" (12): "In the society of consumers," Bauman explains, "no one can become a subject without first turning into a commodity, and no one can keep his or her subjectness secure without perpetually resuscitating, resurrecting and replenishing the capacities expected and required of a sellable commodity" (12). As a successful commodity, the subject quickly replaces the old and outmoded self with the ever-changeable new, where the old is a liability and a source of anxiety. As the old self is fit only for the rubbish heap of history, the old social relations and attachments go with it: "when those objects of yesterday's desires and those past investments of hope break their promises and fail to deliver the instant and complete satisfaction hoped for, they should be abandoned—along with any relationships that delivered a 'bang' that was not quite as 'big' as expected" (36).[4] Social relations thus reappear as full of

---

[4] One might hear again echoes of Walter Benjamin in Bauman's descriptions of the commodity, not only his ideas about the "recently outmoded" that inspired his interest in the Arcades or the famous metaphor of the Angel of History who is propelled "into the future to which his back is turned, while the pile of debris before him grows skyward" (258). Also, Benjamin flashes up in Bauman's lament over lost social relations, uniqueness, tradition, and belonging—what Benjamin calls "aura"— resulting from technological progress and the dominance of the commodity. Writing of the "decay

hostile, menacing, and sinister fiends (of the old social order) responsible for the terrible obstacles in the subject's path to achievement and market success rather than social relations being imagined as the conditions of possibility for that achievement. The commodification of gender in these ways influences, as well, the possibilities for imagining the feminist subject. To rise above the demolition of social life, the feminist subject must model herself on the consumer subject—a self-declared autonomous, resilient, independent master of her own choices, expressions, and differences, which often establishes her ultimate conformity to the system. As Horkheimer and Adorno state quite succinctly, "[T]he economic apparatus endows commodities with the values which decide the behavior of people . . . [and] impress standardized behavior on the individual as the only natural, decent, and rational one. Individuals define themselves now only as things, statistical elements, successes or failures" (21).

Using "sex" and "gender" nearly interchangeably because processes of commodification do not distinguish between them (between, that is, bodies and subjectivities or bodies and abstract symbols), *Gender Commodity* shows that gender is such an objectification of subjectivity, a market-oriented symbolic "thing" that people cling to for security while at the same time producing the conditions of insecurity and precarity by dismantling established socialities. In this book, I use the term "neoliberalism" to address this culture of insecurity where the institutions of social belonging and care that once promoted democratic sociality are presently being undermined or vilified by ideologies that uphold markets as the answer to all social problems. By focusing on cultural and textual examples that showcase gender commodity, I analyze this trend in four areas of importance for feminism: popular feminism,

---

of aura," Benjamin sounds a lot like Bauman discussing the erosion of community: "Unmistakably, [mechanical] reproduction as offered by picture magazines and newsreels differs from the image seen by the unarmed eye. Uniqueness and permanence are as closely linked in the latter as our transitoriness and reproducibility in the former. To pry an object from its shell, to destroy its aura, is the mark of a perception whose 'sense of the universal equality of things'"—by which he means the commodity—"has increased to such a degree that it extracts it even from a unique object by means of reproduction" (*Illuminations*, 223). Or, distinguishing the difference between the storyteller, with his "incomparable aura" (*Illuminations*, 109), and the novelist, who is the product of economic and technological development and individualization, Benjamin writes, "A great storyteller will always be rooted in the people" (*Illuminations*, 101), but storytellers are increasingly rare.

transnational film, the globalization of reproductive technologies, and trans theory. The materials I use range across popular culture genres, from blogs to films, contemporary novels, advertisements and product placements, theory and criticism, current events, mainstream reporting, political discourse, and YouTube videos.

II: Doing Gender With Toys

The commodity makes a promise of security against the insecurities caused by the diminishing powers of institutions of social care. Some feminist media studies scholars have remarked on the way advertising and popular culture are using positive images of women to project narratives of social degradation against which certain products offer a lifeline. By buying, individuals can profess resilience, identifying with the durability of the object as the proof of heroic self-reliance. As Rosalind Gill and Ana Sofia Elias demonstrate, feminism has adopted "love your body discourses" from advertising, particularly from the promotional campaigns of Nike, Dove soap, and Special K cereal. These are "positive, affirmative, seemingly feminist-inflected media messages, targeted exclusively at girls and women, that exhort us to believe we are beautiful" (180)—what Gill and Elias call "emotional capitalism" and "cool capitalism" (180) as they sell femininity to women as a promise of fulfillment. Mostly internet-based but found in a range of media sites, such marketing of emotions, continue Gill and Elias, though apparently "a welcome intervention into a landscape of hostile scrutiny" (183), is still invested in "perfect model ideals" (183), "normative ideal of female attractiveness" (184), "beautiful hair and skin" (184), and "slimming" (184). Likewise, Rosalind Gill and Shani Orgad address "confidence culture," which, just as "love your body discourses," celebrates positive identity by mandating positive affect and sells positive psychological profiles, postures, and gestures, encouraging "individual solutions to structural problems, couched in the psychological language of empowerment, choice, and self-responsibility" (17). These motifs in popular culture—or "neoliberal brand culture" (182)—still reference, say Gill and Elias, "a predictable, stable visual regime of apparently 'natural' women's bodies, and a set of discourses that report on 'real women' talking about 'real problems'" (182). The allure of the commodity is partly, such examples indicate, its promise of stability against the instability that commodities themselves instigate.

Women's magazines, popular feminism, beauty product copy, and "how-to" be successful guides are not the only place where positive gender identities, especially regressive ones, are commercialized as lifelines against precarity. In a June 25, 2019, opinion piece in the *New York Times* entitled "Vaginas Deserve Giant Ads, Too," for example, the writer Jackie Rotman infers that ads featuring vaginas would be the answer to the troubles plaguing New York City's subway, even as subway stories of chronic underfunding, technological obsolescence, bureaucratic malfeasance, and commuter delays littered the *New York Times* headlines for months previously (right before COVID-19 lockdowns). Whereas, she writes, we have grown accustomed to seeing ads about erectile dysfunction products and other types of auxiliaries for male sexual satisfaction, a female sex toy company, Dame Products, has sued the Metropolitan Transportation Authority for violating free speech, due process, and equal protection rights by prohibiting ads depicting vaginas—even ads that symbolically reference vaginas—for their products on the subway. Rotman concludes:

> Today's business policies reflect a broader cultural norm in which women's sexual pleasure is devalued compared with men's. But this shouldn't be, not only because women's sexual well-being is equally valid as men's, but also because it could be equally, if not more, profitable. Sex toys alone are a $27 billion global industry, of which the vibrator market makes up to $6.5 billion and is growing at 13 percent annually. This is multiple times larger than the erectile dysfunction market.

In my estimation, not having our genitals plastered over the train tracks is not clearly a sign of women's degradation. Yet, the writer continues, these tools would clearly help women's sexual and reproductive health. What is really much more important, though, is the potential profitability in the signifiers of women's sexuality. In order for women to be treated equally, these should be given equal space, she continues, not only in the subway but also in other sites that have similarly rejected such ads, like Facebook and Instagram as well as exhibitions, credit card companies, and financial institutions. My vagina is ready to go, to get photographed and enlarged and plastered on those grey tunnel walls to cheer people on their daily commute by forcing the New York Subway to recognize, magnify, and reward women's difference. By using women's difference as an advertising ploy, this editorial typifies the consumer society's moralism that upholds market "choice" as the solution to all social problems.

Time Magazine, as well, has published a Special Edition on *The Science of Gender*, which explains to popular audiences the current state of popular scientific knowledge about gendered bodies, brains, and behaviors. *Time* here follows for the most part in a timeworn tradition of the field of evolutionary psychology, she writes, as Mari Ruti has analyzed it, that gender is *stable*:

> here was a *scholarly* field whose main aim seemed to be to convince non-specialist readers of the *scientific* validity of the worst gender platitudes of our culture. I discovered an entire field built on gender clichés of mind-numbing banality... And there was little effort to hide the fact that evolutionary psychology has, until recently at least, been a white men's club recycling the same worn-out clichés since the time of Darwin. Indeed, what struck me most forcefully was the field's stubborn loyalty to Darwin's pronouncements about gender differences. (2–3)

Even stable, though, genders need to be reinforced by commodified ornamentation and repetition.

The *Time* special issue, as it reviews experiments and discoveries in multiple fields, acknowledges the proliferation of genders beyond conventional binaries while still assuming that genders can be coded in the basic two categories of "men" and "women." In its foray into zoology, "Lessons from Animals," Courtney Mifsud treats as new the old sociobiological dogmatism that sex is about a numerical calculation that reasonable genes do in order to maximize their traits' survival in future generations. In a hostile environment filled with predators and other hazards to reproductive success, what she calls "sexual dimorphism" results from one side of the gender division dressing up pretty. Following in the path of the familiar example of peacocks, humans generally are "grouped into two phenotypes—male and female (with exceptions)" but then elaborate "with adornments as stylized clothing, glittery stones and shiny metals, strategically applied face paint and elaborate arrangements of hair" (28). Makeup assures genetic continuities, as all our genes know! In the next story, "Raising Daughters," Jeffrey Klugar says gender differences "are likely baked in at birth by genes and the womb environment and possibly by subtle differences in sex-linked structures of wiring in the brain" (36). Even so, he notes, these differences exhibit themselves in what toys children play with— for the most part, blowup cars for boys and dollhouses for girls (this is in 2020!), even though there might be a few girls who like playing with toy guns. As the article "Exploring the Gender Divide in the Toy Aisle" elaborates, "Boys will always be boys and girls will always be girls!" but nevertheless, "It's natural for kids to experiment with different toys and identities" (Steinmetz, 94). In other words, the reason we know that gender is real and durable is because commodity identifications and choices are so solid, *Time* tells us, even though they often are not. What connects genes to bombs, cars, and guns is less clear.

Though glossy photos span across the pages of *Time's* special edition with high-tech style and pizazz, the writers are very adamant in their citations of scientific authority, from biology to psychology and sociology, giving lots of statistics and empirical evidence, and, especially when the scientific authority is employed as marketing consultants or the like, embellishing what is tantamount to ad-copy in scientific realism. "Eighty-one percent of Gen Z-ers believe that a person shouldn't be defined by gender, according to a poll by the J. Walter Thomson marketing group" (92). In this final story by Eliana Dockterman, *Time* does allow that different types of gender positions—non-binaries, genderqueer, and so on— are currently pushing out from the binary's stronghold, but mainly motivated by new product lines by Mattel, Lego, Target, and Disney. Not only do we learn that Barbie is not just for girls anymore, we are also introduced to "gender-neutral" and "gender fluid" products, dolls with bleached bangs that can be covered by a blond wig to change gender and that come with "a wardrobe befitting any fashion-conscious kid: hoodies, sneakers, graphic T-shirts in soothing greens and yellows, along with tutus and camo pants" (90). These dolls and others like them create a marketing niche out of a new generation of toy-buyers, granting a progressive gloss to what is otherwise just a familiar corporate practice of market-niche differentiation. One of the problems with such products, though, according to *Time*, is that in parent testing, the dolls have been suspected as "political." The article declares that a progressive gender expression is fueled by sensitive corporate efforts even while insisting that gender is natural and, indeed, *moral* in children so that such corporate interest in selling toys to children is *not* political—no, definitely *not*. Guaranteeing that gender identifications are secured by innovative marketing in innovative play products, the commodity, in this logic, frees us from the danger of politics. In a trick-of-the-hand reversal, politics, it is understood, would be destabilizing (unlike the commodification of subjectivity).

Here, the gender commodity is celebrated as a bulwark against the instability of politics and political institutions. *Time's* liberal progressivism in promoting (albeit slightly) the acceptance of nonbinary gender differences even while sticking for the most part to a scientific fact-ology of binarized evolutionary platitudes borrows what might be seen as a feminist morality to make politics seem not just superfluous but also, more fundamentally, a threat to our children's safety and well-being. In *In the Ruins of Neoliberalism*, Wendy Brown keys into this aspect of the contemporary zeitgeist, where politics and the social are cast away as "coercive, unruly, and arbitrary" (61), and in their place arises a market-based morality. Unlike more familiar social science critics of neoliberalism such as David Harvey and Samir Amin, who focus on central economic building blocks of neoliberalism like privatization, deregulation, polarization, financialization, and the dismantling of the developmental state, Brown starts her account of neoliberalism at the point of its realignment of the politics of democracy. Essential to a functioning democracy, the social, says Brown, "requires explicit efforts to bring into being a people capable of engaging in modest self-rule, efforts that address ways that social and economic inequalities compromise political equality" (27). Therefore, specific rules, institutions, and interventions—what we call "popular sovereignty" or democratic public life— must mitigate social inequalities that compromise the equality on which political participation and deliberation depend: "Freedom without society destroys the lexicon by which freedom is made democratic, paired with social consciousness, and nested in political equality. . . . What happens when freedom is reduced to naked assertions of power and entitlement, while the very idea of society is disavowed, equality is disparaged, and democracy is thinned to liberal privatism?" (44–5). Brown revisits the writings of neoliberalism's original architects like Friedrich Hayek, Milton Friedman, Walter Eucken, and Fran Böhm and finds a deliberate discarding of state social and public involvement—indeed, a disregard of the social altogether, coextensive with a separation of political from economic power—in favor of a seeming moral spontaneity focused on the family.

This spontaneity also, as Brown foregrounds, is founded for these thinkers "neither in law nor in politics, but in the evolved, often inarticulate principles of conduct and opinion forming a cohesive people, principles we 'freely' accept and abide" and that are underpinned by "traditional values" (75). According to the neoliberal pioneers whose philosophies Brown interrogates, liberty, rather than defined as freedom from restraint, is the voluntary exercise of moral codes of conduct and conformity that are ahistorical, internal, and enforced by the traditional family, its religion, and its universal rules. Liberty needs no intervention.[5] In this, Brown follows Melinda Cooper, who, in *Family Values*, has traced the historical politicization of the family as a unit of spontaneous moral activation. Cooper outlines a transition between the late 1960s and early 1970s—when the Nixon administration was moving toward Aid to Families with Dependent Children (AFDC) payments to expand to African American men for the purposes of redistributive welfare and the protection of moral values against market forces[6]—to the mid-seventies, when Nixon, under pressure from Democrats and neoconservatives to back policies opposing inflation, turned course. Part of the reaction was in response not only to right-wing racist agendas but also to a marginal faction of the New Left that wanted to do away with the family wage altogether because of its imposition of sexual controls and norms and find another basis for welfare redistributions besides

[5] Ultimately, Brown ends her book with a mistake. She applies her analysis of the rise of inequalities under neoliberalism and the loss of connection to the political to explain the popular support that got Donald Trump elected as president of the United States in 2016. She then concludes by blaming the Right: "To date," she finishes, "these [affective] remains have been activated mostly by the Right. What kinds of Left political critique and vision might reach and transform them?" Yet, Brown does not clearly specify what she means by "Right" or "Left" here unless the "Right" designates Donald Trump and his supporters and the "Left" everybody else. This view, though, would be an impoverished read on the situation that Brown herself treats in the rest of the text. Neoliberalism does not begin or end with Trump's presidency.

[6] The ideal family's "fundamental values must be actively protected by the state if it is to survive the corrosive force of contractual exchange" (61).

families. In response, neoliberalism's philosophy of the family, writes Cooper, accepts that "the dismantling of welfare represents the most effective means of restoring the private bonds of familial obligation. . . . It is not that neoliberals completely reject the idea of virtue then, . . . but rather that they expect the strictest of virtue ethics to arise spontaneously from the immanent action of market forces" (60). As, for the neoliberals, welfare encouraged a rejection of the morals imposed by Protestant frugality and the work ethic (especially among the working poor), the self-sufficient family is the basic place where market morals can flourish on their own, regulating moral life spontaneously and without aid.

We see here again that neoliberalism positively affirms conventional genders and sexualities as policing against social turmoil and the unleashing of dangerous sexual immoralities. Any political intrusions will disrupt the spontaneous outpouring of the morals that adhere to family conventions as well as market values. Here, gender as constrained by the conventions of the family, as the limit to the political, lends neoliberalism its justification for curtailing the role of the intervening regulatory state. This is where *Gender Commodity* stakes out its territory: As commodity, gender offers a stable social object that promises happiness, fulfillment, belonging, and security within a neoliberal political culture that denies all of that.

III: Social Reproduction and the Marketing of Mothers

Whereas the home may once have been understood as a refuge from work organized around a gendered division of labor in the interests of producing the next generation of laborers, now the home and the family have to be seen as spaces of technological control and primitive accumulation, where children and intimate social forms are ground zero for capital entry. The gender commodity normalizes the extension of market logic into everyday life in its forging of identities, subjectivities, and social relations.

While today feminism celebrates women in popular culture, on T-shirts and bumper stickers, in protest marches, and even among superheroes and, indeed, transgender constructivism is being lauded as the next frontier of civil rights, the question for feminism is whether its advocacy in terms of gender affirmative norms celebrated for their successes in market culture will be adequate to the political emergencies we currently confront. As Susan Watkins points out, the broad "historical context for the new feminist ferment . . . was set in place by the 2008 financial crisis, which gave the skewed outcomes of the neoliberal-feminist era a sharp generational twist" (67–8). Most evident are these areas of gender's commercialization: (1) bodies have come under the domination of market forces (e.g., via surgeries, cosmetics, fashions, prosthetics, sex toys, hormonal enhancers, gene therapies, and, of course, the media); (2) the reproductive economy (or symbolic exchange), formerly related to "women's work," is being redesigned as sites of surplus accumulation. The "reproductive economy" includes surrogacies, media, information, educational systems and technologies, entertainment, mechanization of domesticity and daily life, pharmaceuticals, therapy, children's attention, and bureaucratization as the current locations of subject formation (rather than the home); (3) characteristics associated with women, such as "good at teamwork," "caring," and "seeking flexible schedules," are being hyped as "best practices" for corporate management, bringing the home in line with the market; (4) the commodification of gender influences the possibilities for imagining the feminist subject. *Gender Commodity* asks how gender identities and social relations are being modeled on market cultures and what the implications are for feminism.

Gender Commodity also considers how the production of mass-marketed images and narratives of female-gendered roles like mothers promises solicitude. Offering the feeling that you are being cared for by the objects that you buy, the traditional "mother" image that secured home, health, family, and life contradicts a political understanding of mothers as an obstacle to the free flow of capital. Areas of social reproduction associated with traditional "mothers," like homelife and education, are being targeted by processes of capital accumulation, mechanization, commercialization, and exchangeability. *Gender Commodity* ends by asking how gender can be constructed differently in support of more livable and sustainable social relations.

All identities are intersectional. I start with that assumption. By intersectional, I mean that anyone's particular subjective formation is crossed by many different points of social and cultural identification. Here are examples of this phenomenon as presented in the book: In chapter 3, I note that the commodification of women as machines of reproduction can be traced from the slave trade but now underpins the pharmaceutical industry, often in the business of reproducing whiteness for people with the means, as well as markets in surrogacy, hormones, and sensible pleasures. In chapter 2, I trace feminism's embrace of reproductive rights into a place of difference where it comes into combination and contention in a cultural playing field marked as well by nationalism, industrialization, and religion. The term "intersectionality" is often used as a stand-in for anti-racism, and I certainly intend for this study to be useful to further anti-racist agendas, as the dismantling of the commodity's stronghold on politics and sociality would definitely accomplish. Overall, as is clear in rates of incarceration and police brutality as well as the mistreatment and repression of immigrants for example, people of color have suffered from the alignment of the social with the commodity and will have a lot to gain in a transition of the social away from the commodity's forms.

However, in this book I do not use the term "intersectionality" to talk about race. The reason not to use this word in this study is that it confuses some issues. Not only are all identities intersectional, but also commodities are intersectional, as the ideological underpinnings of mass commodification borrow from existing cultural forms wherever they are set, mixing and matching, combining and recombining. Just look at how advertising targets multiple niche markets at once by selling lifestyle and character narratives, offering sparkling points of identification like "I'd like to buy the world a Coke," "Fly the friendly skies," "Think different," or "You deserve a break today."[7] What may distinguish the commodity from other intersectionalities is which theoretical frameworks and political visions of the future it allows or erases.

---

[7] See, for example, https://kindredmembers.com/insights/intersectionality-marketing/, an advertising industry website headlined "Why Applying Intersectionality to Marketing is Key," which also cites Kimberle Crenshaw (accessed June 8, 2021). The front page boasts that searches for specific products went up from 77 percent (Cheerio's) to 400 percent (Honey Maid) when the companies' ads started to include multiracial and same-sex families.

In this study I favor theoretical terms that I find have more clearly visible political associations and affiliations, like representation, signification, ideology, and, most adequately, hegemony. "Hegemony" is a vital term because it connotes a struggle waged between groups over meaning, where meaning comes out of struggle. Hegemonic views of identity recognize that people have to be educated into subjectivity; this matters politically because it means that people may also be reeducated into subjectivity differently, depending on how the struggle plays out. This "hegemony" is what Stuart Hall is implying in a 1996 article "Who Needs Identity?" when he uses the term "intersectionality" in a way that is slightly distinct from how it has been taken up since law professor Kimberle Crenshaw's coinage in 1989 and 1991. In her 1989 article, for example, Crenshaw writes:

> I argue that Black women are sometimes excluded form feminist theory and antiracist policy discourse because both are predicated on a discrete set of experiences that often does not accurately reflect the interaction of race and gender… Because the intersectional experience is greater than the sum of racism and sexism, any analysis that does not take intersectionality into account cannot sufficiently address the particular manner in which Black women are subordinated. (140)

In 1991, she elaborates:

> I should say at the outset that that intersectionality is not being offered here as some new, totalizing theory of identity. . . . My focus on the intersections of race and gender only highlights the need to account for multiple grounds of identity when considering how the social world is constructed. (1244–5)

While I agree with Crenshaw here, her point is an analytic one that she applies to her interpretations of law and legal proceedings, a method for a deeper understanding of how the social works as it is. The identities in question are given before the start of the analysis, not constructed and reconstructed in response to the historical context and political need. The identities are discrete before they intersect. Intersectionality in itself carries no politics. Only in its use does it articulate with theory and enter a political field. Hall, in contrast, uses "intersection" in his comments on ideological interpellation to address where the psychoanalytic constitution of the subject answers the call to enter its place in the social field in relation to power (7): Identities "are the result of a successful articulation or 'chaining' of the subject into the flow of discourse" (6), and, as such, they are a taking-of-positions, often only for a time. For Hall, "intersection" is not between two identities meeting in a body to account for an experience, but rather it applies to the point where ideology intersects by operating concretely within changing social and symbolic fields.

This book is an interdisciplinary study that brings literary studies into dialogue with the surrounding mediascape around issues of gender, culture, and economy. It therefore shows literature and theory as communicating with a broad spectrum of narratives and images in circulation: on the internet, on TV, in advertising, in political discourse, and in film. It also foregrounds how these media intersect and diverge in constructing women's bodies in social space. In this, *Gender Commodity* implicates literature within a cross-section of popular perspectives and social concerns. It also asks how the symbolic production of gender commodity at home informs an imagination of gender policy as it reaches out globally. As it criticizes gender-affirmative feminism for participating in the culture of the commodity, *Gender Commodity* also looks to feminism to imagine gender otherwise.

Gender Commodity draws on the logic of gender commodity to explain its various contexts. Looking at popular "Third Wave" feminist bloggers Clementine Ford, Laurie Penny, and Jessica Valenti in the first chapter, "Breaking the Waves," demonstrates that the generational narrative of contemporary feminism depends on commodity logic. While outwardly marking a "new" and "improved" version of feminism that corrects the racism and transphobia of past feminisms, the statement of a generational divide serves additional rhetorical purposes: The "prior generation" is accused of being responsible for social alienation—their insufficiencies are blamed for inviting in the scary social world full of sexual predators, social monsters, and the institutions that put them at so much risk by failing to provide security. The new generation is then the feminism that can choose to be independent and, because of that choice, can recognize identities of difference that the "prior generation" and its institutions have buried under a delusional universalism. The autonomy of the "Third Wave" blogger-entrepreneur presents its identity, then, as, like the commodity, a security in the face of a hostile social environment. At the end of this chapter, after calling attention to similarities with the "prior generation" that the bloggers disregard, I link their repudiation of the "prior generations" with their repudiation of their social context by reconsidering the early work of feminist Germaine Greer, the target of much of the "Third Wave" bloggers' dissatisfied condemnations of the "prior generation." I read Greer, in contrast to the bloggers' promotion of heroic autonomy, as analyzing the feminist subject born from the violence and repression that social institutions, attitudes, and ideologies directed at her.

Depicting this feminist subject as a vampire and as an air force officer with her finger on the launch button of killer drones, the second chapter describes the commodity's appropriation of feminism's celebration of autonomy and "choice" to respond to the destruction of social relations. Gender commodity is here exported in international policy to provide security in place of the "failed state" or unproductive local cultures. I review Rick Rosenthal's 2013 TV movie *Drones* and Ana Lily Amipour's 2014 feature debut *A Girl Walks Home Alone at Night*. The first promotes women in the technological workforce through a feel-good narrative about a woman who commands, from a Nevada base, a US Air Force drone assassination operation in Iraq, while the second adulates a vampire-feminist-in-a veil whose sexual autonomy presents an alternative social vision to the deadening industrial landscape installed by the Iranian Revolutionary Regime. Similar to the self-help messages of the bloggers in Chapter 1, these movies call attention to the way social institutions are being depicted as threatening to women's independence so that a heroic new feminist, master of her own choice, can intervene as the savior. I discuss these movies as adapting feminist tropes—the entry of women into the technological workforce in the case of *Drones* and the embrace of sexual autonomy in the case of *A Girl*—into the perfect subject of the consumer society who escapes from social connectedness into adventures of choice.

The third chapter imagines biological, social, and sensual reproduction as a global commodity. Feminist novelist Margaret Atwood is best known for her 1985 feminist dystopian novel *The Handmaid's Tale*, now revived as a TV serial on Hulu and followed up by a 2109 sequel *The Testaments*. *The Handmaid's Tale* tells of a postrevolutionary society where reproduction is centrally controlled by a Christian fundamentalist state. Margaret Atwood is also well known for her *Oryx and Crake* trilogy, where reproduction is manipulated by the corporate security state composed of radical vegetarians, gene splicers, and gamers. Less well known critically is Margaret Atwood's 2016 novel *The Heart Goes Last*. This novel takes on an almost absurd, dystopian task of imagining biological, social, and sensual reproduction "scaled up" as a corporate enterprise. As the novel is set in a corporate prison that the characters "choose" to incarcerate themselves in, this commodification of reproduction is meant to offer safety from financial fallout and ecological disaster that the commodification of the social is causing. Critical of a perspective like the bloggers', *The Heart Goes Last* ironizes blaming the failures of motherhood for social devastation and constructs, as a comical intensification of such a blame narrative, a liberal utopia of a perfect surveillance society that secretly markets autonomous subjective affects like emotions, eroticism, and sensations that it extracts from the unwary consumers who "choose" to be its prisoners. The precarity of social reproduction is given as the cause and justification for technological fixes, surveillance, and bureaucratic and corporate management to infiltrate ever more deeply into bodies, relationships, and intimate spaces, offering security while, in actuality, undermining security. With a nod toward Horkheimer and Adorno, I ask if the gender commodity projects a nature that it proves its mastery by dominating or if reproduction, as Rosa Luxemburg claims (along with some "World Literature" critics who are concerned with "the planetary"), still introduces delays that may divert its total appropriation for commodification.

In the last chapter, I analyze trans theory that understands gender commodities as sources of social instability rather than promises of fulfillment, flourishing, and stability. Some of this trans theory demonstrates how the social world is made scary, inadequate, alienating, and precarious for subjects by the very processes through which the same social world is made adequate for commodity objects, including gender identity. After revisiting both "radical feminist" and poststructuralist feminist perspectives on trans, I engage with Natalie Wynn's YouTube videos, *ContraPoints*, as well as Jordy Rosenberg's 2018 novel *Confessions of a Fox*. *Confessions of a Fox* traces a transgender transition story onto the historical transition from mercantile to commodity and colonial capitalism and then, in parallel, another transgender transition story onto the historical transition from commodity to neoliberal capitalism and beyond. A contemporary literary scholar finds a lost manuscript about eighteenth-century transgender thief and prison escapee Jack Sheppard that tells of the first recorded gender transition surgery. In parallel with Sheppard's series of notorious escapes, the professor then has to flee from the clutches of the neoliberal university and its allied publishing corporation in order to maintain the rights to the footnotes. Transgender YouTube star and "recovering philosopher" Natalie Wynn has been producing videos under the name "ContraPoints" since 2016, staging Platonic dialogues to discuss transgender, the history of philosophy, antiauthoritarian politics, and feminism. As she transitioned after 2016, the transition happened while she was becoming a YouTube celebrity. I read both cultural critics as seeing in the present breakdown of traditional gender identities a transitional moment away from the division of labor that secured the commodity's domination and the opening to an undefined alternative.

IV: Gender Commodity Today

The coronavirus pandemic made glaringly evident the tragic consequences of the neoliberal takeover of social meanings and public space. The political arena was in virtual free fall; the medical system and hospitals lacked the capacity to treat the numbers of patients or to test for new cases, while people were afraid to go to doctors or hospitals for treatment because, with or without privatized health insurance, they may have gone bankrupt. The psychological pressures of widespread lockdowns and quarantine spurred not only widespread depression, especially among teenagers, but also a marked rise in domestic violence against women, with shelters and other services now dangerous or closed. The rollout of the vaccine, once it first came on line, appeared to lack any central organization, authority, or rules, in some places giving rise to chaos as elderly people camped out overnight in Tennessee, for example, only to learn that the provider had run out of doses, or, in Florida, a first-come-first-serve basis for distribution for everyone over sixty-five caused runs on the centers even as phone lines went down.

Schools were unable to provide instruction with safety, and unemployment insurance was being tested at its limits. Since then, a cultural phenomenon called "vaccine skepticism" has inhibited some countries from stopping the spreading of the virus, while other countries lacked the means to negotiate with the corporations for the doses to protect their citizens. Meanwhile, instead of debating about how to fix the institutions that failed to respond adequately, the news incessantly repeated public figures' positions on wearing masks, implying that individual effort alone would resolve the crisis. While politicians rallied over whether unemployment insurance would cover a $200, $600, or $2000 extra supplemental per month during the emergency and whether the extra would disincentivize workers from working, while state legislatures debated whether to restart evictions even while jobs rates remained historically low, the stock market reached record highs while payouts to bail out corporations in relief bills—ostensibly intended to keep people employed—landed instead in stock buybacks. The efforts of those in the US political class to curtail voting rights and overturn elections without any evidence of fraud attests to a general suspicion of political institutions as ineffective. Such suspicion does not belong exclusively to the Right, but at this moment the Right is threatening to end democracy altogether by making it easier to overturn elections.

Though neoliberal logic and its undermining of democratic institutions were what crippled the political system's response to coronavirus, neoliberalism was not an invention of the Trump administration but a long-term, hegemonic project on the part of capital to disinvest in social reproduction—causing widespread social precarity—in order to transfer the accumulatable wealth in social reproduction to the top. As historically feminism has been at the forefront of debates over how reproduction enters into relation with the economy, it must have something to say about neoliberalism. As Silvia Federici insists, reproduction "should be understood as a political, value-positing decision. In a self-governing, autonomous society such decisions would be taken in consideration of our collective well-being, the available resources, and the preservation of the natural wealth" (*Beyond the Periphery*, 19). Feminism needs to be at the forefront of combining a critique of the state with a defense of democracy—to prove the non-paradoxical nature of this paradox.

Some feminism has been a fellow traveler of neoliberalism up until now. One way of thinking about this is that neoliberal ideologies absorb feminism to further an upward redistribution of wealth, recognizing women as having "winning" capacities for their market-based vision of society just as an earlier feminism celebrated women's entry into work outside the home.[8] As Nancy Fraser points out, "Only when decked out as progressive could a deeply regressive political economy [like neoliberalism] become a dynamic center of a new hegemonic bloc" (*The Old is Dying*, 13). In Fraser's account, neoliberalism borrows progressivism's diversity discourses, including feminism, which allows underrepresented and "deserving" individuals to be recognized and affirmed as beneficiaries of a social hierarchy that does not benefit them. By opposing any fallback onto the gender commodity to survive in the situation of social precarity that the commodification of gender itself has caused, *Gender Commodity* goads feminism toward a post-neoliberal vision.

---

[8] Though greater workplace inclusion certainly benefitted many women, particularly professional-class women, it also, when not accompanied by changes in labor laws and discriminatory practices, often enhanced women's exploitation among the working class and racial minorities who quite frequently had always been forced by need into waged work.

1

Breaking the Waves

Sometime in the 1990s, a new wave—the "Third Wave"—of feminism
was declared. This resurgent "Third Wave" labeled itself as "new" and
generational, cut away from the pasts of feminism that they called "Second
Wave" and "First Wave" that were too limiting, essentializing, racist, and
universalizing in their assumptions about women's experience—indeed,
in their use of the word "woman" as a singular category of identity—and
not inclusive enough of different racial, ethnic, national, sexual, gendered,
or non-gendered experiences. I have written elsewhere about the problems
embedded in this generational story,[1] and I am not the only one.[2] The story
of the "waves" has a number of inadequacies and ideological obstacles even
outside of its vagueness, where the boundaries that mark each phase are badly
defined and constantly shifting depending on what the argument needs them

---

[1] See my "Feminism." *Bloomsbury Handbook of Theory and Criticism*. Ed. Jeffrey Di Leo (London
and New York: Bloomsbury, 2018), 125–39, and "Introduction." *Bloomsbury Handbook of Feminist
Theory*. Ed. Robin Truth Goodman (London and New York: Bloomsbury, 2019), 1–18.

[2] There are too many treatments of this topic to enumerate. As a sampling, refer to Nancy Fraser,
Fortunes of Feminism: From State-Managed Capitalism to Neoliberal Capitalism (New York and
London: Verso, 2013), *Third Wave Feminism: A Critical Exploration*, Eds. Stacy Gillis, Gillian Howie,
and Rebecca Mumford (New York: Palgrave, 2007), *Undutiful Daughters New Directions in Feminist
Thought and Practice*, Eds. Henriette Gunkel, Chrysanthi Niganni, and Fanny Sösderbäck (New
York: Palgrave, 2012). Robyn Wiegman analyzes the "Second" and "Third Wave" conflict in terms
of the academic institutionalization of "gender studies" as an imagined progress from "women's
studies" departments: "Gender Studies," she observes, "was touted as more inclusive of difference.
She questions women's studies scholars' self-justification of the move to gender as an "ongoing
expansion . . . that fulfills the political demand for representation and inclusion" (46) and shows
how this rise of gender strips the analytical object "women" of its multiplicities and reconstitutes it as
a political unity in order to pinpoint the "progress" necessary for the new narrative. The "progress"
narrative embedded in the academic institutionalization of identity fields disavows its dependence
on history by condemning history as failure.

to do,[3] and it is not my intention here to do a detailed overview, as many have already done this work.[4] Waves bleed into each other, they tend to set up historical stages as homogeneous and progressive, and they oversimplify fields that are often quite contentious and varied. In this chapter, I explore the "Third Wave" claim that theirs is a generational story.[5] Despite, as Joan Scott remarks, that "maternity has sometimes served to consolidate feminist identification" (2011, 59) and solidarities, some "Third Wave" criticism draws a line dividing the "Third Wave" from its predecessors because of its awareness, its therapeutic usefulness, and its acceptance of difference.

I want to underline here that I am not playing gatekeeper or trying to be a purist about what "really" should count as feminist. Neither do I reject outright the insights of the last thirty years of feminist thinking. Rather, I focus on what Joan Scott recognizes as a "loss of continuity" (2011, 27) in feminism that a generational narrative induces. While this "loss of continuity," Scott goes on, is part and parcel of constructing progressive identities, it

---

[3] The "Second Wave" versus "Third Wave" debate within arguments identified with the "Third Wave" parallels somewhat with the "modernist-postmodernist *paradigm debate*" that Kathi Weeks has characterized: "a history of distortions and a continuing inability by many to recognize the potential of, and the nuances within, the rich traditions of thought that were subsumed into the category of modernism and the equally valuable theoretical frameworks confined by the category of postmodernism" (15). However useful the parallel is conceptually, though, chronologically it works less well, since the "Third Wave" is usually referred to as an internet or twenty-first-century phenomenon, whereas postmodernism is usually identified as a post–World War II emergence.

[4] Responding to such obstacles (though still accepting that the "wave" narrative is already inside institutions and so is inevitable), Nancy Hewitt writes, "The script of feminist history—that each wave overwhelms and exceeds its predecessor—lends itself all too easily to whiggish interpretations" (4), whereas the movement cannot be contained through "discrete and separate waves" because "in reality such movements overlapped and intertwined" (5). Clare Hemmings observes that such feminist "wave" narratives reduce feminism to "progress, "loss," or "return" narratives to frame the past and isolate the contemporary feminist subject in pervasively homogeneous, disconnected, boxed-in "fields" while erasing some of the important political commitments of prior iterations of that feminist subject that might continue to be fervent, generative, and useful. As Penelope Deutscher points out, historical periods are often quite plastic, and a "certain untimeliness always disturbs the contemporary who reassures him or herself in a 'we'" (26), as any categorization of the contemporary is unstable. As a "Second Wave"-identified feminist who comments on the divide, Nina Powers summarizes that she "starts from the premise that we cannot understand anything about what contemporary feminism might be if we neglect to pay attention to specific changes in work" (2).

[5] I believe that the feminism labeled as "Second Wave" is an unfinished project that the feminists calling themselves "Third Wave" tend to define in narrow terms. The questions, observations, critical frameworks, concepts, and protests are still open, developing, and ongoing even as the "Third Wave" wants to close the lid on it, name it, and describe it as a historical event that could and should be bracketed as past.

tends to block, she says, unifying alliances, narratives of solidarity and social belonging, and future imaginings. What interests me here, additionally, is how this generational feminist identity construction borrows the logic of the commodity—of newness and waste—to marginalize and even demonize the social from which the "prior generation" does not adequately protect them. Just as for Marx, the alienation of the worker resulted from the worker putting his life in the object, social alienation results when the social rises before the young feminist as a hostile object that attacks. What I am observing here is that the generational narrative of "Third Wave" feminism imagines the social as a horror film, threatening the existence and security of feminist subjectivity. Revisiting Jean Baudrillard's 1970 book *The Consumer Society*, I suggest that the "Third Wave" rejection of the "prior generation" fundamentally parallels the "housewife" figure who pops up in Baudrillard's descriptions of the excess and waste of the consumer society.[6] Whereas Baudrillard blames the "housewife" for transferring her caring function onto unenduring and disposable marketed products that promise care while denying it, the generational narrative of the "Third Wave" blames the "prior generation" of feminists for social, ideological, and institutional insufficiencies of care that leave them insecure. I foreground a tendency in "Third Wave" generational discourse to reflect adequately on their own brand of entrepreneurial feminist identity as a lifeline promising autonomy from an otherwise precarious and socially horrific world made up of these failing institutions, rapacious criminals, and degrading messaging, causing trauma. Finally, I return to the "prior generation's" term "woman" as a product of social violence, institutional sexism, and repression, and suggest that the term was not intended to ignore difference or universalize experience, as it appears to do now, but invented as a pivotal formation that would reorient institutional violence into revolt.

---

[6] Kathi Weeks warns, "A theory of the subject that rejects its transcendental origins, metaphysical essence, and transhistorical continuity requires a conception of the social order within which subjects are constructed, Moreover, a theory of a gendered subject that conceived gender not as a role that can be discarded at will but as one constitutive element of subjectivity presupposes that gender is in part a systematic effect of a complex set of interconnected social processes. Finally, a theory of a feminist subject requires a conception of the social forces that we want to contest" (164).

My examples of "Third Wave" generational discourse[7] are books of collected blogs written by the best-selling feminist authors Jessica Valenti (American), Laurie Penny (British),[8] and Clementine Ford (Australian)—books which, though explicitly or implicitly in conversation with academic feminism, see themselves as addressing young women on social issues as role models or as advice givers, counselors, therapists, life-coaches, and sympathetic friends. These books are not special but popular examples of trends. The internet may be seen as where the "Third Wave" rose into popularity as a phenomenon in feminism and became marketable by giving itself a name. "Third Wave" temporalization in these autobiographical coming-to-awareness polemics allows for the imagining of a feminist subject who is therapeutic, moral, and heroic, overcoming social obstacles and traumas in an inspired, resilient advance toward an "entrepreneurial" feminism offering a future of autonomy, safety, security, and self-expression. Nina Powers (and many others) has accused consumerism inside feminism of reducing feminism to the individualizing "imperative to feel better about oneself" (27). "Feeling better about oneself" includes a distancing of the self-producing feminist from the social and symbolic frameworks that she inhabits by turning the social itself into *something alien* and feminist identity into a "*subjectivity fetishism*," or the promise of security in the face of threats. In this perspective, feminism is treated as a protective object with which one can identify for personal security, obscuring the causes of social precarity—both ideological and material—that create the need for personal security. In addition, I show here the rise of a commodity logic inside a feminism that creates a new and invigorated entrepreneurial feminist subject by rejecting what it references as its generational antecedents as useless waste.

---

[7] Some critics have noticed a "Fourth Wave" of feminism, and some even see more waves after. I find it confusing to try to determine what the contents of each of these waves are and believe that they, for the most part, follow the same logic I am tracing here. It is not within the scope of this study to pursue this.

[8] Laurie Penny explicitly rejects the "waves" as a way to narrate her relation to feminism: "Feminism, for me," she specifies, "is not a set of waves but a great grumbling tsunami, moving slow, sweeping across a blighted landscape of received assumptions, washing away old certainties. The big wave has hardly begun to hit, and already all of us are changed" (*Bitch*, 19). It does not seem to me that this formulation is used for the purpose of thinking in different than generational terms. The tsunami is the same as a wave, only bigger. The linking of feminism to climate change is provocative and also generational, and, indeed, references to generational change litter the text even after the appearance of this changed metaphor.

One casualty of the generational "wave" story is the term "woman," which has been coated in condemnations that it cannot account for varied experiences of contemporary embodiment. However, even as early as Simone de Beauvoir if not before, the term "woman" was read by feminism as a term that set in motion a set of structural critiques about a social organization put in place through the term. The "wave" story's rejection of the term "woman" is often a turn away from such attention to the social and the ideological, and therefore to modes of social power, and a turn toward individual experience and, in particular, the experience of working on the autonomous self. The untimeliness of "woman" often makes any reference to broad social forces, forms, structures, or categories related to women seem untimely as well. In a Beauvoirian rhetorical move, I might ask: Don't you miss women? What else do we miss when we miss women? Can we still talk about women? What would it be like if women still existed? Would talk about women necessarily imply a repressive universalism? What else would we talk about if we could still talk about women?[9] The questions themselves suggest that the relationship between the gendered subject, on the one hand, and, on the other, the social and political conditions for that gendered subject's continuation and survival have become untimely, less than obvious, and precarious.

I find the reconstitution of feminism along the generational lines of the "Third Wave" carries important stakes in Valenti's, Penny's, and Ford's works. These are (1) as the sign of difference, the feminist body is elevated over ideas; in fact, the body replaces ideas where autonomous meaning, justice, and judgment develop. (2) The body is therefore divorced from the social, especially inasmuch as the body registers pain. Trauma is what divides the body as subject from the social that harms from outside of it. "Women are being killed on a weekly basis by men who hate them so much but want desperately to control them," explains Clementine Ford, for example. "We're raped, violated, abused, pushed around, undermined, ridiculed, mocked, beaten, bullied and degraded" (180). (3) The social works on the autonomous body only through violence,

---

[9] Simone de Beauvoir famously began *The Second Sex*, "For a long time I have hesitated to write a book on woman. The subject is irritating. . . . Are there women, really? . . . But first we must ask: what is a woman?" (xix).

particularly violence as performed by individuals on other individuals. In this, a "radical feminist" tradition á la Andrea Dworkin, which professed that all relations between men and women were sexual violation and pornographic violence (and which seemed to be defeated), surges up again with a vengeance without acknowledging the problems that were attributed to Dworkin's concept in positioning all women as inherently passive victims and all men as rapists. (4) The body and its experience of psychic pain crowd out other parts of the subject's constitution, particularly theory, agency, and social structure analysis. (5) The internet is what severs the old history from the new and the old subject from the new as well as what constitutes the violence of the social. "My mother didn't have the benefit of internet op-eds and women's websites dismantling all this stuff for her" (48), explains Clementine Ford. The imagined transformation of the social into social media affects the way political action can be envisioned, as the internet *is* the agency that opposes violence as much as it is the violence itself. (6) Pre-internet feminism is rejected as a kind of unaware and prudish maternal ancestry, even sometimes monstrous in its unawareness; dismissing this "prior generation" of feminist mothers allows the new generation to rise up on its own, self-sexualized, autonomous, and triumphantly electronic.

The "Third Wave" bloggers not only acknowledge the centrality of the consumer society in their understanding of gender construction but also often introduce elements of the commodification of subjectivity as the means to oppose social violence. Laurie Penny is fully cognizant of how feminism has been commercialized to sell products, that is, "how women's liberation— particularly when gently pried away from its more radical, anti-family, anti-racist, anti-capitalist tendencies—has been used to sell everything from cheap perfume to vibrators" (2017, 160). She mentions how cigarettes were used to display women's "empowerment" in the early twentieth century (2017, 159), and how branding is used to sell feminism's "Fourth Wave" as a new social media sensation (2017, 162). "[W]omen are alienated from their sexual bodies and required to purchase the fundamentals of their own gender" (2010, 2). Commercialization, she remarks, has overtaken not only what women wear but also their social function, including "reproductive capacities" (2010, 2), and their subjective function: "[O]ver 80% of everything that is sold in developed countries is bought by women," she begins her other book of blogs

Meat Market: Female Flesh under Capitalism, "providing a vital engine for the consumption required to sustain neoliberal modes of production. . . . If all women on earth work up tomorrow feeling truly positive and powerful in their own bodies, the economies of the globe would collapse overnight" (2010, 1–2).

In the consumer society, the feminist subject has been reframed from a subject composed of social rights, recognition, political futures, and relations to others into a subject composed through entrepreneurship and consumer rights, or the right to choose that consumption allows as a resistance to conformist impositions of authority. "Part of being a woman," declares Clementine Ford, "regardless of what you look like under your clothes, is the knowledge that other people will assume the right to decide who you are allowed to be on any given day" (21), and feminism, we are meant to understand, will fix that, letting women on their own choose their own image, its expression, and its modes of experience, in opposition to the violence of the social and against the odds. "We need to tell our girls," Clementine Ford reminds us in her definition of the important feminist principle of "self-love," "that their bodies exist for them to use, not for other to look at" (51). Again, I do not want to minimize young women's pain, due to all sorts of social retrenchments linked to neoliberalism: diminishing job prospects, diminishing social supports, rising housing costs, unavailable healthcare provision, increasing polarization, violence, student debt, endemic economic precarity, and the like. Yet the focus on personal trauma instead of social injury leaves out the vital question of social belonging, obligation, and responsibility that Judith Butler has interpreted as defining the mother-child bond: that is, in the face of vulnerabilities, "What leads any of us to seek to preserve the life of the other?" (*The Force*, 67).

Mean Mothers

There are two predominant interpretations of feminism around which I will shape my analysis of Valenti, Penny, and Ford. They believe, first, that what they used to resent about feminism is generational, but their generation will make feminism better, and, second, that the "prior generation's" failures could be named Germaine Greer, as Germaine Greer, even when not specifically mentioned, seems to be the face of what they identify as the "Second Wave's" mis-directions that they reject. "Greer is one of many feminists, some of them well respected," explains Laurie Penny, "who believe transgender people are dangerous to their movement. . . . Greer's comments about trans women exemplify the generational strife between second-wave feminists who sought to expand the definition of 'woman' and the younger feminists who are looking for new gender categories altogether" (206). This inability to account for difference is what makes the "prior generation" fail. "Looking back, though, [on the influence of *The Female Eunuch*]," further ruminates Penny, "that militant insistence on womanhood before everything is part of the reason it's taken me a decade to admit that, in addition to being feminist, I'm genderqueer . . . I grew up on second-wave feminism, but that didn't stop me starving myself" (2017, 203). In other words, *The Female Eunuch* could be the name of the reason young women hesitated to call themselves "feminists," because it could not account for a diversity of experiences under the designation of "woman" and it could not solve their personal problems.

The Australian author of the influential, trend-setting, and revolutionary 1970 landmark *The Female Eunuch*, Germaine Greer, has, indeed, produced public provocations on a number of occasions. Some of these spectacles stick out. In 2006, for example, she opposed the filming of Monica Ali's novel *Brick Lane* in London's East End neighborhood on the grounds that the novel offered an inauthentic representation of London's Bengali community and that Ali, with a background Greer deemed as unconvincingly Bengali, had "created her own version of Bengali-ness" ("Reality Bites"). Greer was thus siding with some members of that community who, she says, "don't recognise its [the novel's] version of their demanding and rigorous minority culture" ("Reality Bites"). For taking this position, Greer incurred the wrath of Salmon Rushdie—among others—who called her opposition "sanctimonious and disgraceful," rebuked Greer for advocating censorship, and denounced her attack on another woman and a feminist as personal.

More recently, Greer came under fire for her statements about transgender women not being women. In an interview at ABC in Australia, she defended her claims by saying, "I'm not saying that people should not be allowed to go through that procedure, what I'm saying is it doesn't make them a woman. It happens to be an opinion, it's not a prohibition" (McMahon). Transgender women, she elaborated, "don't know what it's like to have a 'big hairy smelly vagina'" (*Varsity*). In the face of much pushback, she held fast to that opinion, and subsequently Greer's public lectures at Cardiff University in Wales and at Oxford University were met with student protests, petitions, threats of boycotts, and calls for her cancellation. Both these incidents, but especially the later, exhibit Greer using conceptual terminology that, as it enters into and circulates within the contemporary mediascape, is harmful and insensitive and leads to violence. Indeed, Greer's vilification of transsexuals, and male-to-female (MTF) transsexuals in particular, can be traced through her career, as she characterized her position in 1999: "The insistence that manmade women be accepted as women is the institutional expression of the mistaken conviction that women are defective males" (*The Whole Woman*, 133). This is followed by a condemnation of all cosmetic surgery except when performed as reconstruction after an accident, all in vitro fertilization as dismemberment, and all piercing as "mutilation," because such surgery "is profoundly conservative in that it reinforces sharply contrasting gender roles by shaping individuals to fit them" (*The Whole Woman*, 134). Such views target particular acts of body transformation as responsible for the edifying of patriarchy and as blamable for essentializing and reenforcing conservative norms and gender roles. To me, cancellation shuts down democratic debate, often reduces public figures to politically repulsive decontextualized sound bites and caricatures of themselves, and installs barriers to engaging positively or negatively with any of their ideas at all. The hatefulness of Greer's negative assessments of body modification and transsexual practices provokes a rejection of all her views tout court, even her useful critique of feminist subjectivity's relation to social commodification, alienation, and precarity that creates the identity of "women."

I will return to Germaine Greer later when I look back at *The Female Eunuch* and see what possibilities for feminist interventions are covered up by the popular rejection of her unpopular provocations and refusal of difference. First, though, I address the allegation that the "Second Wave" is a generational thing.

Laurie Penny,[10] for instance, marks a generational split as a mode of explaining feminism's "new" emphasis on identity-talk. She discerns a trend in "young adult" dystopian fiction where, as in *The Hunger Games*, the heroes "cannot rely on any grown-up for help," or as in *Harry Potter*, "we are all doomed," and "adults can't be trusted" (*Bitch*, 433). The dystopian social threat for this new "Third Wave" generation includes older feminists, who, in their estimation, can be blind to what younger feminists know well about difference or who are concertedly racist, exclusionary, or sexually regressive. "My mother was the kind of person who insisted on referring to genitals by their medical names" (67), confesses Clementine Ford. Such sexual repressiveness is an indicator not only of her mother's inadequacies and disregard of difference but also of feminism's historical obsolescence: "When I thought of feminism, I thought of a tired old *movement* filled with irrelevant ideas and even more irrelevant women" (emphasis mine; 1). What made the "tired old *movement*" irrelevant was that it did not acknowledge sex until Harvey Weinstein's crimes motivated women to come forward, and women's expressions of sex then exposed women's differences. The "#MeToo" events opened the floodgates of women talking about sex, harassment, and the media, a newly minted feminism Ford could embrace.[11]

---

[10] Penny engages in a wider range of theoretical, historical, and political thinking and reverts less to autobiography than the other two bloggers mentioned here. For example, Penny starts with this promising statement: "The field of battle is the human imagination. This is a book about the hard stuff, about the painful places where theory crashes into flesh and bone" (2017, 5). *Bitch Doctrine* is a collection of blogs, short vignettes that react to events and engage in public debates and social analysis with a variety of modes of address. In contrast to the other two volumes under discussion here, Penny does cite some theory, which allows her to make connections between different historical, cultural, and social situations. Clementine Ford mentions some of the theory she was introduced to in her undergraduate gender studies course, where she learned some useful vocabulary (like "hegemonic power," "structural violence," and "patriarchy") that was "a throwback to the humourless feminists of old" (24). In the end, she rejects this learning as privilege: "Reckoning with the privileges I have will be a lifelong task, because the assumption that we can somehow transcend the need to have those conversations with ourselves by just reading a few of the right books is where a lot of the damage is caused" (24–5).

[11] Susan Watkins has a different view: "[T]he paradigm within which #MeToo operated, and which gave political form to this powerful but inchoate upsurge of sexual discontent, was largely limited to a variation of the radical-feminist, anti-discrimination, criminal-justice approach that had been naturalized by the campus sexual-assault campaigns: the acceptance of any accusation as de facto *bona fide*; the focus on the post factum penalization of men, and spectacular punishment of some as a deterrent to all, to the exclusion of preventive strategies that foregrounded practical, cultural and material support for women's self-determination. . . . To this was added the new practice of trial by social media, which abandoned any notion of a fair hearing" (73–4).

For Ford, this talking was a sign of women taking control over the body's expression for a diverse aesthetics of diverse tastes: "Look," she asserts, "bodily perfections should not be measured based on the size of our waistbands, the length of our legs, the colour of our skin or the mapping of our genetics. All bodies are good bodies, no matter what shape they come in" (56). The violence of the male gaze for Ford is in imposing a body image that is singular rather than the diversity of sexual expression. "This is what it largely boils down to," Ford informs us, "the power of men to fuck whom they like, when they like, and have the object of their fucking express gratitude for their selection" (200–1). Before having her feminist realization, Ford, under pressure from the gaze that controlled her body, suffered from lack of self-esteem and anorexia.[12] Feminism allows her to understand her body as not what the social gaze dictates: "Part of being a woman, regardless of what you look like under your clothes, is the knowledge that other people will assume the right to decide who you are allowed to be on any given day" (21). Feminism *is* divesting oneself of (Harvey Weinstein's) gaze in favor of many different personal, "authentic" preferences: "small breasts, massive breasts, perky breasts, saggy breasts, augmented breasts, one breast, no breast, wide-set vaginas, small penises, short vaginas" (57), and so forth. "The truth about young women that nobody wants to acknowledge," Laurie Penny explains about the TV show *Girls*,

> is that we are all unique, and the number of stories that haven't been told about our lives is vast, particularly if we are poor, or queer, or if we are not white. It is the telling of many diverse stories, rather than the search for the perfect archetype, that will really challenge the narrative of patriarchy, and I want to see more women's stories told, not just online. (2017, 184)

The idea that the body is a site of difference means that an individual can be authentic and have agency in its being, outside of social interaction, that it is

---

12 "As I continued to shrink, I thought of my body as a monster eating itself. I starved it, because in starving it I thought I could defeat it . . . I looked for nourishment from other things. Appreciative glances from boys in the park" (39).

the aesthetic body in itself that makes its difference. "The body and identity is a wonderfully diverse thing" (108–9), Clementine Ford professes. What is missing is any alternative social sphere to the one represented by the gaze of Weinstein and his ilk—indeed, any *movement*. What has taken the place of the dangerous social (the gaze) is an individualizing of the body based on the body's differentiation. These bloggers clearly feel that their acceptance of difference advances social and cultural inclusion and diversity. I agree that advancing social and cultural inclusion and diversity is an overall social good. Yet their approach to difference is often expounded as a list of surface features of the body or aesthetic physical details. Such a recognition of difference does not take into account alternative histories that influence economic distributions but, rather, envisions all difference as only a sign of difference, nothing more, a better way for me to be me. Instead of diversity, difference here is an empty category that everyone can name for themselves homogeneously and across the board.

Jessica Valenti also turns to autobiography to explore her reactions to an older feminist project and her feelings about the new one. In fact, her sense of the entire social field is composed through her mother's, grandmother's, and aunts' toleration of social spaces that menace women and force them "to live in a body that attracts a particular kind of attention" (65). In her story, similar to in Ford's, her initiation into feminism happens after an initial resistance, followed by a traumatic event, and then an awareness—called "feminism"—about the cause of the trauma, which teaches both that feminism is not the tired, old attitudes that they thought it was. In both cases, the way out of the trauma is through pregnancy and, subsequently, having a child—a daughter—who might be different. Valenti adopts feminism because she realizes feminism can be about women choosing and expressing their sex differently and more diversely than under the control of the gaze. This acceptance of difference sets this type of feminism apart from, say, her grandmother, who blamed the failure of her husband's business on his hiring of Black men, or her mother, who did not admit that she had a disabled brother. Valenti's and Ford's accounts take very similar turns, from a teenage disenchantment and rebellion to a trauma—that Valenti diagnoses as post-traumatic stress disorder (PTSD) (176)—in response to an imposition of a body image that makes them, with a new awareness of difference, understand how different their ideas are from that of their parents. Valenti's grandmother and mother were both molested by members of their families, leading Valenti to believe that this "matrilineal curse" (11), which her "aunts and mom joked about" (11), would inevitably pass down to her and her daughter as well: "men get to rape and kill women and still come home to a dinner cooked by one" (15). Tolerated by her mother, grandmother, and aunts, the experience of sexual assault-haunts Valenti and causes her disaffectedness, as men frequently flash her on the subway, touching her and catcalling: "I started seeing dicks so regularly on my school commute. . . . I started to assume every man on the subway was thinking about showing me his penis" (61). The social, here, is the persistence of the singularizing, punishing gaze that denies difference and that the "prior generation" passively accepted as inevitable suffering.

This constant public assault of male sexual desire on women's bodies takes away women's choices: "We are trapped on the train, in the crowd, in the classroom. If we have no place to go where we can escape that reaction to our bodies, where is it that we're *not* forced" (original emphasis; 65). As with Ford, the problem of men's sexual power gets internalized when, as a child, Valenti feels the pressure to adjust to the gaze by turning herself into a "sex object," obsessing over her nose, feeling ugly, and self-hating for her ugliness. In response, in high school, college, and after, Valenti engages in numerous casual sex acts with numerous partners. Such casual sex is a mark of her oppression by the gaze. She receives numerous online threats and name-calling after a photograph of her meeting Bill Clinton went viral: "The intensity of that abuse has been compounded by the sheer magnitude of the online space" (184). Both Valenti and Ford see the possibility of working to dismantle the gaze in internet engagements that, by rejecting the gaze, admit difference. "It's okay," Clementine Ford permits, "to block men on Facebook and Twitter, to delete their emails without reading them, to tell them to Fuck Off on Tinder and basically to do whatever else you think is necessary to keep their toxic bullshit from seeping into your life" (288). "We aren't granted the flexibility," she explains, "of being able to play characters who can be complicated, messy, irreverent, assertive, admired and angry. These roles are reserved for men" (276). "Social media," Laurie Penny tells us, "allows all people to talk to one another frankly and in elective anonymity about their experiences. Women tell their truths on the Internet" (2017, 366). In this opening to heterogeneity offered on the internet, these writers establish "experience" as the core of an authentic feminism: Feminism is seen here as the imperative to speak of diverse experiences outside of social ideology and norms, to create one's own singular aesthetic. The internet—the source of retaliatory male aggression coming to bear on women who disrupt archaic norms and stereotypes of what a "Woman" "is" for these men—also unlocks experience from social ideology as it bursts forth in experiential multiplicity, in speech.

I find it impossible not to be sympathetic to the pain these women experience. I do not doubt their descriptions of their psychically injurious social encounters with men or the radical effects that these social encounters have had on their physical and psychological health and ultimately on their bodies. They might have turned to the tools and strategies developed by the "prior generation" of feminism for identifying and combating the objectification enforced by the male gaze. For example, Laura Mulvey's famous article on this topic, "Visual Pleasure and Narrative Cinema," was first published in 1975; Luce Irigaray's book *Speculum of the Other Woman*, which addressed the gaze in Western philosophy from Freud back to Plato, was first published in 1974; the gaze is also a formative concept in Simone de Beauvoir's 1946 canonical study *The Second Sex*.[13] Even Germaine Greer notes it: "the woman is tailoring herself to appeal to a buyers' market; her most exigent buyer may be her husband, who goes on exacting her approximation to the accepted image as a condition of his continuing desire and pride in her" (*Female Eunuch*, 41). These young feminist writers might have turned to feminism for its analysis of the effects of sexism on girls' deportments, well-being, and intimacies, particularly after Susan Bordo's landmark *Unbearable Weight: Feminism, Western Culture, and the Body*, published in 1993, addressed issues of body-image dysphoria, eating disorders, bulimia, and anorexia. Yet, instead of drawing connections with

---

[13] Many passages could be cited here; for example: "Woman . . . is even required by society to make herself an erotic object. The purpose of the fashions to which she is enslaved is not to reveal her as an independent individual, but rather to cut her off from her transcendence in order to offer her as prey to male desires; thus society is not seeking to further her projects but to thwart them" (529).

such feminist political and cultural canonical interventions, these "Third Wave" bloggers create a status for themselves as an identity in difference, reinvented as totally new.

Some recent analyses of motherhood as a structural or symbolic problem within the current political climate might provide some insight here. Jaqueline Rose, for example, reads the current social discourse on mothers as blaming them for the fallout of retrenchments of the social safety net or blaming them for immigration rather than blaming the poverty and violence that lead people to immigrate. She asks, "What are we doing *to* mothers—when we expect them to carry the burden of everything that is hardest to contemplate about our society and ourselves?" (1). She goes on, "Mothers always fail . . . there is nothing easier than to make social deterioration look like something that it is the sacred duty of mothers to prevent" (27). Rose looks back at antiquity and spots such negative depictions of mothers in Greek tragedies, philosophy, and after, but, as Angela McRobbie has stipulated, this targeting of mothers for criticism and blame is a particularly potent trope of our neoliberal moment.

McRobbie shows how right-wing politics has absorbed aspects of feminist thinking, upholding the appropriately meritorious feminist mother as a bulwark of seemingly progressive, professional, entrepreneurial, self-help ideology. "Feminism," she writes, "is no longer despised but given some new life through an articulation with a specific range of values pertaining to the project of contemporary neoliberalism" ("Feminism, The Family...", 120). In commercial messaging like Sheryl Sandberg's "lean-in" feminism, the championing of family-career balance in various TV, radio, magazine, and other media outlets under the mantra of individualism and competition, the entrepreneurial mom for McRobbie is the example of success that demeans the mother who is dependent or unsuccessful in terms set by market culture, the one who fails to "have it all." "[V]ulnerability and dependency," she continues, "are . . . equated with personal carelessness, with being overweight, and badly dressed" and eventually with "inadequate life planning" and "mismanaged lives" (122). Against stories of most women's distress, the entrepreneurial mom proves that *it can be done*. Masking the dependence of "successful" women on their own families, social systems, or domestic help, such emphasis on affluent women's ability to "have it all" by their own ambition, effort, and excellence faults the women who do not have much for their own social precarity and, as well, is an alibi for cuts to social supports or a reason for the denial of social rights and provisions.

McRobbie reviews some past feminism's serious engagements with "cross-border solidarities . . . and anti-racist struggles" (*Aftermath*, 9), as well as with working-class movements, and highlights that the "Third Wave" treatment of the "Second Wave" revises this history: "Feminism's wider intersections with anti-racism," she notes, "with gay and lesbian politics, are written out of the kind of history which surfaces even in serious journalism, and the feminism which is then vilified and thrown backwards into a previous era, is a truncated and sclerotic anti-male and censorious version of a movement which was much more diverse and open-minded" (*Aftermath*, 9).[14] In McRobbie's reading, the glamorized entrepreneurial feminist mother, in her glorious autonomy, is a corralling of feminism in the service of confirming class identity, and it rewrites the past to take out the political edge, erasing the influence of multiple social movements as they transact in the construction of the feminist subject.

Additionally, the three bloggers see themselves as entrepreneurs, self-employed writers, their self-employment and creative labor a big part of what empowers them as feminists and as mothers. Indeed, the entrepreneurial character is what separates their own motherhood from the motherhood of their mothers and grandmothers who were dependent housewives without the same work opportunities—it is the mark of their independence. This entrepreneurial self-characterization is central to the way they express their experiences of motherhood.[15] Clementine Ford talks not only about establishing her career as a feminist before having children but also about her work as a blogger about women on social media being "the ones who

---

[14] In fact, as Rashmi Varma has elaborated in detail, starting in 1924 with the International Conference of Women, twentieth century feminism had a much closer alliance with anti-imperialist struggles than today's feminism which is "aligned with a dilution of genuine internationalism as borders close on refugees and migrants" (464).

[15] The exception is Laurie Penny who believes that pregnancy would be an obstacle to her career: "I love babies, but not enough to make the work, the pain, the worry and the lost opportunities involved with it for me—not right now, and maybe not ever. I live in a commune, I date multiple people, and I'm focused on my career" (*Bitch Doctrine*, 43).

overwhelmingly experience pregnancy and abortion, and it's vital that we wrest back control of the narratives of both" (128). As Catherine Rottenberg has noticed, neoliberalism invested in motherhood as the entrepreneurial subject's orientation toward the future: Entrepreneurial mothering "is based not on the management of future risks, but rather on the promise of future individual *fulfillment*, or, more accurately, one based on careful sequencing and smart self-investments in the present to ensure enhanced returns in the future" (original emphasis; 83). In keeping, the last section of Jessica Valenti's blog series links a very difficult premature C-section birth to an incipient independent writer's career. While the birth debilitated Valenti with anemia, depression, weight loss, and other physical ailments, her baby Layla endured breathing problems, eating problems, a feeding tube, a blood transfusion, an oxygen machine, and a collapsed lung but triumphantly came through. Layla, though, is left speechless. Like for the feminist body, the injuries sustained by Layla's body coming into the world speak of her difference as a triumph over trauma. Coaxing out her daughter's words in the face of a violent society and against the odds, Valenti becomes a feminist, both a mother and an entrepreneur.

Maternal Ambience

In the bloggers' self-assessment, their recognition of difference will elevate them to a new, better, and more secure awareness, a feminism that the "prior generation" could not develop because of its focus on the singularity of "woman," a focus that needs to be discarded because it confirms the male gaze. The "prior generation's" denial of difference in "woman" and espousal of singularity as "woman," according to them, built the conditions for the violence of the social, where the gaze takes away women's choice of difference, bodily aesthetics, and the expression of individual experience. For them, feminism demands autonomy from the social: Self-expression—being able to wear what you want to go where you want—will make us all into the difference that the "prior generation" could not accept, dismantling the power of the gaze to decide for us. This perspective is apace with descriptions of the consumer society: "The consumer," Jean Baudrillard expounds, "experiences his distinctive behaviours as freedom, as aspiration, as choice" (61).

In *The Consumer Society*, Baudrillard blames a prior generation of women for indulging in a type of conspicuous consumption that offers salvation in reducing difference to homogeneous codes and perpetual shopping while inciting "nuisance effects" of social and environmental degradation to proliferate abundantly and without hindrance. "[W]hat we are seeing very generally today," Baudrillard goes on, "is the *extension of the feminine model to the whole field of consumption*" (98). Heavily criticized by feminists of the "prior generation,"[16] Baudrillard creates a "housewife" character that takes on the features and roles that make society into the consumer society: As the

---

[16] Baudrillard's track record on gender issues has not been favorable. "[T]here has never truly been any sexuality" (43), he notes in *Forget Foucault*, and, in his 1979 volume *Seduction*, he writes, "Freud was right: there is but one sexuality, one libido—and it is masculine" (6) and "[t]he feminine is not found in the history of suffering and oppression imputed to it" (6–7) and "the feminine has never been dominated, but has always been dominant" (15) and "the feminine is not a sex" (21). Feminists have identified *Seduction* as a particularly egregious text: The thesis is that feminism erred in celebrating "women" as the embodiment of a positive identity, and instead women should manipulate "femininity" as seduction and play, as "femininity" has no positive form and can therefore undermine (or deconstruct) the fake referentiality of the patriarchal code that secures the real. Indeed, the feminist response to Baudrillard throughout the 1980s and into the early 1990s was one of distancing and disgust. At the forefront, Jane Gallop—who had written her own book on the problem of seduction in feminism but three years before Baudrillard's book commending seduction as anti-feminism—calls Baudrillard's "rather rabid attack on feminism" an "insult" (113). Gallop upbraids Baudrillard not only for declaring that "woman is only appearance" (113), and not only for persisting "in seeing feminism as stupid, wrong, mistaken" (114), but also, even more appallingly, for maintaining that he "knows the truth of the feminine and the masculine and can thus, from this privileged position beyond sexual difference, advise women how best to combat masculine power" (114). In her very short review of *Seduction*, Luce Irigaray faults Baudrillard on an array of fronts. She takes him to task not only for relegating women's power to artifice but also for assuming, following Kierkegaard and neglecting the painful alienation of the victims, that rape was a game or a strategy, a resistance against the code erected by and for men. She also lambasts him for positioning women outside of power, sovereignty, and sexuality (defined narrowly, as the source of identity), in fact outside of any existence within the real, in an undefined elsewhere. See also Alice Jardine, Sadie Plant, and Teresa de Lauretis. A noted exception to this feminist consensus is Victoria Grace's *Baudrillard's Challenge*, which Baudrillard himself endorsed. In it, Grace champions Baudrillard because of his "refusal of the fetishization of 'women'" (4); according to Grace, he radically challenges the foundationalism in the real, particularly the real that produces (gender) identity as a positivity (or essence), proving it instead to be contingent and fluid like signification, escaping the control of the code by undermining the code's stability, and ready for circulation or iteration. Baudrillard, she concludes, "considers simulation to be in less accord with a paternal, phallic law of identity/difference . . . and more in accordance with a kind of 'maternal law,' characterized by an implosive collapse, engulfment, and the displacement of any oppositional term" (126). Gender, in Grace's reading of Baudrillard, takes on the same formation as the commodity which, because it gets its character within exchange as sign, is undermined by its own signifying structure.

prototype of the feminist "entrepreneur," she asserts value in the difference of the new by discarding the old as waste; she offers the promise of affection, security, and a simulation of care in the objects that she buys to mask the absence of social welfare; and she revels in the status that objects and identities confer through their difference from other objects (recognizing status in these objects), even as such difference is an empty signifier exchangeable with other like signifiers. For Baudrillard, "woman" traffics in waste, and the example of wastefulness par excellence is the "housewife," who indulges in stupid leisure, making herself up in mass-marketed cosmetics for mass-marketed appeal by buying into allures of prestige and status that sustain the system. The "housewife" gains status by engaging in continually choosing the signs of difference: "[w]hat mother has not dreamt of a washing machine specially designed for her alone," Baudrillard reads in an advert. Similarly, by rejecting the "prior generation," the bloggers adopt the consumption of identities of difference that, according to Baudrillard, is the appeal and motivation of the consumer society. As they declare their own difference, they are manipulating identities like the "housewife" manipulates objects, "as signs which distinguish you" (61).

Baudrillard wrote *The Consumer Society* three years before his signature critique of Marx and the paradigm of production in *The Mirror of Production* and eleven years before his more well-known work in *Simulations*.[17] The argument in *The Consumer Society* goes like this: In an age of abundance and infinite growth, consumption is not about the satisfaction of need or use, as Marx theorized it; rather, the objects of consumption function as markers of difference or signs. In a consumer society, Baudrillard notes, purchasing objects that have no function

---

[17] In the wake of *Simulations*, Baudrillard has been severely criticized for his idealist claims that an economy of signs and images has overtaken production and work that were the basis of industrial society. Criticism of Baudrillard has nearly amounted to total dismissal, as his ideas about the rule of the code rubbed against the premises of poststructuralist thought (or, some say, took it too much to the extreme of its own logic), inspiring Deleuze, as Sylvère Lotringer points out in his "Introduction to *Forget Foucault*," to make it "known around Paris that he saw Baudrillard as 'the shame of the profession'" (20). Nature does not exist except as a sign of nature, the energy crisis is but a simulation of over-production, and there have never been "real shortages" (*Symbolic Exchange*, 175). "We are at the end of production" (*Symbolic Exchange*, 102), Baudrillard declares; "the unions and parties are dead, all that remains for them to do is die" (153), and therefore "there is no longer any prospect of revolution" (104).

except to be signs of status and distinction compensates for a general lack of the means to make life better, satisfy needs, or produce satisfaction. That is, in the ideology of the "affluent society" (of the late 1960s), where signs are equated to other signs to make all value into exchange value (social relations have been totally subsumed under market logic), commodities have lost all use value except for bestowing the promise of status (in differentiating) while engineering—as signifiers unmoored from reality—total conformity. Objects have become subjects, and the ultimate object, the body, has been reduced to only its "aesthetic/erotic exchange-value" (*Consumer Society*, 136) as defined in films, mass literature, and advertising. The "liberation" of this body is just a "managed 'emancipation'" (*Consumer Society*, 138) that leads to deeper servitude. "Consumer products thus present themselves," he proposes, "as a *harnessing of power*, not as products embodying work" (32), and the body is *nothing but the sign* inside a system of exchange, not productive but reproductive.

"The invitation of self-indulgence," says Jean Baudrillard in *The Consumer Society*, "is mainly directed at women" (95). Like the "Third Wavers," Baudrillard attributes this denial of difference not only to sexual repressiveness and censorship tied to old-fashioned mores but also to the replacement of subjects with objects. "There is no woman, however *demanding*, who cannot satisfy the tastes and *desires of her personality* with a Mercedes Benz!" Baudrillard cites from *Le Monde*. Baudrillard places women, and in particular housewives, at the center of what he identifies as an economic and cultural sea change. The housewife, he notes, is responsible for the waste and obsolescence that fuels the consumer society; she is "*the lubrication of social relations with the institutional smile*" (161). As the manager of the private sphere, she is the one who adorns it with objects, reducing everything to the simple function of managing difference within a universal system of signs of difference. Through this relation with the "housewife," such objects take on a maternal protective character that he calls "a *beneficent*, maternal *ambience*" (192) or "*functional femininity*" (*Consumer Society*, 96), "a continual consumption of solicitude, sincerity and warmth . . . even more vital for the individual than biological nourishment" (*Consumer Society*, 161). "It is the smile of everyone who has already spent an enjoyable time at one of our hotels" (*Consumer Society*, 161), Baudrillard cites in an ad for Sofitel professing that the hotel fills in where the wife and family are absent, producing "intimacy where there is none" (161). Within the context of the failure of social institutions like social security, aid to families, retirement, and unemployment benefits that might have propped up the home, the "housewife" appears instead, in the guise of generosity, charity, sympathy, and security, the sign of redemption in a world that is happy to leave you bereft. The "housewife" dresses up systemic inequalities in such codes of aesthetic difference for status, says Baudrillard, by personifying the failing of social redistributive institutions in a character offering protective solicitude.

By focusing on the mother or "housewife" as the point of the consumer society's entry into intimate social relations, Baudrillard privileges symbolic reproduction over production as the overriding site of surplus accumulation. This contradicts some feminist Marxist perspectives on reproduction that still sees reproduction as "necessary labor" that responds to a natural need at the transitional border between nature and culture. Sylvia Federici, for example, an advocate of wages for housework, takes Marx and Marxism to task for not sufficiently addressing the economic contributions of reproduction because Marx thought reproduction would eventually disappear, absorbed into the productive economy as technology and commercialization take over domestic tasks. In contrast, Federici asserts, "the reproductive work that Marx's analysis bypasses is, to a large extent, work that cannot be mechanized. . . . How can we mechanize washing, cuddling, dressing, and feeding a child, providing sexual services, or assisting those who are ill or the elderly?" (2020: 162). For Baudrillard, capital has been successful in infiltrating into private space and nature in order to capture excess reproductive time, and, indeed, most of the care-tasks that Federici lists have become or are becoming economic and technological functions. In the ascendance of media, information, educational systems and technologies, entertainment, mechanization of domesticity and daily life, pharmaceuticals, therapy, and bureaucratization, commercialization, says Baudrillard, enters the home and its most intimate social relations. "Production is dead," he proclaims, "long live reproduction!" (*Symbolic Exchange*, 160).

Baudrillard acknowledged that the turn of capital toward symbolic exchange (reproduction) entails an intensification of consumer markets in bodies, subjectivities, intimacies, and social relations. The body, in other words, *becomes your job.*[18] "We are reaching a point," Baudrillard concludes, "where the group is less interested in what it produces than in the human relations within it. Its essential work may be, more or less, to *produce relationship*" (*Consumer Society*, 171). With the purchase of cosmetics, pharmaceuticals, manicures, fitness products, health products, hygienic products, dieting products, food, tattoos, vitamins, cosmetic surgeries, tanning, medical visits, trips to the salon, lifestyle adventures, and sex toys, norms are managed in the body, the home, and intimate relationships by a constant resource extraction that consumers do to themselves for the profit of others in the name of difference. The "huge system of solicitude," Baudrillard continues, masks "the spread of the abstraction of exchange-value into the very heart of daily life and the most personal relationships" (162). As much as Freud marked the early twentieth century as the time when the historical subject was embodied, Baudrillard's "housewife" frames his contemporary historical moment as one where market culture is embodied. Consumption gives birth to and cares for objects and signs as though they were subjects.

Baudrillard's "housewife" borrows from Georges Bataille's theory of excess, where, in the real economy of endless growth, the "general movement of exudation (of waste) of living matter impels him [man], and he cannot stop it . . . it destined him, in a privileged way, to that glorious operation, to useless consumption" (23). Opposing the Marxist emphasis on accumulation through surplus, Bataille is known for his theory of general economy, where societies and cultures find adhesion in the often-ritualized destruction of surplus. For Bataille, productive growth of both life and production exceeds the spatial limits available, and the destruction of excess, uselessness, and waste is therefore necessary for forms of life to reproduce themselves. A part is cut out to destroy.

---

[18] What is *not* the case for Baudrillard is a "real" body that is overlaid and added onto by various embellishing products, as Laurie Penny interprets Baudrillard to say: Citing *The Consumer Society*, Penny agrees that "Young people growing up with pressure to perform in every aspect of their lives find themselves aping a robotic capitalist eroticism that has little to do with their own legitimate desires" (*Meat Market*, 10). Baudrillard, however, does not believe that there is a "real" or legitimate body or desire underneath the commercial coverings but rather that the commercial body is the "real"—"sign material being exchanged" (*Consumer Society*, 132); there is no other one, no outside imposition, no difference between the signifying body and the one signified.

Baudrillard agrees, "All societies have always wasted, squandered, expended, and consumed beyond what is strictly necessary for the simple reason that it is in the consumption of a surplus, of a superfluity that the individual—and society—feel not merely that they exist, but that they are alive" (43). This is true of the bloggers as well. Whereas the "housewife" spends wastefully on an excess of objects in order to reproduce her difference in signs, destroying her old and useless objects, the bloggers destroy, as well, what they deem as useless ideas, attitudes, and dispositions represented as the "prior generation" in order to surpass their perceived limits and remake themselves as examples of a growing culture of feminism. The function of the tired old attitudes of the "prior generation" parallels that of the "'disposable panties' which, 80 per cent viscose and 20 per cent non-woven acrylic," Baudrillard quips, "can be put on in the morning and thrown away at night, and need no washing" (46). The uselessness of the consumer product is built into the system, says Baudrillard, "a wastage built into them and, therefore, obligatorily *consumed* as fragility, their built-in obsolescence, their condemnation to transience. What is produced today is . . . produced . . . with an *eye to its death*" (46). The sparkling new thing is a repeat of the recently outmoded object, discarded but recycled and repackaged as different. Just as the "housewife" repudiates her past by disposing of its objects, the bloggers repudiate the "prior generation" by censuring its subjects.

As well, Baudrillard's "housewife" is recognizable in the bloggers' "entrepreneur." In this era of human capital, Catherine Rottenberg has demonstrated, motherhood is reworked "in increasingly managerial terms" (139), with self-help and therapy professing a "happy work-family balance." The entrepreneurial "housewife" would combine motherhood with work while demanding constant work on the self, facilitating "the transmutation of the self into a business enterprise" (146) through fashion choices, time management, retraining, and constant change: "market competition is central to her vision" (158), even for solutions to family problems. The entrepreneur is thus, for Rottenberg, like the "housewife" for Baudrillard, the point of entry for the market into the home and its intimate relationships. Baudrillard likens "the housewife"—the arbiter who selects objects for the home as signs of differential status—to the receptionist, the social worker, the public relations consultant, the advertising pin-up girl, the shopkeeper, the bank clerk, the sales girl, the representative—in fact, to the service industry as a whole, including information services, promoting, packaging, marketing, and merchandising human relations (161)—in other words, to the incipient, twenty-first-century feminist "entrepreneur." Baudrillard is prescient here: Like his "housewife," the "entrepreneur" dresses up the failures of social institutions and security in a triumphant, super-heroic, smiling solicitude.

Baudrillard's "housewife" shares with the "Third Wave" "entrepreneur" a crucial function in the economy of signs: "[k]nowing how to choose and not to let one's standards slip" (96), she is the purveyor of difference in the adventure of the same. The "housewife's" role is to respond to the need for differentiation and status, to stand before the "Shop-Window," answer the free gift offers in magazines, or follow what the stars are wearing this season, where dressing right is the road to social integration, social ascendance, and security. Also, though, the logic of fashion, with its hierarchical code of values and its quick turnover of tastes and styles, acculturates everyone to social homogenization where, for Baudrillard, "*the real differences* between human beings" (89) have been abolished. I do not agree with Baudrillard that there are no longer real differences between human beings or that signs have been emptied of real meaningful and historical content. Yet the gesture of discarding the "prior generation" as just so much waste because it allegedly allowed the violent imposition of the singularity of the gaze similarly reduces difference to aesthetics, that is, to visible signs of difference. "All bodies help us in varying ways," Clementine Ford tells us, defensively, "thick hair, sparse hair, hairy armpits, hairy bush, hairy toes, hairy belly, hairy face, no hair . . . bodies that look like nobody else's bodies at all—the list goes on and on ad infinitum because of the beautiful, diverse complexity of the human race" (56–7). Such surface differences, much like differences in a fashion catalog or a "Shop-Window," refer to difference itself and, as differences devoid of context, are all the same.

Mother's Mouth

The history of feminist theory offers examples of mother-child relationships that follow other logics besides the logic of the consumer society and where the line between generations is not a line of division with one part portrayed as waste in order to uphold the other as durable and resilient as it singularly overcomes trauma in expressions of difference. The trend in feminism to separate from a prior feminist generation and to represent that generation as inadequate and compromised waste—as "ethnocentric," universalizing, heterosexualizing, ableist, deterministic, and essentializing, indelibly white and blind to otherness—leads to a depoliticizing of the feminist past and a charge of past failures as the naïveté (or worse, e.g., racism, heterosexism, and imperialist formation) and ignorance of feminism's "Second Wave" pioneers. Not only does such a perspective decontextualize feminism, blaming feminists for the political, social, and discursive limits imposed on them by the historical moment, but it also upholds a new feminist identity as heroically escaping from its traumas onto a new plateau of security: sophistication and personal pride, purity of experience, fashionable self-awareness, self-expression, self-appreciation, and limitless cultural sensitivity. Such a move of separation from the past, unwittingly, does not separate these contemporary feminist outlooks from the standpoints of the past against which they pose themselves. There are many productive points of intersection between the many feminisms past and present. In fact, the debasing of the mother is a site that continually appears in feminist theory in different forms. Julia Kristeva is a case in point, where the mother needs to be beheaded in order to allow the child access to the Symbolic and to speech. Feminist rhetoric has been built upon mother hatred as early as Freud's patient Dora[19] and the feminist appropriation of her for her hysterical defiance and schizoid speech.[20] Freud's conclusion that Dora hated her mother out of jealousy for the father,[21] though preposterous, allowed

---

[19] "From the accounts given to me by the girl and her father I was led to imagine her as an uncultivated woman and above all a foolish one, who had concentrated all her interests upon domestic affairs, especially since her husband's illness and the estrangement to which it led" (13).

[20] Hélène Cixous writes, "I could not keep from laughing from one end to the other, because, despite her powerlessness and with (thanks to) that powerlessness, here is a kid who successfully jams all the little adulterous wheels that are turning around her and, one after the other, they break down. She manages to say what she doesn't say, so intensely that men drop like flies" (279). Catherine Clément answers, "[I]n Dora's case, Dora is in the place of the boss' wife: the mother is set aside. She is dead, she is nothing, and everybody has agreed to bury her. Including Freud. Not for a moment does he analyze the reports given him about the mother" (281).

[21] "Dora's jealousy of her mother was inseparable from the group of thoughts relating to her infantile love for her father which she summoned up for her protection" (82).

him to attribute her despair to psychic imbalances, thermodynamic currents, language experiments, and personal failings rather than, as the case implies, to social alienation and socially sanctioned domestic and sexual abuse.

Simone de Beauvoir, as well, is well known and well criticized for her scorn of motherhood. For Beauvoir in *The Second Sex*, motherhood blocks women from fulfillment, liberty, and mutual recognition, as mothers reduce women to the hated particularity of womanness, seeking "eagerly to sacrifice their liberty of action to the functioning of their flesh: it seems to them that their existence is tranquilly justified in the passive fecundity of their bodies" (*Second Sex*, 495). After all, Beauvoir ruminates disdainfully, "It is in maternity that woman fulfills her physiological destiny; it is her natural 'calling,' since her whole organic structure is adapted for the perpetuation of the species" (*ibid.*, 484). As mothers are trapped in the immanence of the body, prototypes of women's situation, Beauvoir also derided her own mother on her deathbed: "Only this body, suddenly reduced by her capitulation to being a body and nothing more, hardly differed at all from a corpse—a poor defenceless carcass turned and manipulated by professional hands, one in which life seemed to carry on only because of its own stupid momentum" (*A Very Easy Death*, 20). Reduced to mere life without morality or decision, the mother is pure body.

As the "foremother" of what is identified as the "Second Wave," Beauvoir's reduction of women to the immanence of the body might seem to "prove" that the "prior generation" of feminists singularizes women's experience. Yet the critical record has not settled on that interpretation. Susan Hekman, for example, argues that Beauvoir is challenging the entire tradition of Western philosophy by introducing, through Woman, a split in the philosophical subject, philosophy's relation to the Other: "What Beauvoir seems to be suggesting . . . is that the question of women does not fit within the parameters of the philosophical positions she has been espousing. What this entails is that the question of woman requires a radically new approach that jettisons previous philosophical methods" (13). Hekman's insightful point here is that Beauvoir introduced the question of the Other for feminism by introducing women as Other into the philosophical tradition. What gets called the "Second Wave" was born from the recognition of difference. This meant that "woman" for what the "Third Wave" is calling the "Second Wave" was always split in multiple directions by the various positions its outsidedness had in relation to the dominant. In keeping, Beauvoir's memoirs are much more conflicted about her mother than her negativity about motherhood in *The Second Sex* would imply. As Beauvoir despises the bourgeois conformism of her family life, represented by her mother's frustrations,[22] she also sees her mother as the point of resistance, the line that lures her from the unintellectual confinement of her conservative provincial childhood toward the freedom that she seeks in philosophical and artistic practice. "The principal function of . . . Mama was to feed me" (*Memoirs*, 6), she remembers, because "The world became more intimately a part of me when it entered through my mouth than through my eyes and my sense of touch" (*ibid.*, 6). Her mother's feeding not only reduces Beauvoir to a biological need but also provides an access to an other knowing beyond her inert, enclosed biological body. The mouth is the point of entry for difference. Identification with the mother's body leads both to a hated regression into the atrophied, nonautonomous experience of her past *and* to a transcendence, the break into the future in an other sensible, material, and intellectual form: "my own mouth was not obeying me any more: I had put Maman's mouth on my own face and in spite of myself, I copied its movements. Her whole person, her whole being, was concentrated there, and compassion wrung my heart" (*A Very Easy Death*, 31). Such an image does not depict separation from the mother and the social in entrepreneurial expression but rather a reaching out toward otherness—a speaking of difference that distorts the self—exemplified in a relation to the mother.

Yet the "Third Wave" rejects any solidarity to be generated in this "prior generation's" reach toward the other. Laurie Penny, for instance, laments: "the

---

[22] Beauvoir's biographer Kate Kirkpatrick discusses how Beauvoir as a young woman grew to resent her mother Françoise for opposing her study of philosophy as a career and pushing her to marry her cousin Jacques Champigneulle: "One night, frustrated after a proposal-less dinner with the Champigneulles, Françoise returned home. She paced for several hours, then screamed that she would deliver her daughter from disgrace and left the apartment. . . . Françoise stopped in front of the Champigneulle residence, shouting. The noise woke Simone, who rushed down to the street. The daughters silently escorted their shrieking mother back inside. From the vantage point of the twenty-first century, this story—if true—raises questions about Françoise de Beauvoir's mental health. Later, the female characters in Beauvoir's works often felt trapped, sometimes hovering on the verge of madness" (61).

knowledge of how different things could have been if I'd known as a teenager that I wasn't alone, the thought of how else I might have lived and loved and dated if I'd the words and the community . . . opens cold fingers of longing somewhere in my stomach and squeezes tight" (2017, 208–9). Penny goes on to acknowledge how proud she is, ultimately, for overcoming obstacles and traumas on her own, as though the experience of the trauma and its overcoming grant her feminist credentials that are unique to her. For feminist historian Joan Scott, motherhood provided such a sense of community for feminism, a common reference point as well as a humanity-focused urgency: "The fantasy of maternal love has provided feminists with a way of establishing a commonality based on unconscious associations, despite their differences, and this has been its efficacy" (66). On the other hand, by reconciling contradictions for the purposes of political solidarity and its enabling fantasies, such a consolidating image confirmed some essentialist versions of "woman."

An example of feminism constructing such unifying ideals, the feminist poet and theorist Adrienne Rich began her study of motherhood with the famous statement "All human life on the planet is born of woman" (11) in her canonical work *Of Woman Born,* first published in 1976. Rich understood the topic of motherhood as a pathway into a social, cultural, and institutional critique about how patriarchy controls the construction of a woman and her social roles. From our perspective, starting from motherhood might seem essentializing as it ties women's place to a biological function. After all, we now know, with transsexual birthing, that all human life on the planet is not born of a female and that human life, in order to be born, is already connected to machines,[23] media, and political inequalities that testify to how the attribute of "human" is discriminately applied.

---

[23] Rosi Braidotti writes about post-human feminism, "contemporary science and biotechnologies affect the very fibre and structure of the living and have altered dramatically our understanding of what counts as the basic frame of reference for the human today" (40). Donna Haraway has also analyzed how "[b]oth the whole earth and the fetus owe their existence as public objects to visualizing technologies. These technologies include computers, video cameras, satellites, sonography machines, optical fiber technology, television, microcine-matography and much more. The global fetus and the spherical whole Earth both exist because of, and inside of, technoscientific visual culture" (*Modest_Witness*, 174).

Actually, though, Rich is aware that women are being made into women by an institutionalized impressing of reproduction onto them and does not agree that this should be the case: "Woman's status as childbearer has been made into a major fact of her life," she qualifies. "Terms like 'barren' or 'childless' have been used to negate any further identity" (11). She explicitly discards genetics as forming gender, instead attributing gender to experience, the weather, and organizing (xv). Rather than seeing maternity as an inherent and essential function that all women share, she implicates it as a patriarchal imposition that unifies women symbolically. The maternal bond serves to politicize structural discrimination against itself: "[t]he affirmation of the mother-daughter bond is powerfully expressed, not primarily in terms of a dyad but as a facet of a culture of women and a group history that is not merely personal" (xxviii). Recognizing that the symbolic unity for the mother-daughter bond does not necessarily account for every experience in the same way, she goes on: "There are, of course, wide variations of culture and history, framed by the fact of racism and of the positions occupied by women of color in a racist and sexist economy" (xxviii) and, she includes too, variations of language, nation, and ethnicity. Yet the diversity does not preclude a common rhetorical place, dictated by the social structure, from which a critique could be established and an orientation through which a protest could be lodged: "Until a strong line of love, confirmation, and example stretches from mother to daughter," she concludes, "from woman to woman *across the generations*, women will still be wandering in the wilderness" (emphasis mine; 246).

The Female Eunuch

The idea that a transvestite feels like a woman or wants to be a woman has had a variety of interpretations, ranging from assessments of her as essentializing and conservative to celebrations of her as radical. Let us start with Jasbir Puar. Puar writes, "there is no trans" (56). She does not state but could add "there is no woman, either." I take her to mean that the designations "man" and "woman" are arbitrary, due to an assignment at birth; the assignment might be more or less arbitrary, taking into account the appearance of genitalia, or chromosomes, or what Freud called "secondary sex characteristics," whether or not all these features through which gender is interpreted line up clearly and correspond clearly with the expectations in the category signifier. Analyzing the appearance of trans within the Americans for Disabilities Act (ADA), Puar shows that claiming a gender normative identity for trans people was attached to a strategy of accessing medical needs (which does not make such a claim less real or substantive): Those appealing for rights and treatments had to demonstrate behaviors and sensibilities from childhood that conformed to the opposite gender's "normal" practices within specified parameters. In contrast, Puar's is a logic of "becoming." For Puar, "becoming," which develops out of their thinking on Deleuze and Guatarri's "dividual," depends on "subindividual capacities" (57) or piecing. In line with a neoliberal economy that favors flexibilization, plasticity, fluidity, "porous boundaries" (36), and a "fragmentation of the body for capitalist profit" (36), piecing, Puar elaborates, highlights how bodies, all bodies, under constant modification as bodies, "are malleable as composites of parts, affects, compartmentalized capacities and debilities, and as data points and informational substrates" (50). As "a multi-sectional market" (45), a body, divided into pieces, each with a potential for enhancement of profit and productivity, is always transforming and never coming to rest, finally, in terms set by a particular set of identity-defining traits or combinations of traits or in a specified linear development bound up in a particular predetermined identity name, like "woman." A body is multiple from the inside.

Germaine Greer's framing of her concerns is similar. Though Greer is considered out of sync with new forms of popular feminism and often hated or severely criticized by young feminists, she was a trendsetter, giving feminism pizzazz and personality while drawing on rich anthropological and psychoanalytic traditions to show gender as imbricated in culture and answering to historical needs and so fundamentally multiple and available for repositioning. For this, her insights opened up feminist analysis to a searing critique of the formation of the subject inside sociality. Greer would never say that "there is no such thing as a woman," but she does demonstrate the various and varying social forces through which something we identify as a "woman" gets made. Though, like Baudrillard, on the cusp of a turn to neoliberalism rather than, as with Puar, in the midst of its flourishing, Greer traces the institutional and economic conditions that create gender identity by piecing together its parts and elements for enhanced profit and production.

Greer is not precise, consistent, or careful in her vocabulary referencing transvestites versus transsexuals or homosexuals, so "transsexuality" and related words are often used in various and even contradictory ways, sometimes friendly and other times not. Her opening gambit, just like Beauvoir's, is to ask what about the body accounts for gender dimorphism, and, after examining the cell structure, bones, curviness, hair, chromosomes, tissues, genitalia, and even menstruation, she concludes: "The 'normal' sex roles that we learn to play from our infancy are no more natural than the antics of a transvestite" (33). In this and comparable allegations, Greer is, indeed, maintaining that a "transvestite" is not a "woman," a similar position to the one that will become the reason for attacks on her over fifty years later. Her meaning here is twofold: (1) that the attribute "woman" is not a body-type but a set of conditions and experiences, so it cannot be made by alterations of the body, like surgery or pharmaceuticals, just like a "transvestite" is also a social position rather than a body-type, also made by a combination of pieces of culture and biology; (2) both "woman" and "transvestite" are "sex roles," a phrase from Margaret Meade's anthropological studies referring to cultural diversity in sexual expression rather than innate biological, cross-cultural conformity. "Woman" and "transvestite" are both made, but they are made differently, just as some "women" are made differently than other "women," depending on culture, and both "women" and "transvestites" are inherently diverse because of the many ways they are touched by the social.

In keeping, her harsh critique of "transvestites" centers on performances that she sees as degrading to women. "Another kind of humorous insult that women take in good part is the drag artists' grotesque guying of female foibles," she writes.

> Some of the transvestite acts are loving celebrations of the sexless trappings of femininity, and should be chiefly of value in pointing out how little femininity has to do with actual sex and how much with fakery and glamour-binding. Many more of them are maliciously conceived caricatures of female types ogling and apeing women's blandishments. (304)

The problem of the "transvestite," according to a description like this one, is that a "transvestite" could trap "women" in a derogatory and damaging social image. For Greer, what she calls the "transvestite" is the embodiment of the male gaze. By recreating a male fantasy of what he would expect a "woman" to be, the "transvestite" projects an image of "woman" that is the objectification of either a singular fantasy or a negative fantasy that ridicules or punishes "women" for stepping outside of the code set by male desire.

The political climate has changed since Greer's interventions here, reshaping some mainstream perceptions of trans, particularly in the face of the terrible abuse, discrimination, hostility, and violence that trans people frequently confront. In Puar's sense, trans may be understood now as having multiple relations to the norms of the gender system. There is no way to defend Greer from a dominant reading where she is saying that the "transvestite" is nothing but a singular term for a cruel ruse to insult women, to keep them in their place, and to expunge any differences that might exist between them by submerging them in a caricature. As a projection of a regressive female sexuality from which any progressive feminist movement would need to separate, the "transvestite" here holds the same inestimable position that the "prior generation" or the "Second Wave" holds for Penny, Ford, and Valenti.

As with the "prior generation" for Penny, Ford, and Valenti, as well, Greer bewails the "transvestite" because it, by definition, serves to stifle women's diverse sexuality. Unlike for Puar, who believes that what makes a body zone ripe for profit is its generating intensification of meaning, for Greer women are made as women by social actions upon them that cut into their being. Like Penny, Ford, and Valenti, Greer can spot the stereotype of repressed femininity that women espouse in response to the male gaze, which she sometimes calls "transvestite," "female eunuch," or castration and says that it alienates women from their womanhood, but unlike them, she does not believe that women can therefore just step out of the society produced by the gaze in an empowered eruption of self-aestheticizing, self-focused, self-expressive, super-heroic speech. Affecting all aspects of a woman's relation to others, repression is inflicted by many different pressures—ideology, psychoanalysis, stereotypes, education, entertainment, advertisement, poetry, family, humor, fashion, religion, medicine, romance (contemporary and classical), marriage, conditioning, art, modes of child rearing, employment, housing, and labor needs (including temp work and domestic labor). For Greer as for Bataille in his theory of general economy,[24] repression is "the suppression and deflection of *Energy*" (18)[25] that creates sociality (based loosely on Freudian repression from *Civilization and Its Discontents*). "[N]ot so very different after all from the impotence of feminine women, who submit to sex without desire" (72), the "transvestite" is a caricature of the production of a socially negating image-meaning. When Greer insists that "transvestites" are not "women," then, she might be suggesting that the "transvestite" is an abstract machine of the gaze that enforces women's social marginalization by reinforcing a stereotype of females whose sexual *Energy*—her difference—is deflected.

For Greer, *Energy* as sociality is suppressed and depleted in all sorts of ways in the enforcement of civilizational norms, but the suppression of *Energy* through the sexual repression of women does not just lead to trauma or individual unhappiness but to a total depletion of civilization (in a Freudian sense): morality, responsibility, modes of living together. Tied to social institutions and signifying systems, loss of *Energy* is de-sexualization, de-intellectualization, and de-socialization at the same time.

> [I]t is exactly the element of quest in her sexuality which the female is taught to deny. She is not only taught to deny it in her sexual contacts, but . . . in all her contacts, from infancy onward, so that when she becomes aware of her sex the pattern has sufficient force of inertia to prevail over new forms of desire and curiosity. (78)

---

[24] "That as a rule, an organism has at its disposal greater energy resources than are necessary for the operations that sustain life (functional activities and, in animals, essential muscular exercises, the search for food) is evident from functions like growth and reproduction. Neither growth nor reproduction would be possible if plants and animals did not normally dispose of an excess. The very principle of living matter requires that the chemical operations of life, which demand an expenditure of energy, be gainful, productive of surpluses" (27).

[25] Bataille writes, "I insist on the fact that there is generally no growth but only a luxurious squandering of energy in every form!"

Desexualization is anti-sociality, accepting immobility, inertia, and predictable modes of behavior without imagination or curiosity. Repression is countered by *Energy*. Energy is not an individual pursuit, a personalized security system, or an expression for self-gratification or self-enrichment. Rather, by including what "older sisters might teach us what they found out" so that we "learn from each other's experience" (369), it is a gathering of knowledge in excess of the "congenital pathological condition" of "egotistic morality" (83).

Neither an individual experience nor an entrepreneurial one, *Energy* is revolution, and what such a revolution entails is women's quest for sexuality and joy that would, at the same time, destroy the restraints of dimorphous sex roles, redistributing rights, power, and association in the interests of freedom. Freedom, she notes, is "insecurity" (274)—that is, the shedding off of familiar sex roles that deny life and getting rid of habits that provide stability by refusing the unknown. "Women should reject the advertising that seeks to draw millions of pounds out of them each Christmas" (364), she explains. Also, women must no longer have the sole responsibility for childrearing, and if "women are to effect a significant amelioration in their condition it seems obvious that they must refuse to marry" (358), and therefore the "cunt must come into its own" (356). Revolution might mean that there is no longer "woman," and for this, Greer revisits the "transvestite" more sympathetically, as a potential breaker of the social structure that depends on the sexual subordination of women: The "transvestite," Greer acknowledges, "may be understood as revolt against the limitations of the female role of passivity, hypocrisy and indirect action, as well as rejection of the brutality and mechanicalness of male sexual passion" (330). Yet this "transvestite" does not go far enough in opposing normality by unleashing difference, because the violence, insult, and shame inflicted on her impose a relation to the norms of a gender-dimorphous sociality and the repression of *Energy*. Revolution would, then, be an opening toward freeing the difference inside from the violence that wants to keep it static under static social and symbolic sexual form.

The regressiveness that the "Third Wave" attributed to the "prior generation" corresponds considerably with the repressiveness that Greer identifies with the social structure. For the structural analysis that Greer and many other feminists engaged for understanding the domination of women, she therefore borrowed social scientific methods, including social philosophers' informing the New Left. Freud's model of civilization depends on a thermodynamic balance of energy, where energy is withdrawn from sexual function so that it can be used toward not only civilizational processes like work but also neurosis and psychosis. Energy is an expression of a human need for security developing from infantile helplessness. In Freud's account, women, as expenditures of energy, stand in the way of men's use of energy for civilizational purposes and so are "forced into the background by the claims of civilization" (51).

Like Bataille, Frankfurt School thinkers like Herbert Marcuse and Erich Fromm adapted Freud's energy model for political analysis, asking why "men"—as Fromm posits the problem—submit their "vital energy" (5)—creativity and freedom—to oppressive political forms like Fascism. Fear of what Freud labels the "irrational"—of drives, instincts, passions, anxieties, aloneness, freedom, and the Unconscious—according to Fromm, leads "Man" to sublimate this Energy in culture and sociality, for the purpose of self-preservation and security, and both the solitude and the reaction to it intensify in modernity. The increasing isolation induced by modernity—its loss of community and a resultant increasing individuation—generates a crisis out of that fear and a growing insecurity as well as a search for security. Often "man" puts his fear of loneliness and insecurity onto a punishing outer object, inducing feelings of powerlessness by projecting overwhelming power onto this outside force. This "inner compulsion" is "effective in harnessing all energies to work" (94). At times, too, it is harnessed onto not only political symbols that promise everlastingness but also commodity objects and energy fields—atomic, mechanic, cybernetic, industrial (xiv) —that, in the name of planetary self-preservation, could lead to total annihilation. One of the causes Fromm cites to explain such sublimation is "the so-called castration complex in women" (9).

The Female Eunuch represents Germaine Greer's investigations into the social forms taken by the sexual repression of women and the sublimation of their *Energy* into various social and cultural objects of oppression. Fromm does not study "Man's" psychology separated from a sociality in the mode of the bloggers, but rather he studies "the specific kind of relatedness of the individual towards the world" (10), which changes over time in response to historical productive needs and the related "*differences* in men's characters" (original emphasis; 10). In keeping, the freedom of character *differences*, in *The Female Eunuch*, is connected to the historicity of the social system itself with its division of labor, its damaging stereotypes, its restrictive moral codes, and its modes of ideological conditioning. You are a woman or a man because of social repression, not in spite of it; you will be *something else* once the *Energy* finds different outlets. *The Female Eunuch* describes the social system that comes about, at a particular historical moment, through the repression of a multiplicity of needs, drives, and energies and their sublimation into a form of authority—the symbolic structure called "woman"—that dominates them. Greer's point, like Fromm's, is that modernity makes freedom into "an unbearable burden" (Fromm, 35) that can either, repressed, energize the current oppressive social relations formed around the realization of "women" as waste or create *something else*.

If Greer represents a form of feminist thinking from a "prior generation," then the "Third Wave" has a lot more in common with it than the "wave" paradigm of history admits. Her idea that the sexual repression of women is what creates "women" as a social category, erasing differences, dovetails significantly with the "Third Wave" idea that sexual experiences are controlled by others, through violence and the gaze. Yet the dissimilarities between the two viewpoints are also noteworthy. In the "Third Wave" outlook, social violence can be countered by aesthetic expression, body love, therapy, resilient self-help, inspiration, independence, or writing as a feminist (which is all of these things), whereas, for Greer, the sexual repression of women takes on many guises in many images, narratives, and the institutional organization of signification (including the history of literature, art, and philosophy) and can only be countered by informed feminist social movements. Whereas, for the bloggers, "feminism" is a therapeutic lifeline that gives individuals security against the social violence targeting them from the inheritance of the "prior generation," for Greer, "feminism" would create insecurity, as it would overturn durable language forms that secure identities, social hierarchies, and institutions inflict. Whereas, for the bloggers, the social can only be violent and against them—a punitive, overwhelming power partaking of some of the same features as the castrating phallic mother of psychoanalysis—for Greer, violence is repressed by social institutions, the language that organizes and controls them, and the subjectivities they engender, and so can be de-sublimated as *Energy* and unleashed in revolt.

Feminism has certainly been strengthened through analyses that recognize the diversity of experiences and the various ways that identities are made for the purpose of intensifying productivities. Yet a politics of identity and difference, as Nancy Fraser has argued, has combined with a meritocratic politics of choice and self-reliant subjects shackled to the hegemonic forms of market energies. The idea of the feminist as an isolated monadic hero with a keyboard and a modem set to fend off the monstrous, repressive forces of social castration shares a general outlook with a broader neoliberal culture where the resilience of the subject stands alone and apart from the sociality that brought that subject to be and still conditions that subject's survival. There is no doubt that gender is radically changing and reorganizing and, at the same time, that feminism is having a resurgence. Even as not long ago, in the early aughts, Governor Jeb Bush of Florida could proudly proclaim to marchers and activists that the Equal Rights Amendment (ERA) was outdated like bell-bottoms, young women and men today are wearing T-shirts and "pussy hats" extolling feminism, putting pro-feminist bumper stickers on their cars, Black Lives Matter has captured the headlines and the streets, and the ERA is back on the table. The United States has just elected a female vice president for the first time. Even *The New York Times* marked International Women's Day in 2018 by recognizing that women die too and their deaths should be honored in *New York Times* obituaries. Indeed, on International Women's Day in 2018, 5.3 million Spanish women stopped working, causing an economic slowdown. In Ireland, voters approved a referendum that legalized abortion. There have been marches of thousands of women in Brazil, large movements against sexual violence in India, crowds of women turning up in protest to argue against their government's repressions of reproductive freedoms in Poland, and the "Ni Una Menos" (Not One Less) movement in Argentina (against femicides and domestic abuse) has succeeded in bringing abortion legalization bills to the legislative floor. A number of social movements have arisen around the world that reference feminism and women's rights, including one in Saudi Arabia, where women were finally allowed to drive, to travel without permission, and to jog in public (even though women's rights activists remained incarcerated). Women protestors at the US Supreme Court were right to hold up red signs saying "Feminists Are the Majority."

The question that confronts us is whether the sort of feminism that has arisen in the political emergency of our present is adequate to that emergency. With sexual harassers being called out and women "leaning in" to achieve work-family balance, more women being elected to political office, more women CEOs, and superheroes like Wonder Woman, Furiosa, and Katniss Everdeen kicking the world's butt to secure the world's survival, why would "Third Wave" blogger Andrea Long Chu still define "female" as "the part of ourselves that we hate most," that is, "any psychic operation in which the self is sacrificed to make room for the desires of another" (22)? What does it mean that "the part of ourselves that we hate most" is the part of ourselves that relates most to others, the social now portrayed as our enemy?

2

Uses and Abuses of "Choice" Feminism

This chapter looks at two recent US films—Rick Rosenthal's 2013 *Drones* and Ana Lily Amirpour's 2014 *A Girl Walks Home Alone at Night*—to discuss the intersections between feminism and neoliberalism. It argues that images of feminist-influenced independent women promote neoliberal ideologies of resilience and public-sector critique, glossing with a glowing, optimistic aura neoliberalism's policies of privatization, technological expansion, reproductive control, and cuts in workforce supports. The protagonists of both these films are feminist "success" stories: In *Drones*, Sue works as a combat pilot, a commanding officer in the US Air Force serving as a drone operator in the Iraq War; in *A Girl*, the vampire rises above familial, religious, and cultural controls on women by means of sexual dominance. In both cases, this feminist inflection of their characters drives the plot by creating a conflict between the character and her social and cultural environment, which she leaves in ruins. In both cases, as with the "Third Wave" bloggers of Chapter 1, the feminist hero needs to separate from her social context because the social context itself is a death-dealing horror show, whether in war as in the case of *Drones* or in environmental degradation due to the fallout of industrialization in *A Girl*.

These feminist "success" stories integrate with neoliberal success stories, as the feminist victory is also a neoliberal victory: In *Drones*, Sue's professional autonomy, her acceptance into the technological workforce, overlays the victory of technological means over local cultures and kinships; in *A Girl*, the vampire's sexual autonomy is the means of defeating the backward industrialist policies of the Iranian Islamist/nationalist regime and launching an economic opening that would include deregulation and population control. By "neoliberalism," I mean the ideological backing of policy directed toward reductions in state, regulatory, and developmental supports, increased financialization and austerity, and the transfer of public functions into private—mostly corporate—hands: the shrinking of the "soft arm" of state policy in favor of the "strong arm" of military and police violence, allowing the transfer of wealth upward.

Though the *effects* of what I call "neoliberalism" are different in different regions, its messaging tends to promote some narrative features that the "Third Wave" bloggers of Chapter 1 also embraced: a heroic individualism available to everyone, despite their differences, by their own efforts and a social system that, on its own, is ineffectual, falling apart, and trying but failing, through horror film tactics, to kill the individual's initiative and choice. I am certainly not inferring that *all* feminism is neoliberal; instead, I am arguing that neoliberal hegemonies absorb cultural tendencies, like feminism, as points of identification. Like the commodity, such cultural tendencies, repurposed for neoliberalism, offer stability, happiness, and fulfillment for a subject caught inside a world in the process of destroying stability, happiness, and fulfillment through war and technologization, in the one case, and deindustrialization and economic liberalization in the other. Feminism needs to invigorate success stories that do not grant triumph to neoliberal autonomy or inclusion against a social system that neoliberal ideologies have vilified and framed as destructive and wasteful.

The neoliberal appropriation and redesign of feminism are certainly under the critical radar. As Catherine Rottenberg, for example, remarks, even as they reduce public supports for an equality that would allow most women to "have it all," neoliberal ideologies advance within images of women who "have it all" in "work/family balance": "The dizzyingly [*sic*] pace at which so many high-powered women have embraced feminism is unprecedented. No form of feminism has ever been welcomed and championed by iconic, mainstream, and highly visible figures as the current form" (13). In fact, the popular belief that feminism is all about "work/family" balance in the professional workplace is so widespread that Kim Brooks in *The New York Times* ridiculously declared the "failure" of feminism when the coronavirus pandemic exposed—as never before, she infers—the "work/family" balance as unachievable. Brooks finds evidence for this framing of feminism in the 1980s Hollywood blockbusters *Aliens* (with Sigourney Weaver) and *Baby Boom* (with Diane Keaton). Brooks' opinion piece testifies to *The New York Times*' sudden discovery of what most women knew already: that Hollywood's version of feminism had very little affinity with most women's experiences with work and life. Feminism is not only—and not even predominantly—about creating more opportunities for women in an exclusionary professional workplace invested in maintaining the hierarchies of a class society, and it is not only—and not even predominantly—about individual achievement and advancement in a rigged meritocracy but also—Brooks seems unaware—about opposing both a geopolitics of gender-based inequality and the ideological support maintaining that geopolitics.

The misuses of feminism to build neoliberal hegemony are legion. One example is *The New York Times*' celebration of Saudi Arabia's embrace of "women's rights" in an article that lauds the achievement of women's entry into the workforce as baristas, low-earning and low-skilled service to a cosmopolitan consumerist elite. *The New York Times* recognizes this change, using feminist vocabulary, as a boost to "self-esteem" (Yee) because it gives women workers a choice of what to wear. As Susan Watkins explains, feminism has been absorbed as "a mantra of the global establishment" (5), becoming an ethical rallying cry for the expansion of global power and losing some of its critical edge even as its following surges. Though Catherine Rottenberg recognizes that what she calls "choice feminism" has become "increasingly compatible with neoliberal and neoconservative political and economic agendas" (11), by fostering a calculative rationalism in lifestyle choice, a neoliberal use of feminist themes must also be understood as helping to fuel the projection of US corporate and military power around the world.

This chapter looks at feminism's visibility as it is appropriated to shape neoliberalism's self-image. While in the late 1970s we may have learned from Laura Mulvey that the masculine cinematic gaze fetishizes woman-as-image, we are now seeing neoliberalism itself fetishized as feminist by the woman in the image. I analyze this phenomenon in two recent films where neoliberalism's ideologies appear as feminist. The first, *Drones*, stars Eloise Mumford as Sue Lawson, daughter of a four-star general, who, as a recently commissioned US Air Force lieutenant, gets assigned as a drone operator because of a physical handicap. Her main duty is to monitor inside the home of a family in Iraq as the members are projected on a screen in a trailer at Creech Air Force Base in the Nevada desert. The film shows the success of the feminist ideal of including women in the professional, technological workforce as officers. The second film, *A Girl Walks Home Alone at Night*, is a 2014 début feature directed by British filmmaker of Iranian descent and US resident Ana Lily Amirpour in the mode of the Iranian New Wave (her parents fled Iran after the Revolution and arrived in Kent; they moved to Miami when she was eight; her first trip to Tehran was in 2003). Shot in Farsi from Taft, California, and funded through crowd-sourcing on *Indiegogo* (where Margaret Atwood was one of the first to donate part of the initial $57,000[1]), this movie captures the postindustrial landscape of post-Revolutionary Iran in a spaghetti-Western, ghost-town, avant-garde aesthetic with a vampire theme. Whereas *Drones* takes up the problem of feminism as women enter the workforce, *A Girl Walks Home Alone at Night* shows how feminist discourses of sexual autonomy work to make sense of neoliberal hegemony, making women responsible for controlling population. While extolling women's sexual and reproductive autonomy in the face of local culture and religious controls over reproduction, the film presents the reproducing body as blamable for social deaths caused by public disinvestments. Both films offer neoliberalized feminist identities as a stability against social chaos, even though neoliberalism would be the cause of such social chaos. I argue that images of feminist-influenced independent women advance neoliberal ideologies of resilience and public-sector critique; its policies of privatization, technological expansion, and cuts in workforce supports; its heroic hyperindividualism; and its policies of depopulation and dispossession. With their striving for ethical, sexual, and economic autonomy against oppositional forces of social control, feminist characters offer a means for neoliberalism to capture reproductive economies as apparent points of freedom within its unfree consumerist, market logics.

Images of feminist women can unleash the ideological forces behind neoliberalism's hegemonic rise. Indeed, neoliberal ideologies *use* women, and particularly feminist women, to affirm social relations that attest to its

---

[1] Much of this filmography information is cited from Danny Leigh's interview with Amirpour: "The Skateboarding Iranian Vampire Diaries," *The Guardian* (May 7, 2015), https://www.theguardian.com/film/2015/may/07/skateboarding-iranian-vampire-ana-lily-amirpour-feminism-porn-girl-walks-home-alone-at-night.

ascendance and proclaim its success,[2] especially where "social" and "natural" reproduction can be seen as the frontline of the struggle over resources and the formation of subjects. Contemporary feminism supplies an array of visual and narrative tropes that exalt women's autonomy and resilience as an "advance" beyond socially embedded reproduction—often coded as local, traditional, or unreasonable (non-calculating)—or an overburdened, overreaching, regulation-saddled nationalist state.

On a global scale, neoliberalism is modeled as feminist primarily in five areas: neoliberalism profits from feminism's interest in bringing women into the workforce, especially into the technological workforce; from feminism's interest in women exercising control over their own sexuality and reproductive rights with the outcome of lower birth rates, especially in poorer nations; from feminism's criticisms of the reproductive economy's relationships to the productive economy and the state in the age of industrialization, welfare, and after; from feminism's critique of the state; and from feminism's affirmation of positive identity to support these prior agendas.[3] By "reproductive economy," I mean here the relics of the (usually unpaid) arrangements—or intimate relations—that, under industrialization, prepared the worker for the next day of work and also assisted in preparing the next generation of laborers, as well as the welfare state's supports and protections for such socializing processes. As Aihwa Ong has shown, under neoliberalism, such private, domestic, reproductive identities are manipulated into exchangeable privatized "work." For example, as women professionals in, for example, the tech economy have been absorbed into production in tech-rich countries like Singapore, women "care" workers are recruited from poorer nations like Malaysia and the Philippines, their identities reenvisioned with "moral guarantees of biological welfare"

---

[2] As British cultural theorist Angela McRobbie, for example, observes, girls' "capacity, success, attainment, enjoyment, entitlement, social mobility and participation" have all become export values proving the value of economic resilience in neoliberalism's ideology of self-reliant meritocracy. "Nowadays," she notes, "the young woman's success seems to promise economic prosperity on the basis of her enthusiasm for work and having a career" ("Top Girls," 722).

[3] Lisa Duggan, for example, highlights how corporatist agendas have strengthened and spread partly by hardening identity hierarchies: Neoliberals, she maintains, "make use of identity politics to obscure redistributive aims" (15).

(179) by prohibitions on sex, promotion of affective dispositions associated with submissiveness, and policed leisure time. As Fraser, Bhattacharya, and Arruzza phrase it, "the making of people is treated as a mere means to the making of profit" (22) as this system "free-rides on nature, public goods, and the unwaged work that reproduces human beings and communities" (17). Today, as evidenced in, for example, the "work/family" balance, the tasks of social reproduction are being increasingly left to the individual with a superpowerful individual responsibility divorced from social bonds or supports. Dumping responsibility for socialization singularly on mothers and their caregiver surrogates overburdens women with extending the promise of future social well-being and security both nationally and internationally even while the withdrawal of public resources to support socialization and care has led to increasing precarity and insecurity. Women can appear "feminist" for taking on by themselves responsibility for global political failure.

In fashioning the superpowerful and super-responsible individual, neoliberal feminist ideology works to erase the social bonds that form the conditions for the social reproduction of that individuality. Mothers can be blamed for all sorts of crises that are intensified in the absence of social bonds and their socializing institutions. Particularly in film, a deficiency of social provisions for safety and security is made visible and narratable through the mother's failures, as is a skepticism about the reproductive economy's abilities to care for life's precarities. Promoted by Hollywood, stories of escape from the mother—the outcome of the individual's effort and excellence, and the road to autonomy—extend globally as a "feel good" moral gloss, a defense for a global politics of shrinking government supports and the shrinking developmental state. For example, in the wake of revelations of mogul film producer Harvey Weinstein's decades-long serial sexual assault of women in the industry, the list of 2018 US Academy Award nominees included four films focused on maternal abuse of daughters: Greta Gerwig's *Lady Bird*, Allison Janney's *I, Tonya*, Martin McDonagh's *Three Billboards Outside Ebbing, Missouri*, and Sean Baker's *The Florida Project*.[4] In

---

[4] The top awards finally went to (arguably anti-feminist) films with men-directors (Guillermo del Toro won Best Director for his childish fantasy-film saccharine romance *The Shape of Water* that also won for Best Picture).

these films, the mother provides an inadequate response to the burgeoning feminist character's internalized emotional or developmental pain, suggesting the marginalization of the social (and the inadequate mother too) to the daughter's triumphant narrative. The films recognized by the Academy also held mothers responsible for not creating a safe world for their daughters, where these mothers appeared marred by their obsessive ties to sociality: The "prior generation" was deficient, negligent, unaware, and even complicit in patriarchal violence, and their daughters can only escape by, for example, becoming a global figure-skating celebrity in *I, Tonya* or running off to Disneyland in the case of *The Florida Project*, or the crimes against them can only be adjudicated with recourse to traditional modes of advertising or in arbitrary vigilante violence as in *Three Billboards*. Through undoing the maternal function, the Academy's preferred films thus blamed traditional and socialized structures of reproductive labor and family control for a host of social ills—from malaise and sexual frustration to financial tightening, physical endangerment, alienation, murder, rape, and poverty—and offered instead commercialization and spectacle as a future of greater safety and inclusion for the maturing girls.[5]

In a context where imperial interventions have been executed professedly for the defense of women's sexual freedom,[6] where birth control including

---

[5] In neoliberal cultures, the maternal bond replaces the social bond, thereby holding individuals such as mothers and women workers responsible for social ills ranging from overpopulation, poverty, and dependency to educational failure, unemployment, and marginalization. We see this in the language of immigration, where mothers are held responsible for illegally bringing their children across the border when the violence inflicted on their home communities was what was responsible for putting their children at risk. Feminist theory does not need to and should not accept the terms neoliberalism offers of a feminism threatened by social bonding. One technique for rejecting neoliberalism's anti-maternalism would be to refuse the frame, as does Chantal Akerman in her 2015 film *No Home Movie* about her mother's death. In that film, the mother is often filmed off to the side, in low angle, outside of the frame or in partial frame, through a video screen, or from the back, and finally disappears from the frame altogether as the living room is filmed too low and off to the side but empty and the camera lingers, as though the emptiness was always there and waiting. The mother is never situated inside a narrative of causation—as, for example, the *cause* of the daughter's pain and rejection. Another example might be Taylor Sheridan's 2017 *Wind River*, which got no mention from the Academy though it came out in the same year as "#MeToo" and, like the films named above, foregrounded a critique of sexual abuse and murder of young girls, but, unlike the films named above, blamed it on US racist policies in relation to First Nations, on corporate exploitation of nature and greed, and on development policy rather than on mothers.

[6] Talking about the news coverage leading up to the start of the US war in Afghanistan as well as First Lady Laura Bush's address to the nation, anthropologist Lila Abu-Lughod emphasizes, "What is striking about these . . . ideas for news programs is that there was a consistent resort to the cultural,

nonconsensual surgeries is often used on marginalized women in order to curtail population growth, where women employees still get paid 0.75 on the dollar and often have no recourse from harassment, and where microfinance has often indebted women through their work, Hollywood's response to "#MeToo" commodifies feminist autonomy and feminist dissent as fixes to the problems that a socially embedded and publicly supported reproductive economy inflicts on children. As a popular feminism has recharacterized the victories of feminism's past as social dangers, feminist sexual and work autonomy is appropriable for spreading the message of the benefits of US imperialism, corporate expansion, and market fundamentalism. This chapter considers global cinema's vision of a neoliberal feminism that transcends social-embedded reproductive economies in favor of a resilient, commodified independence.

Neoliberalism and Feminist Critique

Some recent feminist scholarship is concerned with how the construction of gender in feminism, but not only in feminism, reorganizes gender to facilitate neoliberalism's advances into reproductive economies, often to the detriment of women. Neoliberalism has different effects in different settings, but it spans geographies on the back of hegemonic ideas. Such ideas usually pit the individual against society, repackaging this relationship as if society were a death-delivering bloodsucker out to stifle the individual's economic potentials. As Nancy Fraser aptly puts it, "the cultural changes jump-started by the second wave, salutary in themselves, have served to

---

as if knowing something about women and Islam or the meaning of a religious ritual would help one understand the tragic attack on New York's World Trade Center and the U.S. Pentagon" (784). She goes on to draw a connection between this coverage and the history of colonialism in the region: "Many who have worked on British Colonialism in South Asia have noted the use of the woman question in colonial policies where intervention into sati (the practice of widows immolating themselves on their husbands' funeral pyres), child marriage, and other practices was used to justify [British] rule" (784). Laura Bush had said in a TV appearance: " 'Because of our recent military gains in much of Afghanistan, women are no longer imprisoned in their homes. They can listen to music and teach their daughters with fear of punishment. . . . The fight against terrorism is also a fight for the rights and dignity of women'" (784).

legitimate a structural transformation of capitalist society that runs directly counter to feminist visions of society" ("Cunning," 99). For Fraser, not only was feminism's critique of culture and the social adopted into neoliberal ideologies (and twisted to blame that culture for inequality), but it also took up feminism's critique of economism (framing social questions as market issues or acceptance into a hierarchical economic system as it stood) and the family wage, an ideological cushioning for neoliberalism's "reducing state action *tout court*" ("Cunning," 111). Women were disproportionately absorbed into low-pay or low-skilled jobs, while the NGO-ification of services, short-term financial investments, and microcredit in the Third World filled "the space vacated by shrinking states" ("Cunning," 111) by incorporating the home into production and marketing. The "independence" that feminism sought for women was likewise appropriated in the growth of contract labor and eventually the gig economy: Workers would be more responsible for supplying their own work provisions, conditions, and tools (without contracts or unions), while worker supports and benefits would cease being the responsibility of employers within a public regulatory framework. Feminism's critique of state-organized capitalism helped "to legitimate the flexible neoliberal capitalism of our time" ("Cunning," 109). In short, says Fraser, "capitalism periodically remakes itself in moments of historical rupture, in part by recuperating strands of critique against it" ("Cunning," 109).

Looking at the global context of feminism's rise, Susan Watkins, as well, chronicles a feminist agenda from the early 1970s to restructure existing institutions and think differently about the social reproductive spheres— to "include" women in public life and grant them sexual and economic autonomy. This feminist common sense dovetailed with a neoliberalism that needed more labor flexibility and more self-reliance for reproducing labor. A feminism that set out to dismantle institutions based on unfair social redistributive policies thereby turned into an antidiscrimination feminism, according to Watkins— sponsored by the Ford Foundation, among others— that advocated for women to enter existing institutions without substantial changes: "what might be called actually existing neoliberalism—the practice of corporations committed to shareholder agendas," notes Watkins, "—came to see advantages in the active promotion of women" (15). As the social world into which women entered was reshaped along neoliberalist lines often counter to most women's needs, women and feminism both became an integral part of that power structure.

The feminism that gained steam in the 1970s when numerous women entered the workforce coincides with the history of neoliberalism that David Harvey, among others, dates likewise from the early 1970s, with its Milton Friedman-esque anti-statist market fundamentalisms taking shape in response to the bankruptcy of New York City, the oil crisis, the end of the developmental state, the war on crime, and cuts to the regulatory state.[7] In response to the crisis, workers were forced to give up their share of profits through losses in wages, health care, retirement provisions, and other parts of their reproductive employment compensation, and make up the difference by borrowing it back. For this, neoliberalism, as David Harvey has remarked frequently, needed the military,[8] as much to capture public and productive territories as to capitalize on the generation of subjects and control citizens.[9] One of neoliberalism's techniques is the inclusion of women in the technological and combative workplace, which was gradually achieved from the 1970s on.[10]

As women were lured into the workforce by neoliberal ideology's false promises of fulfillment through autonomy, capital openly made incursions into domestic space, family intimacies, and population development. Additionally, the feminist espousal of birth control as opening the possibilities of women's sexual autonomy has been reinterpreted to mean that women alone are

---

[7] As Harvey explicates the main difference between liberalism and neoliberalism that arose in the seventies: "under the former lenders take the losses that arise from bad investment decisions, while under the latter borrowers are forced by state and international powers to take on board the cost of debt repayment no matter what the consequences for the livelihood and well-being of the local population" (29).

[8] "The coercive arm of the state," notes Harvey, meaning the police, the prisons, and the army, "is augmented to protect corporate interests and, if necessary, to repress dissent" (David Harvey, *A Brief History of Neoliberalism* (Oxford, UK and New York: Oxford University Press, 2005), 77).

[9] See my *Gender for the Warfare State: Literature of Women in Combat* (Routledge, 2016).

[10] At the same time, militarization shapes identities and interprets bodies. As Jasbir Puar states, "Militarized bodies are crafted through the dissemination and diffusion of control" (*Terrorist Assemblages*, 156). In neoliberalism, Puar continues, people acquire an intimacy with enforcement mechanisms, an intimacy which prepares bodies and minds for participation in containment policies.

responsible for the repercussions not only of their sexual acts but also for the full range of reproductive care perhaps once widely understood as a social concern. Even though both Angela Davis and Adrienne Rich warned that a feminist movement for reproductive rights needs to be careful to disassociate itself from the eugenic racism of "population control" in sterilization campaigns (Rich, xix) like the one in 1960s Bolivia, today population as a pressure on the environment has elicited a feminist response that makes women responsible for depopulation as part of global feminist agendas. A feminist as prominent as Donna Haraway has saddled feminism with reducing population in the face of environmental collapse, burdening feminism with the onus of planetary redemption by advancing the slogan "Make Kin Not Babies!" (*Staying with the Trouble*, 102). In the face of structural adjustment programs enforced by the International Monetary Fund (IMF) and the World Bank as well as credit crunches under the Volcker plan—worsening economic conditions disproportionately to women—World Bank and US policy has sought to use "women's empowerment" as a mechanism for boosting economic growth by reducing fertility rates. While First World feminism's emphasis on liberation through sexuality ushered in population control through birth control to the benefit, as Susan Watkins points out, of Big Pharma (45), sterilization was often imposed on women of color and women in poorer countries[11] to control the numbers of what Marx called "the reserve army of labor" and to diminish state and corporate responsibility for the economically marginalized and the dispossessed. Concern over population, as Hannah Arendt pointed out, involves a decision over "who should and who should not inhabit the world" (*Eichmann*, 279). Arendt was protesting Eichmann and the Nazis' illegitimate sovereign appropriation of this decision, leading into her lifelong thinking on participatory politics. Twisting feminist politicization of reproductive rights issues, this sovereign decision over population has been refashioned, under the dominance of neoliberal ideology, as a responsibility of mothers and the

---

[11] "An integrative feminist politics of reproduction was reduced to decorative support for pharmaceutical companies and population controllers. Numerical targets for implants and sterilizations—the polar opposite of a woman's right to choose—still drove policy on the ground." Susan Watkins, "Which Feminisms?" *New Left Review* 109 (January/February 2018): 45.

excessive fecundity of their reproducing bodies, thereby positioning mothers as blamable for social failure.

In the neoliberal response to overpopulation, feminism has become an alibi for public disinvestment. According to Susan Watkins, the belief that the US-led global feminism is a myth; actually, during a time in the early 1970s when the price of oil was high and the United States was still reeling from defeats in Vietnam, African and Arab feminist movements called for national control over resources to defend against the incursion of foreign corporate interests. A corporate backlash and appropriation ensued, consisting of a World Bank "feminist turn" focused on private-sector growth with the extension of microcredit and contraception as its stated goals, thereby targeting religious states primarily. "'[W]omens empowerment,'" Watkins sums up the World Bank's position, "would boost economic growth and could help to reduce fertility rates" (41). In particular, the 1994 Cairo Programme "directed the bulk of funds towards long-acting contraception programmes" (44) without any improvements to health care, child mortality, or social services. In this logic, women's bodies as reproductive capacities are at fault for the bloated budgets that have led to both economic and ecological decline, not corporate-favored policies of upward redistribution, tax cuts, social spending cuts, privatization, deregulation, and the like. The World Bank solution is to put onto women the responsibility for securing future productivity by bearing fewer children. As Rashmi Varma has argued, this moment of feminism "rolls back the many significant gains that were made in those earlier decades by anti-imperialist feminists, a decline that meshes with the more general diminishing of the Third World project today and is aligned with a dilution of genuine internationalism as borders close in on refugees and migrants" (463–4).

There have been a number of critics who have interrogated how maternity circulates as an ideological lever for neoliberal cuts, economic restructuring, and individual responsibilization. As Jacqueline Rose asks, "what are we doing to mothers—when we expect them to carry the burden of everything that is hardest to contemplate about our society and ourselves?" (1). "Sex and sexuality now are not the essential property of the subject," Paul Preciado explains, "but rather the product of various social, discursive technologies, political practices of controlling truth and life. . . . Maternity is just one possible use of the body, among others. It's not a guarantee of sexual difference, or femininity" (*Apartment on Uranus*, 99). Catherine Rottenberg has, too, noticed a corporate messaging seizing feminism and mothering within neoliberal ideals in "the commodification and the depoliticization of motherhood" where "parenting problems are the result of problematic individual choices" (113). Angela McRobbie, meanwhile, equates the "rehabilitation of feminism" ("Feminism, the Family. . . ," 120) under neoliberalism with a maternalism that emphasizes "self-responsibility, entrepreneurialism" to "enhance the core values of the neoliberal project" ("Feminism, the Family. . . ," 121). Particularly non-white mothers, Sophie Lewis adds, "can practically do no right and carry the blame for every social problem even as they receive no economic incentive whatsoever to perform motherhood 'better'" (114). Neoliberalism's corporatism spreads across the globe, according to McRobbie, by making mothers responsible for the insecurities ensuing from the gutting of the social safety net. McRobbie specifies that the "empowerment" of the entrepreneurial mother is in part, after 9/11, formed in opposition to "the imagined other, the Muslim woman assumed to be oppressed and subjected to various forms of domination and control" (("Feminism, the Family. . . ," 121–2). In this view, the entrepreneurial mother is envisioned as an evolutionary step upward, on top of the hierarchy, because she is able to "have it all" in a "work/family balance," superior to the woman whose choices and mobility are the targets of religious fundamentalist regressive patriarchies with their regulations on the family. With the nationalist state as a foil for the "freedom" promised in neoliberal ideology, constituted as commanding the growth of families in excess to what its command-economy can provide, the passive backwardness of the Islamist woman without choice is, in this logic, the proof of secular progress elsewhere promised in market integration.

There have been few treatments of how the birth rate and population controls are filters for neoliberal ideas, where women's bodies are invested with the interests of capital in removing the birth of the unwanted and the dependent from habitation in the world. One exception may be Penelope Deutscher. She asks, "how does reproduction come to present as a mode of responsibility toward 'population' or its future?" (78). Her interest is in the production "of female subjects understood as having the capacity to propagate death" (65).[12] Though Deutscher talks about how unhealthy situations are attributed to "deficient mothering" (93) and "deficient mothering" is held responsible for "the quality of the population and the nation's strength" (96). Through this, she foregrounds the ideological role of the mother under neoliberalism in making lives precarious. Women's reproducing bodies here constitute a division between desirable and undesirable lives, and women can be blamed for economic scarcities—particularly ones that target precarious populations like immigrants—that should be laid in the lap of bankers and financers. My interest here is in how such a heroic feminist narrative around the capacity of women's bodies to populate, depopulate, and work justifies neoliberalism's transnational productivities by transferring the responsibility for negative externalities and social decline onto local cultures.

Drones

> No government exclusively based on the means of violence has ever existed.
> Even the totalitarian ruler, whose chief instrument of rule is torture, needs a
> power basis—the secret police and its net of informers. Only the development
> of robot soldiers, which, as previously mentioned, would eliminate the human
> factor completely and, conceivably, permit one man with a push button to
> destroy whomever he pleased, could change this fundamental ascendency of
> power over violence.
>
> —Hannah Arendt, *Crisis of the Republic* (149)

Drone warfare is seemingly bodiless. One might argue that this is its point. As Grégoire Chamayou has contended in his philosophy of drones, drones

---

[12] Deutscher looks at neoliberalism with a different frame than mine, though still useful. Her focus is on understanding reproductive and abortion rights politics as about not just a transfer of sovereign decision from the state to the individual but also a biopolitics or "thanopolitics," a politics of death. "[T]he family," she writes, "is a zone of risk. As the space of the child's desirable survival, it also becomes the context for calculating its likelihood of death" (93). She goes on, "I have argued that to see reproduction and parenting taking shape as technologies targeting the health and optimization of individual and population futures is to see them concurrently taking shape as parallel technologies of death, with corresponding conducts including averting, managing, gridding, stimulating, predicting, distributing, and proliferating" (114).

make it "a priori impossible to die as one kills" (13). Drones, as Chamayou defines them, are "flying, high-resolution video cameras armed with missiles" that "allow you to project power without projecting vulnerability" (12). In accordance with the neoliberalism that is part of their historical context, drones are an instrumentalized (militarized) replacement for democratic political sovereignty, removed from human affairs, destroying their law. Because of drone warfare's bodilessness, states engaging in it, Chamayou continues, can disengage from needing to convince citizens that the ideological causes of the war are worth the sacrifice. In other words, militarized states take over the role of reproducing bodies for work formerly assigned to softer socialized sides of the apparatus. Chamayou called this "democratic militarization": "Once warfare became ghostly and teleguided, citizens, who no longer risked their lives, would no longer have a say in it" (188). Drone warfare is the ascendance of a means-ends logic of violence over politics and the sociality of subject reproduction that, says Chamayou, has already changed the political landscape.

In terms that Chamayou shares with Hannah Arendt, drone warfare leads to the automation of violent means that are justified by their own recurrences rather than by ideological constructions: Violence takes over the social. Bypassing the need to call out citizens' consent, this substitution of means-ends logic for politics and sociality promises both foreign and domestic policies steeped in command, retaliation, and effectivity. What concerns Arendt (and what Chamayou underscores as already present) is that technological rationality—total militarization—could take over all rationality, thinking, deliberation, and education. She particularly worries that when matters of the body or of identity surface as inside the means-ends logic of tools, politics—indeed, life—gets shut down: "The most powerful necessity of which we are aware in self-introspection," she notes in her discussion of historical turns against the politics of freedom,

> is the life process which permeates our bodies and keeps them in a constant state of a change whose movements are automatic, independent of our own activities, and irresistible—i.e., of an overwhelming urgency. The less we are doing ourselves, the less active we are, the more forcefully will this biological process assert itself, impose its inherent necessity upon us, and overawe us

with the fateful automatism of sheer happening that underlies all human history. (*On Revolution*, 49)

In other words, the reproduction of subjectivity is seen as becoming automatized, causing the demise of identifying with the political. Military social relations become social relations tout court. That is, the instrumentalized social replaces intimate social relations of the family and the local culture—instead of the individual attaching to social relations as a type of origin, connection, or subjective identification, the individual is threatened or endangered by them.

Militarization is, then, a metaphor for a vast historical movement toward the mechanization and automization of social, political, and economic life— both productive and reproductive—under authoritarian governance, when citizens—taking refuge in isolated identities—surrender their responsibility to make decisions together over how to share the world with others. There is no need here for deliberations or for interference in the social for the purposes of creating a greater equality. Like the authoritarian state guided by instrumental reason, the military state, resumes Chamayou in a similar vein, can stand outside of the political and social life of the nation and reduce the lives of its citizens and enemies alike to predictable patterns on a panoptical screen and deviations from those patterns. These patterns can appear as calculations and probabilities—or "data"—and be "objectively" cataloged as degrees of suspicious activity or deviance from norms. People's lives become automatic processes, administered as mechanical inferences on charts and graphs and through algorithms. In other words, the mechanization and technologization of identities link the identities up with something bigger and more durable to offer stability in a world made less stable by that mechanization and technologization.

The 2013 film *Drones* creates a biography for a commodity by showing the absorption of feminist subjectivity into that commodity. The film is about the militarization of gender or the seizure of feminist autonomy inside the means- ends logic of reproduction within a military apparatus. *Drones* at first presents feminism as an obstacle to the militarization of conscience, as feminism stands for an affective relationship to a sociality that creates the conditions for equality and that needs to be cast aside for furthering the necessary work ethic of the instrument. Yet feminism moves from being aligned with social relations embedded in the family to being motivated operationally. In particular, the death of the mother and the crushing of "traditional" modes of reproduction signal the weaponization of reproduction in line with capital's command.

Read in a certain way, *Drones* is also a tale about militarization as a means to economic control in the reproductive sphere through loss of political decision. Earlier films were made about drones, before drones had entered quite so resoundingly into political dialogue, popular culture, and consumerist speculation for faster deliveries. One such film, Rob Cohen's 2005 film *Stealth*, introduces the idea of the automation of state violence in the drone as a gender-defining issue. *Stealth* presents the drone as self-operating, making its own decisions in human expressions of personality and will, having human biological features such as "blood," "veins," "nerves," and "skeleton." Three expert Navy pilots are joined in their flying missions by an "Unmanned Combat Aerial Vehicle" (UCAV) named EDI, who, we learn from the commander, "flies all by himself." The first pilot rejoins, "You mean 'itself,' don't you, sir?" Maleness in such conversations is meant to display itself in biological instrumentalism—"You know what? I'll call it a 'he' when it gets out of its cockpit and takes a piss, how's that?"—whereas femaleness means emotion, sympathy, ethics, and a desire to avoid collateral damage on civilians. Later, we learn, "War's about tools. Think about it. . . . The best guy with the best weapon wins."

Eight years later, *Drones* envisions gender, all gender, merging with a means-ends logic of the apparatus, where the command to do your gender right—to use your gender like an instrument—replaces judgment, moral feeling, or politics. "We're not getting paid to bake oatmeal cookies and make babies," Airman Jack Bowles informs his commanding officer, Lieutenant Sue Lawson, on her first day on the job. The statement brings out many qualities that Jack sees in his job: first, it is a job (not a conviction nor a vocation, nor an act of patriotism, nor a moral or ethical duty, nor a defense of the Constitution, nor political); second, it is not work that "real" girls do; and third, having a job means that "the colonel tells you who to take out and you do it." To do the job of fighting the war right, one should follow the command to do his gender right. The point returns in a later scene when Sue is resisting following orders to drop hellfire on the Iraqi suspects, including twelve civilians and two children; the colonel tells her, "I understand you're feeling emotional. There's nothing wrong with that, but it means you're not equipped to make cold, calculated, strategic decisions. Fortunately, that's not your job. That's for men like your father." Being a "woman" means having autonomous emotional and ethical reasoning that blocks "men" who know better from executing orders or from reaching targets—the term "woman" operates as a form of economic regulation on the self-fulfilling, naturalized, male freedom of the self-functioning, calculating command economy. The film's point is to instrumentalize the conventions of *female*-attributed traits in the same way that masculinity has been turned into a military job.

Though the film's title suggests that the film is about a new machine of war that ushers in a new way of waging war without bodies, the filmmaking itself emphasizes the gendered body as the film's focus, the secret the film will reveal. The problem the film poses is about the relation of gender identity to militarization. The plot's premise—where a woman is being tested as a commissioned officer in the US Air Force—is basically also a test for a type of mainstream, affirmative action of feminism that demands "equality" in women's inclusion in the workforce: whether or not a woman can do the job that the new neoliberal military economy demands. The film's opening addresses this question as a question of body identity, that is, of whether *this* body can be imagined as belonging in the world of violent instruments.

Drones begins at daybreak in a small empty town, a train crashing through the frame of the film, first with its booming sound even before the image appears. The camera then creeps up the street, following the ensuing silence toward the only noise, heavy breathing and rhythmic thumping coming from the gym at the end of the street. The camera advances through the window with its display of lighted red lettering and approaches, from behind, a solitary trainee in a hooded sweatshirt at the punching bag. The camera pans around the figure and then advances forward toward its first shot of Sue's face, partly concealed by the hood, making sentimental cause—even pausing in emphatic shock—over the fact of her womanness. Here at the gym, bodies matter, and Sue is soon displayed in the shower, steaming and wet, in full makeup (which, miraculously, does not run), face turned upward in post-workout bliss, eyes closed, water dripping. This eroticized post-workout cleaning ritual is interrupted by a boom of airpower as the camera pans toward the window where an aerial formation flies over the desert, opening the question of a metaphoric connection between the visibility of the female fighter and the invisible weapon.

What astonishes later is that this film is not about bodies; it is, rather, a film about machines that move sensual bodies out of the frame. Instead of worrying about war and bodily risk, Jack continually warns Sue that the biggest danger they face is thinking, because thinking blocks the instrumental resolution of the war. The question of the body raised in those first shots is then asking not only whether the female, feminist body can manage in the violent work-world of machine-society but also whether or not feminism can sustain the type of reason necessary to hit the targets the command sets, whether women can carry out commands, even unethical ones. Autonomous, bodily (affective) female thinking would deviate from the calculation of the machine command, Jack warns, as machine command requires an identity that adheres resolutely to the rules and calculations of the job. Time and again, he cautions her: "Don't think too much"; "The colonel tells you who to take out and you do it. Some people are good at that and some people aren't because they think too much"; "I can tell that you're obviously a smart individual. It's kind of what I'm worried about"; "Don't think about it"; "We just gotta blast the terrorist son of a bitch and fly away"; "Obey orders from and trust the chain of command like they're god." Thinking, Jack informs her, distracts; it cannot be absorbed in the mechanism; it is what killed her predecessor, as he succeeded in taking out a Highly Valued Target, drank ten shots, and drove off a cliff. The problem of gender in work is a problem of autonomous forms of thinking, particularly women's embodied ones: feeling, sympathy, and the like. "Men" here constitute the identity of the worker who can follow the means-ends reason necessary for neoliberal economics, while the place of "women"—especially "feminist women" (women who hesitate to follow possibly unreliable orders because they have feeling and relate to the intimacies of others)—is questionable, perhaps even a challenge to the calculating machine. As bodily sensibility, "women" dangerously introduce politics into work.

The question that arises in relation to feminism is whether this work can sustain its instrumentalized rationality when accommodating this other type of thinking, sensibility, social relationality, or politics aligned with feminism. The problem of politics in war becomes a topic of conversation for Jack and Sue as together they debate the meaning of what they are doing. In each of their cases, the physical body is made incommensurable with the war. Jack claims pride in doing a service for his country without putting himself at risk, projecting power without physical vulnerability, not wishing to sacrifice to war the possibility of a rich sensible life: "I'm only twenty-two," he says, "I don't want to die before I've had a threesome" (specifying nervously that it should only be with girls). Here, Jack is projecting body sensibility into the future. Soon, Jack and Sue turn on the image-console and watch the Iraqi couple having sex on the roof. For Jack, sensual fulfillment is therefore anticipated and postponed in separation from the present of calculating reason, while familial relations and intimacies are likewise projected elsewhere or into another time. Sue, meanwhile, wistfully remembers stories her father told her about flying over Hanoi, with his friend Tommy going down in flames. Whereas Jack postpones his feelings into the future, and the screen projects feelings from the Gulf, Sue places hers in the past, in conventional plots of the last war and attachment to her family. In contrast to the body's sensible experience in some other time or place, the body in the present is funneled into the job of war. As Jack reminds Sue, "This isn't about being a hero like him [her father] and his pal [Tommy]. It's about winning the fucking war, doing our job."

Sue's autonomous thinking does threaten the mission at the same time as it puts limits on the smooth executions of orders in the military hierarchy. For example, though the colonel on screen tells her he wants "indisputable visual confirmation," this is clearly *not* what the military command wants, as the colonel continues throughout the film to yell at and threaten her when she disputes the meaning the military command has given to the visuals—he wants her to read the signs on the screen as confirming his already established sense of the facts on the ground. Military command next tells her to fire on the car driving toward the house as her target, but again, instead of just accepting the interpretation of the visual sign as self-evident, she steps back, compares the photographic capture to an older file photo and rejects the identification, incurring the wrath of her higher-ups. Sue's ability to change perspectives and interpret is a metaphoric rendition of her physical ailment: She has a partially detached retina, due to a boxing accident while at flight school. She has, literally, taken her eye out of her eye socket, moved its position, and become like a camera, and her camera-eye grants her the capacity to witness and interpret social relations. As a result of Sue's deviations from what is given in the image as military fact, feminism is glossed as short-circuiting the means-ends advance of military logic with interpretation.

Drones shares the feel of Samuel Maoz's 2009 début Israeli film *Lebanon*. As in *Drones*, where the drone *is* the film apparatus, *Lebanon's* mise-en-scène is an armored tank moving into the war zone on the first day of the 1982 Israeli invasion. Most of the action takes place in the claustrophobic, dark, hot inside as the soldiers, in terror, lose their reason, trying to make the weapon work— amidst leaks, loose wires, and electrical failures—while, like a stalker, the weapon's crosshairs frame—in circles and squares and bullseyes—fragments of the war outside: destruction, ruins, confusion, civilian murders, animal torture, atrocities, casualties, betrayals, confessions, and threats. The body of the soldier is locked inside the machine, watching the politics of supplication of those in the tank's crosshairs and of the infrastructural collapse glimpsed through the shutter. The soldiers in this film eventually experience physical, moral, and emotional meltdown.

In *Drones*, the trailer replaces the tank as the inside-camera space: The mise-en-scène registers disembodied voice and command in window-like openings, not to the immediate outside as in *Lebanon* but to half a world away. The body and its social context are separated by both military machinery and space. The screens showing the war are like still frames next to machine controls in the trailer where Jack and Sue are stationed in the Nevada desert. The trailer's air conditioner is broken (the body that the new technology is supposed to make obsolete is constantly being recalled in its sweat). Nobody else enters except, briefly, somebody delivering a pizza. There are only brief moments when the film moves outside. The machine-box contains nearly the entire action of the film, as though we were watching a play rather than a film, with only a single set and dialogue. Most of the film editing splices shot-reverse-shot sequences, with the camera occasionally dropping to show their fingers typing swiftly but decisively on the keyboards. To interrupt the banality of the closed, dull, dank, and gritty industrial space (where nothing actually happens except repetition and typing), sometimes the shot-reverse-shot sequences are broken by interspersed moments when one of the characters throws a glance at the grainy terminal screens, and we see kids playing soccer in the Iraqi sun far away, grown-ups dancing or cleaning, barbecuing, everyday domestic family life in Iraq.

The main action of the movie is not the dominant visual set. The dominant action, instead, flickers through windows and screens on the control panel as fragments of reproductive life elsewhere. The machine itself—its operating keyboards, levers, wires, and switches—is the primary point of close visual identification, suggesting that the tech crews, prop managers, and camera operators—the laborers behind the project—are the dramatis personae of war, turning the film inside out: What is usually invisible becomes all the more visible, as instrument of work and war. Because of this reversal, the usual appearances of sensibility and subjectivity formation are projected onto the past and future rather than absorbed and naturalized onto bodies, and the social is disconnected, located in the distance, and digitalized. Sue can identify on the screen heroic actions and feelings similar to what she imagines her father's were in the last war; similar as these are to her own experience, they do not belong to her. Watching the Iraqi kids anticipate their father's return, she remembers waiting for her own father's return many years before on his birthday. Sue experiences feeling in her own body as given to her in distant appearances and projections of reproductive life.

Whereas sensibility is alienated, identification with the machine is a historical necessity, the film suggests, as it produces the neoliberal subject aligned with a now triumphant feminist autonomy. The conflict of Sue's newly evolved subjectivity is resolved only through the death of the mother: Her mother's death is what allies her with military command and secures her professional success. Like a god, the face and voice of Sue's father, the four-star general, now comes on the screen to tell Sue that the target Mahmoud Kahlil was one of the masterminds of 9/11 and thus responsible for killing her mother and her brother David in the attack, and that Kahlil is planning another chemical attack that would have even more devastating repercussions.

She has the responsibility of stopping him from causing such pain to others, her father says. Here, the face of the father challenges the family structure from one of care and alliance to one of conquest. Oversized and domineering as his face is enlarged on the screen, Sue's father enjoins her autonomous decision-making to be a retaliatory arm of state violence.

Sue knocks Jack out of the way; she seizes the controls, the light in the trailer turns red (as in the gym), and a symphonic, religious screeching sound crescendos. The film cuts to the screen she is watching: Replacing the father's enlarged face is a grainy image, mysteriously marked with a target and bathed in red light, of Kahlil pushing his kids on a swing set. This gives way to direct bright sunlight, as we follow the path of the missile crashing. The sound turns off and ten seconds pass with Kahlil and his kids playing happily, mostly in silence, until the bomb hits, and the film cuts back to the flames wiping out the family scene, with Sue and Jack watching through the video-screen in the Nevada trailer. Another cut puts us back directly into the bright Iraqi sunlight at the site of the explosion, amidst the drifting rubble, as a happy birthday/welcome-home banner floats down on the debris and burns, the bodies buried in desert dust. The film ends with a close-up moving in on Sue's face, devilish in the red glow of the launch but victorious.

A Girl Walks Home Alone at Night

Drones hails feminism as ultimately absorbed into the imperialist/neoliberal machine by offering women and feminism inclusion in the military/technological workforce. In this, it separates out social context and intimate relations as a disturbance to feminist autonomy and the possibility of the feminist heroic individual. As well, *Drones* shows feminism as making women responsible for a politics of death, where the mother/family as social and affective political reason is replaced with an apolitics of instrumental reason. Both *Drones* and *A Girl Walks Home Alone at Night* demonstrate the absorption of the feminist subject and its autonomy into the economic rebirth promised in neoliberalism. This section considers further how neoliberal ideology reshapes feminism's oppositional rhetorics to gloss neoliberalism as oppositional to imperialism, religious conservatism, and authoritarianism. In other words, feminism is being used for neoliberalism's purposes in order to make neoliberalism seem as though it is oppositional to the global Realpolitik that it practices.

Whereas *Drones* presents neoliberalism as absorbed in command and control, *A Girl Walks Home at Night* casts a female character to plot neoliberalism and market exchange as an escape from patriarchal control and industrialism's techno-rational control together. Rather than as military efficiency, techno-rational control is here an authoritarian holdover that neoliberalism as feminism will topple: a religious fundamentalism linked to a nationalist industrial economy shown as a historical relic surviving past its viability. *A Girl Walks Home Alone at Night* returns us to a moment when Iran is moving toward a 2015 international agreement with the member states of the United Nations Security Council—to restrict its nuclear enrichment and reprocessing capacities in exchange for an easing of sanctions. In US political positioning of the time, Iran was seen as a nation-state that denied individual and market freedoms through an isolationist religious fundamentalism—represented in part in the West by the veil and its control of women—held in place by economic stagnancy and regression that, in this logic, only market fundamentalism could resolve. Whereas the Obama administration and its allies negotiated to bring Iran more in line with mainstream economic liberalization, anti-terrorism, and peace initiatives, including controlling its energy markets, the Trump administration—against Europe and most of the rest of the international community—subsequently surrendered such an alliance, following instead their more right-wing Saudi and Israeli counterparts by continuing instead an Iran policy based in economic and political marginalization of Iran. The Obama era treaty may have opened Iran up for normalization, financial investments, and the advancement of credit, while Trump's policy, ushering back in a draconian regime of sanctions, bolstered up the more conservative wing of the Iranian political establishment. The period I am considering is before Trump changed the US course.[13]

---

[13] Now in 2021, it is still too early to tell how the United States's Iran policy will proceed during the Biden administration. The United States has posed blocks to the negotiations by continuing the sanctions and demanding more concessions from Iran even as the United States was the party that broke the treaty.

In my argument, culture plays an important role in creating consent and implementing neoliberalism's hegemony, showing that neoliberal reforms make sense only after intervening in and asserting dominance over the prevailing mix of local political and cultural ideas. The film imagines a substantial difference between liberalism and authoritarianism through the figure of the liberal woman. In this, the feminist in her quest for freedom is positioned as directly resisting the regime's economic industrial control by means of her sexual autonomy in the same way that neoliberal reforms promised by the signing of the treaty were supposed to break up the old Iranian power block. Contingently, feminism is defanged, so to speak, from resisting neoliberalism's platforms that have impoverished women, subjecting them to debt and austerity and making them responsible for the care of population in the absence of state and social supports.

Because the film is staging a conflict between ideas of free markets and ideas of state regulatory control, it refers back to the 1980s as the point of origin, using the feminist vampire as the free agent and revolutionary momentum who breaks through the deadening stronghold of the old economy even as the Revolution was breaking the stronghold of Western imperialism and free markets with the nationalist rhetoric surrounding its regulatory policies. After the opening credits, the main character, referring to his car, asks a boy, "Do you know how many days I've worked for this car?" and says, "2,191 days"—exactly six years, dating his working life as ending around the time of the Revolution.[14] The decline of the protagonist's work-life—the film's dead zone—points to the 1980s, the Iranian Revolution and industrial decline, as the time period when the horror began. *A Girl Walks Home Alone at Night* imagines feminism as carrying forward neoliberalization into Iran's social landscape made into a deathscape by the Revolution's economic and political policies. The feminist in her quest for freedom is positioned as directly resisting the failing Iranian regime's control by means of her sexual autonomy in the same way that neoliberal reforms

---

[14] I deduct 1986 as the date the film is supposed to take place because of the date of many of the references.

allowed by the signing of the treaty were supposed to break up the old Iranian power block. The liberated feminist in a veil in *A Girl Walks Home Alone at Night* embodies the conflict between the religious fundamentalist state and the ideologies of the free market, while also embodying the possibilities of social cohabitation of Iran with liberal statehood and an international community.

Though there are many social, religious, economic, and political issues that might be seen to separate Iran from the international community— including, of course, issues surrounding their development of nuclear power—the central problem that *A Girl Walks Home Alone at Night* poses for Iran's international conciliation is the conflict over women's rights. From the very beginning, *A Girl Walks Home Alone at Night* represents the barren industrial economy (represented in the heavy-equipment-laden dead landscape) as marginalized within the frame of its narrative of reproduction. In *Drones* the unraveling of the family structure leads the girl to pursue the accomplishments of a professional career supported by feminism, and the "Third Wave" bloggers in Chapter 1 the feminist subject needs to separate from the regressive family that offers no protection from social perils and the menacing gaze because of its denial of difference. In *A Girl* meanwhile, familial dissolution is caused by the weakening fiscal power of the regime and equally propels women into sexual mobility. The movie favors this sexual liberation from culture and family as a defining trait of its hero. Whereas *Drones* understood the dissolution of the family as an opening for the family to be replaced by the efficiency of the state-productive machine in the hands of the feminist-influenced subject, in *A Girl Walks Home Alone at Night* the familial dissolution brings to light an association between women's freed sexuality and the demise of the Iranian regime that, in the film's logic, builds its power in part through familial control. In its contrast to the fundamentalist regime in demise, neoliberalism is the condition of possibility for the exercise of free sexuality on the part of the individual woman.

The film's opening sequence establishes this central political conflict between the sovereign Islamic state and its economic decline, on the one hand, and the sovereign individual woman, on the other. A series of spliced-together shots tracks the male protagonist Arash on his way home with a found cat: deserted streets lined with shuttered up middle-class homes; a fenced-in work site with trucks, barrels, and other equipment but without workers; in front of the fence, a close-up of the prostitute, her lipstick applied, shadows over her face, her eyes lifted seductively in reaction to Arash, and her eyelids blinking over a half-smile as he passes, ignoring her; the camera pulls back on three white silos at the back of her, dwarfing her. The next shot reveals, on the side of a highway, a pit strewn with dead bodies, curving around, with a set of electrical wires crisscrossing overhead, followed by another shot of the same setting with Arash walking by it in the opposite direction to reveal a pile of corpses (we only learn quite later that this is the pit where the vampire dumps the bodies after she is done with them). Indications of industrial work and power poles without actual workers here hang over a pile of corpses, as though industrial development had been death-inflicting rather than life-enhancing. The movie is shot in black and white with sharp contrast and deep shadows, creating an eerie, after-life quality.

The feminist themes and themes of sexual autonomy in *A Girl Walks Home Alone at Night* have received less critical attention than themes of genre and its cultural hybridizations, especially given the film's central visual concern with the veil. The critics of *A Girl* have mostly been interested in Amirpour's experiment with genre translated into a new and exotic national setting. "*A Girl Walks Home Alone at Night*," writes, for example, Sheila O'Malley in *Rogerebert.com*, "is a film about film, a fresh and exciting re-imaging of a well-worn oft-told genre."[15] Mary Ann Johanson of *Flick Filosopher* excitedly comments: "The Iranian skateboarding vampire feminist spaghetti western we have all been waiting for, creepy cool and gorgeously sinister, engorged with suspense and desire."[16] And Sheila O'Malley says, "They all live in Bad

---

15 Sheila O'Malley, "A Girl Walks Home Alone at Night (2014)," *Rogerebert.com* (November 21, 2014), https://www.rogerebert.com/reviews/a-girl-walks-home-alone-at-night-2014.
16 Mary Ann Johanson, "A Girl Walks Home Alone at Night Movie Review: Blood Pressure," *Flick Filosopher* (March 31, 2015), https://www.flickfilosopher.com/2015/03/a-girl-walks-home-alone-a t-night-movie-review-blood-pressure.html

City, an Iranian town filled with bad bad vibes, surrounded by pumping oil drills, seen like galumphing prehistoric beasts, going up and down, up and down."[17] The film, however, does more than just play off the strangeness of seeing a Muslim culture within a familiarly sexualized genre, an interpretation that would overindulge the film's conventional Orientalism. The film uses the deathlike quality of the industrial landscape to highlight the failures of the authoritarian Islamic Republic, with giant, slow-moving, metallic machines bending into the dust. At the same time, the film raises depopulation as a result and social fallout caused by the failing economic policies of the Islamic Republic's authoritarianism. Islamic fundamentalism with its death machines creates the death landscape from which the liberated woman must escape. This is a far cry from the "reproductive futurism" that Lee Edelman says repeats the future in the oppressive social and cultural hierarchies of the present;[18] instead, the future is premised on the woman's capacity to deny reproduction and interrupt the nation, to set it on a different path. Nonreproductive and death-dealing, the vampire embodies independence and becomes a figure of rejuvenation, a feminist hero freed up from the stagnation of authoritarian nationalism, religious dogmatism, economic retrenchment, and sluggishness, and familial and cultural traditionalism in order to pursue entrepreneurial adventurism.

On top of the exoticizing aesthetic that critics have observed, *A Girl Walks Home Alone at Night* uses cultural difference as the visual sign of a historical transition from industrial capitalism controlled by a developmental nationalist state to open consumer markets. The film's visuals span between the dark outside with pounding machines and the internal lair of the vampire, with

---

[17] O'Malley.

[18] Edelman explains, "In its coercive universalization. . . , the image of the Child, not to be confused with the lived experiences of any historical children, serves to regulate political discourse—to prescribe what will *count* as political discourse—by compelling such discourse to accede in advance to the reality of a collective future whose figurative status we are never permitted to acknowledge. . . . That figural Child alone embodies the citizen as an ideal, entitled to claim full rights to its future share in the nation's good. . . . Hence, whatever refuses this mandate by which our political institutions compel the collective reproduction of the Child must appear as a threat not only to the organization of a given social order but also, and far more ominously, to social order as such, insofar as it threatens the logic of futurism on which meaning always depends" (11).

its many references to Western popular culture. The film alludes to the 1980s through its consumer culture's time-period references: from the turntables, to the cassette tapes, to the posters of Michael Jackson's *Thriller* (1983), Madonna, and the Bee Gees collaged on the lead female character's bedroom wall to the vampire's confession that her favorite song is Lionel Richie's 1984 release *Hello Hello* (a song that might not easily be associated with vampires) and the song in the almost-sex scene—a 2009 White Lies piece called *Death*, part of a British goth revival of early 1980s sounds produced by bands like Joy Division.[19] So Mayer, from the British Film Institute's (BFI) *Sight and Sound*, points to cultural references like Jim Jarmusch's *Only Lovers Left Alive*, which similarly alludes not only to the early 1980s in its score but also to *Down by Law* and Gus Van Sant's gritty queer cult flick *Mala Noche*, both from 1986.[20] The vampire, her sexual autonomy, and feminism are, through these constant citations of 1980s' Western culture, linked to open internationalized markets, cultural exchange, international easing, covered up by the veil. Unlike the machines, the vampire is, like the pop culture icons, unattached to the ground of the nation, sometimes seeming to float in on her victims on the wings of her veil like a bat.

The many reminders of imported 1980s commercial culture are not the only insinuations of cultural opening and movement linked to the vampire, her veil, and her detachment from the immediate setting. Visually correlated to consumer culture, the vampire is also untethered from the nation's social and cultural landscape in her refusal to repopulate. Her non-reproductiveness is like a cut, a disassociation from the nation, and Amirpour treats the failures of the regime's industry as castration. The cut after the opening sequence reveals a smoky dark sky bearing over giant drills pounding into the black earth, the equipment in dark silhouette. The presence of oil extraction returns in scene after scene as still, smoky, inhuman transition shots, deathlike, with the monstrous machines bearing into the ground-like rapists. This

---

[19] I thank Barry J. Faulk for this interpretation of the soundtrack.
[20] So Mayer, "Film of the Week: A Girl Walks Home Alone at Night," *Sight & Sound* 25, 6 (June 2015), https://www.bfi.org.uk/news-opinion/sight-sound-magazine/reviews-recommendations/film-week -girl-walks-home-alone-night.

exploitation of the earth is echoed in the vampire's murder scenes when she replicates the motion of the borer. In the first murder, like the phallic mother of psychoanalysis she bares her teeth, sticks them deep into the pimp's finger flesh for a cut, sucks his finger as though giving him *fellatio*, and then bores her sharp incisors down into him (like the oil drills) till he falls away screaming, and she slowly slides the severed finger from her mouth. The pimp dies in that scene. A typical feminist reading might interpret this scene as instigating a psychic terror caused by the female reversing the order of gender domination and seizing the phallus, where the narrative trajectory would then be to punish the woman in order to restore the correct order of power. The film, however, sides with the vampire as she rises in a feminist victory of revenge for the pimp's evil control of women. Against the control of the pimp, the family, and the industrial machine, the vampire orchestrates a punishment against patriarchal power and the control of women by controlling the gaze—she herself chooses to wear or not wear the veil, either way for the purpose of her seductions.

This imagery can be seen as a reversal of Iran's film codes and a direct critique of the regime. Iranian post-Revolutionary film has, as Negar Mottahedeh argues, used the veiled woman to counter the imperialist gaze. One method for changing what Ayatollah Khomeini objected to as women's sexualization in the imperialist gaze in realist film conventions and to purify the Islamist body was by covering women, blocking the gaze—that Laura Mulvey had argued allowed identification with the camera and the subsequent objectification of women—through a nonnarrative interruption, a dense black mark, a fetish. "[V]eiled female bodies," Mottahedeh notes, "were generated to stand against the contaminating influences previously introduced into mediating technologies" (2). Yet Amirpour restores castration in the gaze to oppose the logic of the regime, using the veil as a screen that gives away the secret. The chador that the vampire wears could read as Orientalist exoticism, but it also, more glaringly, with the veil in silhouette, gives the back of her head the same shape as the industrial grinder biting into the soil for its life-blood. The vampire-woman often appears out of nowhere, accompanied by a drumbeat, landing when an unaware character turns around, or breaking the continuity of a street or a wall, creating an eerie shadow, stopping the motion with her speechless stare. The camera takes her in as a break in the stilled, regularized rhythm and symmetry of the industrial mise-en-scène, an opening, within the shot, that suggests *something else* not in the shot and outside of its pattern, a dark empty break. Amirpour teases with the veil and then removes the veil, emphasizing the body's sexual empowerment, her autonomous sexuality breaking through the regime's controlled social and economic program.[21]

The unproductiveness of production of the Islamists' boring machines therefore directly corresponds to the unreproductiveness of reproduction of the vampire, the decline of the family, and the subsequent rise of female sexual autonomy (feminism). In *A Girl*, the family buckles under the pressure from too much social, economic, and indeed reproductive control by a bloated political hierarchy, freeing the woman for sexual adventure. The degenerate corruption of political/ruling-class families leads toward uncontrolled female circulation in the form of female domination, female choice, female seduction, female desire, female reason, female autonomy, and even female killing. Arash is employed as a groundsman for what looks like a ruling-class family with impressive jewelry and a luxurious compound, when the TV breaks and the daughter invites him up to her room to fix it. As she lounges on her bed in a loose-fitting slip, he asks that she leave, as her parents (though apparently not home) would think it inappropriate for the

---

[21] Alison Phipps has remarked on the veil as a symbol of both patriarchal, religious oppression and of resistance to it: "The veiling-as-resistance narrative has become a common refrain among Muslim women in the West and can be seen as partly produced by the dichotomous nature of contemporary politics and efforts to avoid making alliances with neoconservative projects or inflaming anti-Muslim prejudice, discrimination and harassment" (63–4). In this she follows Joan Scott. In her book about the French controversy over the headscarf, Scott makes it clear that French feminists who supported legislation to ban the veil because it did not allow the visibility of women's sexuality were the same feminists who thought that the excessive visibility of women's bodies in Western culture was an expression of accessibility and an objectification that was also an oppression. In addressing the Lévy case before the Stasi commission in 2003, Scott documents that the Lévy sisters had a secular upbringing and their parents opposed their choice to wear ,the veil: "Theirs were individual decisions," writes Scott, "which while religious might well be read also as exquisite gestures of adolescent rebellion, or as attempts to challenge mainstream society as the girls' parents had, though in a completely different idiom from the left-wing politics of the older generation (a politics no longer available in a postcommunist age). Indeed, one sociologist, commenting on the headscarf controversies, suggested that for young dissidents in the twenty-first century, identifying with Islam was the functional equivalent of the Maoism of the 1960s or 70s" (*The Politics of the Veil*, 32). The most famous example of the veil as resistance is Frantz Fanon's well-known essay "Algeria Unveiled": "Removed and reassumed again and again, the veil has been manipulated, transformed into a technique of camouflage, into a means of struggle" (61).

two to be alone. She laughs and teases him, touches him from behind. This is the only work scene in the film; however, it is not a scene of workers making things but rather a scene of unveiling where a worker seemingly (though unconvincingly) tries to fix broken things—including the family and the veil—and fails.

Like commercialism and exchange, feminism's sexual autonomy tears apart the family and its reproduction in parallel to industrialism's extraction tears apart the earth. The film shows many instances of the family unraveling while the regime's industrial machines burrow down. Admitting that the exchange of cash is an alienated transactional or commercial rather than familial sociability, the pimp scolds the prostitute for not having children as he guides her head down toward his lap, reminding her that she is old and should want a family. Arash's father, sick with addiction, flings the photograph of Arash's missing mother across the room, breaking the glass. The TV intones, "Your husband brings home the money. But be prepared. One day, everything changes." When Arash approaches the vampire from behind over the turntable, embraces her, and caresses her neck, the scene cuts to the prostitute dancing with a balloon in industrial wreckage, suggesting death, dispossession, and developmental decline as the *sexual* byproduct. Most terrifying of all, the vampire accosts a boy alone on the street at night and blocks his way, appearing in a series of jump cuts and close-ups right in front of him no matter which way he turns; she asks him multiple times if he is a good boy, and when he insists that he is, she puts her face up to his, tells him not to lie, bares her incisors, and steals his skateboard, threatening—in an echoing, devilish whisper—to take his eyes out of his skull and feed them to the dogs, while he cries and runs away, and she licks her lips. As the inverted mother, the title character shatters any sense of a naturalized reproductive femininity, showing instead feminist femininity as destructive, petrifying, and murderous, especially to children. Female sexuality turns the reproductive family into a death machine in as much as the Revolution detaches the fruits of industry from enriching the cultural ground on which it intimately stands.

Meanwhile, the feminist signals authenticity; freedom of the body, its movement, and its sensations unmoored from religious dictates, coded restraints, and dress codes. The vampire's veil conceals a secular, authentic feminist underneath—a crop-haired young rock 'n' roll sex-seeker, living alone, wearing a tank top or nothing at all, with lipstick and eyeliner, penetrating seductive eyes (often in close-up), and hip-waving dance moves. The regime's failures allow the independent woman to engage in sexual and cultural actions that surpass the obsolescent industrial order, religious fundamentalism, nationalism, or traditionalism. In *A Girl Walks Home Alone at Night*, autonomous female sexuality triggers a post-regulatory escape. Arash, the vampire, and the cat drive off in the car into what should be the sunset but is, rather, the neoliberal future. There are no repercussions for the girl's murders—including the killing of the father—as industrial automation and vampiric fear take the place of any semblance of government presence, state regulation, social responsibility, or police. In the deadened landscape, the film gives no sense of the road ahead offering anything but more of the same: "If there were a storm coming right now," Arash asks the vampire under the smoke from the refining station, "a big storm, from behind those mountains, would it matter? Would it change anything?" With the family and the local economy both left in ruins, the film's concluding nihilism could be read as a menacing warning that the industrial economic policies of the Revolutionary regime with its Muslim cover need to turn the page from small-town mentality and national inwardness that led to political and ecological collapse toward, instead, an outward, expansive, global opening to the world, or else face a deadly bloodsucking. In front of this threat, this opening to the unknown future begins with feminism and economic liberalization, as we watch the two main characters through the windshield, the free male worker and the smiling veiled female vampire now travelling forward on the open desert road.

As I have elaborated throughout this book, neoliberalism exploits reproductive economies as much as productive economies, finding methods of reconceptualizing domestic spheres and intimate relations as work sites, places of consumer subject formation and social organization, networks of consumer demand, ideological pressure points, or points where agents of global profit directly extract surplus from local poverty. In industrial economies, as feminist scholar Leopoldina Fortunati observes, "while production both *is* and *appears as* the creation of value, reproduction *is* the creation of value but *appears otherwise*" (8); yet neoliberalism has remade reproduction to *appear as* the creation of value—as a commodity. In this, the socially autonomous woman who leaves behind her culture, in the dead of night, to die from its past—like the autonomous woman who, identifying with new technologies, kills a family that looks like hers—offers the promise of survival, the fetishized feminist subject enduring against social disconnection, wreckage, and waste.

To rescue feminism's political edge in a neoliberal context, feminism needs to wrest itself from being used as an ideological bulwark in the struggle between fundamentalist nationalism, on the one hand, and market fundamentalism or imperialism, on the other. Fundamentalist nationalism positions women as the internal culture that imperialism threatens, while imperialism, by justifying itself on freer markets and more microcredit loans to women, promises to rescue women from the injustices of a violent, "backward" culture and an oversized authoritarian state by putting them to work, often for foreign interests. Giving very little sense of a viable economic future beyond domination by either markets or the overreaching regulatory state, neoliberal hegemony also gives very little sense of a viable future beyond sexuality and population regulated by the family or by the state, on the one hand, or freed up by markets, on the other. The struggle over the symbolic meaning of "woman" is caught up in conflicting positions over the politics of reproduction, not just the politics of profit extraction and production. In the name of "freedom," imperialism wants to increase population controls in its areas of wealth extraction so that it is not burdened with costs of reproduction, while authoritarian nationalism wants to shift responsibility of reproduction onto traditional family structures in the name of nationalist self-determination policies. The "woman question" marks how the ideological clash between neoliberal imperialism and authoritarianism is part of a broader struggle over the exploitation of sexualities and reproductive economies. It should be clear that an espousal of independent sovereign heroic resilience at the expense of social attachment does not oppose authoritarianism but rather gives it another life while not offering any suggestion that the social could be anything but the sucking of the life-blood of others.

3

Gender Commodity in an Age of Financial Ruin and Environmental Disaster

The premise of Margaret Atwood's 2015 novel *The Heart Goes Last* is ridiculous: The novel attempts to envision what reproduction looks like "scaled up" as a global commodity but can only do so through absurdities and contradictions. In the novel's terms, reproduction "scaled up" in commodity production would create an appearance of security and control against the collapse of social organization: the absence of jobs, wide-scale crime, a real estate crash, and environmental unsustainability. Starting in a city gutted by financial crises, mass homelessness, home foreclosures, unemployment, sickness and disease, and pollution, the two main characters, the hardworking upwardly mobile Stan and Charmaine, having lost their house to bank foreclosure, are living in their car, threatened by roving urban gangs; they volunteer to go to the corporate prison Consilience/Positron and sign a life contract that promises them security and long life; there, initially happy, they soon unwittingly fall in with human organ traffickers, euthanizing bureaucracies, makers of schlock, and Elvis- and Marilyn-impersonating sex-robot escorts in Las Vegas who, though at first tormenting them, ultimately assist them toward a resolution of happy marriage in the suburbs with a baby that they always wanted. It is no wonder that the novel has received almost no critical attention, even at a time when Margaret Atwood herself has again been honored with explosive accolades on both the literary and popular culture scene for her other recent TV and literary forays, including a second Booker Prize win.

Nevertheless, this novel has keyed into under-theorized issues and concerns embedded in the public unconscious. Like Atwood's other novels— *The Handmaid's Tale*, its sequel, her second Man Booker prize winner, *The*

Testaments, the *Oryx and Crake* trilogy, and even her first Man Booker prize winner *The Blind Assassin*—*The Heart Goes Last* is a novel about reproduction. Its focus on reproduction draws it toward some of the themes and dialogues engaged in *Gender Commodity*'s prior chapters, in particular where the mother is targeted as a "subject at fault" for social dangers or the absence of care, aspects of neoliberal hegemony that serve to justify redistribution of rights, income, and wealth upward and thereby create more social dangers that the mother is supposed to fix.

The Heart Goes Last turns the mother into a function, and a mechanized function at that, a corporate machine set up to drive investment profits at the expense of the social, cultural, and natural environments. In this novel, she is no longer the "cause" of failure, unhappiness, and insecurity that contemporary feminism wants to load onto its past, nor is she the character form of the regulatory state, blamed for the problem of economic stagnation that only—the logic goes—the free market will solve. Here, rather, the mother-function is constructed—quite explicitly, out of "brick-and-mortar," wires, plastics, electronics, and labor—as a remedy to all that, a machine of profit that will fulfill the needs of a society, under neoliberal authority, left bereft by disinvestments and capital flight.[1] Charmaine as the aspiring mother demonstrates too many character fallibilities, and so her social and sexual role is replaced by mechanized reproduction in Consilience/Positron. Consilience/Positron will fulfill the promise of modernity, ending violence and want by taking over the mother's role. Indeed, *The Heart Goes Last* depicts the technologization of reproduction as the result of capital's penetration into intimate relations and sensibilities, its exploitation of the mother-function

---

[1] Sophie Lewis writes, "Narrating capital's evolving history . . . becomes a matter of revealing a web of surrogacy relations at the heart of empire, reaching into every intimate abode. Social reproduction theory becomes a matter populated by a whole raft of 'surrogates': provisioners, test subjects, helps, and tech supports. 'Surrogate,' more than 'reproductive' or 'feminized,' might be a word that proves useful for that field in bringing together the millions of precarious and/or migrant workers laboring today as cleaners, nannies, butlers, assistants, cooks, and sexual assistants in First World homes, whose services is figured as dirtied by commerce, in contrast to the supposedly 'free' or 'natural' love-acts of an angelic white bourgeois femininity it in fact makes possible. Surrogacy, in its current connotation, is the lie and the truth of their situation. It speaks of the millions of living bodies secretly crouching inside the automatons" (56).

redesigned for technological rationalization and profit extraction, and its violent usurpation of conventional socializing roles through surveillance.

By "reproduction," I do not intend to draw a line between biological bodies that replicate themselves through "natural" processes, on the one side, and social and cultural processes that ensure that everyone continues to be put in their place within relations of production, on the other. A tradition of feminism once saw women's relegation to the domestic sphere for the purposes of reproduction and its "necessary labor" as the source of their oppression and violence against them, but currently it is becoming clearer that the source of women's oppression is shifting, even if the association of women with domesticity continues to play a part. By presenting reproduction as having reached a transitional stage beyond its domestication, *The Heart Goes Last* takes seriously an insight like Lise Vogel's when she asserts that "The social relations through which necessary labour is carried out therefore cannot be postulated independently of specific historical cases" (149–50), where the family and its sexual division of labor take on certain reproductive functions only at the historical moment when such a form is needed. A prevalent source of oppression can now be seen instead in the commodification of reproduction.

The "necessary labor" of reproducing labor for the next day of work and the next generation now merges into the machine. What gets lost in the mechanization of reproduction in *The Heart Goes Last* is a state of the political that is not just about the liberal state's authority in securing life but the means by which technology makes the decision about who and what gets reproduced into a seemingly value-free project, erasing the other side of the liberal contract: the political input of citizens over the social organization of the reproduction of life. As Grégoire Chamayou has recognized, in a state of total and permanent war, where security through mechanization has become the protocol of state power, politics is more about calculation, repair, automation, and efficiency than about the ethics of decision-making, consensus-building through argument, negotiations with power, or debates about the good life. For Chamayou, against current practices of securitization by any means necessary and available, the right to decide over war has participated in a political tradition of democratic engagement where leaders have to appeal to citizens. Until now, that is, the decision to go to war has ideally, within democratic culture, involved the right to decide over which subjects' lives are put at risk, exposing the state itself to a *"political vulnerabilization"* (184), or "the possibility of it becoming the object of a critique or some kind of limitation" (184). Total mechanization takes the political relation away, meaning that the powers of securitization have become invulnerable to political critique, not having to answer to the opinions of the governed about when life is worth risking or, in the case of *The Heart Goes Last*, when, how, and for what ends the reproduction of subjects should be controlled or protected toward the apparent goal of minimizing social risk.

The division between, on the one hand, the reproduction of bodies and subjectivities and, on the other, the reproduction of the social system has been a fervent and vexed point of feminist engagement and contention, from activists like Selma James, who advocated for paid housework, to writers like Shulamith Firestone, who insisted that babies be cultivated in test-tube laboratories in order to free women from the burdens of domestic life, to analyses, like Donna Haraway's, acknowledging that "women's work" was always inside the circuit (often called the "feminization of labor")—that is, economic and technological forces were already extrapolating surplus from reproductive "women's work" that was devalued in its ideological separation from commodified labor, depressing the wages of labor as its reserve army. If social reproduction reproduces the race, class, and gender hierarchies that distribute bodies for the maximal output of the global productive system, then the job of reproducing bodies is no different than the job of reproducing social subjects, as much current feminist scholarship attests.[2] As Horkheimer and Adorno explain it, "The blessing that the market does not ask about birth is paid for in the exchange society by the fact that the possibilities conferred by birth are molded to fit

---

[2] See, for example, Sophie Lewis, who writes of pregnancy "as a contingent material process shaped by structural antagonisms. In particular, too few of the speculative ectogenesis texts grappled at all with the relationship between social reproduction and reproduction of capital—the unequal distribution of technology, and the limits of (the desirability of) automation" (28). Lewis links pregnancy to sex work and to work in general. "I don't just mean," she qualifies, "that the products of gestational labor are intimate aliens confronting their makers; I mean that the process itself is necessarily going to estrange the laboring body in every society except a society where that labor's independent existence is wrestled into *maximal* gestator control" (139–40). More specifically, Lewis stipulates, "The regime of quasi-compulsory 'motherhood,' while vindicating itself in reference to an undifferentiated passing-on of 'life itself,' is heavily implicated in the structures that stratify human beings in terms of their biopolitical value in present societies" (21).

the production of goods that can be bought on the market" (9). Additionally, the overtaking of the mother-function by capital, bureaucratic mechanization, and instrumental rationality can be seen as Atwood's thinking through of a relationship between feminism and the environment. For Horkheimer and Adorno, the disappearance of nature results from its imitation by calculative machines that assume an impossible reconciliation between nature and society. In the novel, the reduction of the mother-function to growth calculation similarly links social reproduction to the disappearance of nature. The novel defines reproduction's natural referent as the empty place of politics: The current vulnerabilities of "necessary labor" result from a withdrawal of politics from the care of socialized nature. Perfect technological control falsely assures security against what is posited as nature's—or women's—riskiness, decay, unpredictabilities, and indeterminacies" in reproduction.

In the case of *The Heart Goes Last*, social reproduction fuses into the commodity, ghettoing off nature by appropriating its power. This commodification inflicts subjectlessness while disguising its productive circuits as desiring subjects. One job of social reproduction over which Atwood troubles is that some political projects, including feminist ones, treat it as though natural reproduction came first and social reproduction is a corrupted overlay or supplement put on top as an improvement, replacement, or fix in the face of its catastrophes. In such a scenario, nature persists in its natural form underneath the commodity and can be rescued or retrieved.[3] Atwood rejects this view.[4] In *The Heart Goes Last*, overcoming nature is, for

---

[3] Catherine Rottenberg, for example, has also noted that neoliberalism's dominant political imaginary is troubled by reproduction. For Rottenberg, liberal democracies exist through a division of space between private and public domains, and because neoliberalism "has neither lexicon nor framework for addressing unwaged work or activity within the family" (100), therefore "reproduction has presented a quandary and a 'remainder'" (101). However, private and public domains were never credibly separated except ideologically and symbolically for the purposes of materially distributing bodies in space and profiting off of unpaid reproductive labor. Neither Atwood nor I agree that the private domain can be set off from work or from neoliberal commandeering of reproduction.

[4] Atwood is not the only one. Judith Butler also understands nature—or "sex"—as a byproduct or aftermath of the social construction of "gender." Dismantling the "sex/gender system" that had been so central to feminist analysis might be said to be one of Butler's primary contributions to scholarship, accounting for the wide interest in and popularity of *Gender Trouble*. For example: "The sexual politics that construct and maintain this distinction are effectively concealed by the discursive production of a nature and, indeed, a natural sex that postures as the unquestioned foundation of

the commodity, proof of its progress, so the commodity has to project "nature" backwards to triumph over it. In the novel, commodification, as Horkheimer and Adorno might have understood it, needs "to break the compulsion of nature by breaking nature" (9), where the commodity evokes a vision of nature as resisting commodification so that it can conquer nature and prove its own total domination. "Natural" reproduction is, then, an outcome of the commodity's projection of nature onto an "outside" or a "before" internal to the commodity and is just a part of the commodity. The commodity culture that Horkheimer and Adorno analyze understands nature—represented in part by "woman in bourgeois society" (56)—as its outside, its promise, its condition of endurance that it makes and then must come to dominate, what they call "the vain lie of power": "As a representative of nature, woman in bourgeois society has become an enigma of irresistibility and powerlessness. Thus she reflects back the vain lie of power, which substitutes the mastery over nature for reconciliation with it" (56). Horkheimer and Adorno see the subject, with nature, as disappearing but not yet disappeared, so the subject is an irreconcilable disturbance, a nature that speaks even as it is remade as a dead object (as a commodity).

I am not saying that Atwood finds a radical feminist response to total commodification (neither do Horkheimer and Adorno find a radical response). Rather, I am addressing the allusion to "nature" in the descriptions of a totally commodified world as a placeholder for a disruption within the commodity itself, a time delay, a politics, or a gap where it becomes apparent that the commodity cannot reconcile with itself, where the commodity comes up against its internal contradiction. Instead of returning to a naturalized nature as the commodity's Other, its predecessor or its aftermath, *The Heart Goes Last* tells a tale of a totally commodified reproduction that incites sexual autonomy and choice—celebrated by feminism—as a mechanism of control. "Choice" like nature is not an escape from the commodity but is, rather, the

culture. . . . The analysis that assumes nature to be singular and prediscursive cannot ask, what qualifies as 'nature' within a given cultural context, and for what purposes? Is the dualism necessary at all? How are the sex/gender and nature/culture dualisms constructed and naturalized in and through one another. What gender hierarchies do they serve, and what relations of subordination do they reify? If the very designation of sex is political, then 'sex,' that designation supposed to be most in the raw, proves to be always already 'cooked'" (*Gender Trouble*, 51).

condition for the intensification of its power. Atwood's text then challenges feminism to see itself as part of a totally commodified world, and yet she does not give feminism up to the commodity. Instead, she suggests there is a feminist time—a concern for reproduction and its economies—that contradicts the logic of the commodity even if it cannot find its way outside.

This chapter teases out the troubling that reproduction—or nature— presents when intimated within reproductive processes that are totally commodified and mechanized, as Atwood speculates. In this analysis, the naturalized subject is the realization of what Mark Fisher calls "capitalist realism,"[5] where capitalism has been made to seem like the only reality possible:[6] The naturalized body is the resting ground for the sprawling contradictions that reproduction is unleashing culturally as the status of the biological is increasingly indistinguishable from global inhuman practices of calculation, public disinvestment, and appropriation for accumulation. *The Heart Goes Last* tells a tale of reproduction that, articulated as "world" commodification, shows the precarity in this relationship: Subject reproduction is still irreconcilable with its absorption into "world" production.

This chapter begins by addressing various critical settings where feminist theory foregrounds the cultural effects of intersections of reproduction and commodity, that is, where capitalist technologies have infiltrated reproduction and made the imposition of power and profit appear as a mechanical process in much the same way as Atwood's Consilience/Positron does. Then, this chapter is divided into two additional sections. The first section discusses reproductive politics taken over by the commodification of life itself; the second section

---

5 "[T]he widespread sense that not only is capitalism the only viable political and economic system, but als0 that it is now impossible even to *imagine* a coherent alternative to it" (2). And further: "Capitalist realism as I understand it . . . is . . . like a pervasive *atmosphere,* conditioning not only the production of culture but also the regulation of work and education. . . . An ideological position can never be really successful until it is naturalized, and it cannot be naturalized while it is still thought of as a value rather than a fact. Accordingly, neoliberalism has sought to eliminate the very category of value in the ethical sense. Over the past thirty years, capitalism has successfully installed a 'business ontology' in which is it *simply obvious* that everything in society, including healthcare and education, should be run as a business" (16–17).

6 In a rare through brief mention of *The Heart Goes Last* in criticism, Annika Gonnermann characterizes the novel in this way: "The protagonists . . . make themselves comfortable within the conceptual limits offered by the system" (37).

addresses the contradictions involved in current theorizations of "world" in world literature criticism with respect to the "scaled up" reproduction of subjects in time. By "world literature," I am referring to a field in literary studies whose origins are most commonly attributed to Goethe's cosmopolitanism and the internationalization of Marx's bourgeois revolution but have since become a meeting ground for many contemporary issues ranging from migration and exile to translation. Much of this scholarship links up the production of literary texts with broader global social, cultural, and economic trends, particularly in terms of world systems theory and the inequalities between nations resulting from histories of imperialism and the integration of different regions into global finance and trade. In reading Margaret Atwood's text, this chapter considers the commodification of social reproduction as a "scaled up" world system and what this means for feminism.

Reproduction "Scaled Up" as Global Commodity

The undeniable entwinement of biological and social reproduction must be a foundational point of engagement for any feminist future. Especially in the current climate with scientific interventions like gene and hormone therapy, gender reassignment, tissue implants, prostheses, erectile dysfunction remedies, early viability, fertility drugs, commercial surrogacy, biotech, and the ubiquity of pornography, the idea that the biological and the social reproduction of subjects could be mutually exclusive in any legible way—or that one is more "original"—has become all but mute, and the idea that biology somehow provides a primary natural bonding between infants and parents for the purposes of socialization has been similarly refuted.[7]

---

[7] Sophia Lewis, for example, notes that biological reproduction under capitalism often does the opposite, severing social bonds instead of affirming them: "When and how does gestation under capitalism generate . . . an *absence* of bonds between infants and adults; a genuine wish . . . not to mother the infant you've borne? . . . A sense of alienation from the baby, and even dislike or disgust, is a massively common experience" (123). Lewis believes that the only difference between surrogacy and what we think of as natural pregnancy is the wage (44): "Work is alienated labor, and it seems safe to say that . . . the vast majority of human gestation is at least somewhat alienated in a

A number of feminists have studied reproductive practices in ways that show the consumer society's embeddedness inside of them. For Paul Preciado, the commodification of gender and sexuality not only creates the means of total control but also generates and intensifies differences that could, potentially, disrupt the system. As he puts it, "the present technological revolution, marked by genetic manipulation, nanotechnology, the technologies of communication, logistics, pharmacology and artificial intelligence, impacts the processes of reproducing life. In the current industrial mutation, the body and sexuality occupy the place occupied by the factory in the nineteenth century" (*An Apartment on Uranus,* 40), including the proletarianization of particular biological and neurological parts. Preciado universalizes gender alienation, a disability of the Sick Society—a type of precarity or incapacity affecting everyone and that needs constant fixing or work, driven by a commerce in technotherapies, biomedical exchanges, and constant assembly and reassembly. He goes on: "Homosexuality and heterosexuality, intersexuality and transsexuality do not exist outside of a colonial, capitalist epistemology, which privileges the sexual practices of reproduction as a strategy for managing the population and the reproduction of labor, but also the reproduction of the population of consumers. It is capital, not life, that is being reproduced" (*Ibid.,* 29). For Preciado, the consumer society's stimulations and ejaculations—"the conversion of life into information" (*Testo,* 278)—are the energy the economy runs on—an intense and constant stimulation of energy in the body that is released as excess: Work is "destined to cause a hard-on" (*Testo,* 293).

Not all interpretations understand this extraction of surplus from the body as quite so potentially "subversive." Processes of reproducing the body, its sensations, its arousals, its intimacies, and its sensibilities may have once been relegated, as natural, to the outside of economic structures, to the home as refuge from the violence of productive spheres; now they

---

world in which people of all classes are equally free to starve" (74–5). Lewis uses examples like the technologization of all birth, not just surrogacy, the need for social supports like migrant workers for childcare assistance and schools, as well as the way children are often seen as commodities—investments for the future, branded products, scientifically and legally contracted (18).

are acknowledged to be markets and often quite exploitative ones. There is growing trade not only in organic parts but also in subjectivities: affects, sensibilities, and experiences, much like "the feelies" sold total sensory experiences to drugged-up populations in Aldous Huxley's 1932 novel *Brave New World*. We are, Jasbir Puar admits, "composites of information that splay the body across registers of disciplinary space and time. The target is data" (2017, 57).[8] Genes, like finance, have been made abstractable, commercializable, and exchangeable, even amenable to be turned into investment grade financial instruments and bundled up in speculation. Body process, thought processes, and intelligence are also being artificially replicated, integrated, and distributed. Likewise, as in *Brave New World*, questions are raised about the meaning and status of nature even as—and *Brave New World* predicts this as well—nature is seen as ever more at risk in its relation to the commodity. Nature, even projected as its outside, seems tied into the commodity, controlled by the commodity, as well as threatened by the commodity.

Markets in body parts, prosthetics, cosmetic enhancers, genetic products and therapies, cells, organs and tissues, as well as mediated emotions, pills for arousal, menstrual cycle control, puberty inhibitors, sexual climax, clinical inseminations, and egg fertilization: Reproduction transpires in multiple intersecting exchange circuits and markets. In her book *Life as Surplus*, feminist theorist Melinda Cooper has noted that exchange society inhabits the body—the discipline of the life sciences, she shows, was developed in the late eighteenth century alongside the discipline of political economy. In the nineteenth century, she suggests, when "the economy begins to grow for the first time," also "life comes to be understood as a process of evolution and ontogenetic development" and "[h]enceforth political economy will analyze the processes of labor and of production in tandem with those of human,

---

[8] Data and information, as Alexander Galloway has pointed out, exist "first and foremost as number" (88) that carries "*no necessary information*" (89)—formal graphs and diagrams, disconnected from raw particulars. For Galloway, this particular tendency of world imagining is the one meted out by military domination, a diagram of lines of influence, forces, and alliances that cancels out the sensible lives behind the data the way the Kantian subject overcomes his confusion and fear of the sublime.

biological reproduction" (7). Cooper demonstrates that exchange circuits are immersed not only in organicities but also in psychologies and subjectivities: our knowing, being, feeling, and experiencing. Markets in life, she says, currently integrate with markets not only in organs, tissues, and other body parts but also in subjective reproductive and data processes —all of these cut up, functionalized and mechanized into differential sectors of commercial exchange. Under neoliberalism, the imbrication of life science and political economy has become even more pronounced.

Like organ and tissue markets, labor markets have also invested in making traits to meet reproductive and health needs. In fact, Christopher Chitty has shown how, since the end of the Middle Ages, capitalist development included the incentivization of male homosexualities to support proletarianization, encouraging work outside of traditional family ownership as in dockyards and ships, and homosexualities' de-incentivization and regulation in periods of instability: "the commodity form has transformed the essential coordinates of human sexuality" (90). The construction of genders and sexualities to meet capital's needs for labor continues alongside a marketing in other naturalized dispositions like ethnicities. Feminist anthropologist Aihwa Ong traces the genome project in Singapore where researchers in pharmaceutical companies like Biopolis are using the human genome to develop markets in health programs and therapies for particularly Asian diseases. Where the political and scientific proponents of the Human Genome in the West advertise the universality of the human gene, their Singaporean counterparts are developing remedies, insurance, and information banks that respond to diseases designated as particular to ethnicities in Asia. Biopolis is founded on the premise that "biovalue" materializes "as a signifying power that gathers up diverse local components bound up with health and wealth" (2016, 15), a "logico-semantic maneuver" (2016, 15) by which (ethnic) difference is remade as contextually generated exchangeable value in biomaterials.

Our bodies, minds, relations, emotions, excitements, and genders are, Preciado thinks, the metaphoric appearances of the consumer society in our differences, what Baudrillard might call its "maternal ambience." Instead of a birth or a parental line tracing her origin, Preciado poses hormonal manufacture, the fabrication of technology for gender construction and planning, the taking of pills: We are born from the commodity. Preciado sees the consumer society perpetuated through the integration of media in the body, making birth into the generation of a global circulatory system of signs, messages, information, pornographies, and excitements. "Marilyn and Elvis were two perfectly plastic bodies," he concludes,

> carburized by drugs, just as plastic as the vinyl that would capture their voices. . . . The new Hollywood prototypes of masculinity and femininity were already so artificial that nobody would have bet a dollar that Elvis wasn't a drag king or that Marilyn wasn't a silicone transsexual. . . . That's how it was. . . . Ordinary consumer products, prosthetic legs, and silicone breasts were produced on an industrial scale using similar design, production, and sale procedures. (*Counter-sexual*, 165–6)

The Heart Goes Last is a novel predominantly about those perfectly plastic bodies that are now us. This commercialization of reproduction in Atwood's experiment generates a sense of nature as prior, primitive, broken, and unstable, demanding investments and complex finance even as investments and complex finance in it were what made it unstable in the first place.

Asking about nature and therefore reproduction within the culture of the global commodity with its destruction of social life, the novel sets up an alternative controllable commercial nature as a replacement nature in order to escape from the horrors of what had become of the natural and social world. The nature of the everyday world has become too prone to its own forces of destruction, and another manufactured one could repair all the glitches, avoid all the hazards, and include fail-safes (even if they end up failing). *The Heart Goes Last* picks up on the old dream of mechanizing reproduction, a dream about removing women's bodies from the reproductive process (i.e., *Frankenstein*), because women's bodies, in whatever their form and derivation, introduce inequality, vulnerability, and precarity as a disturbance at the heart of commodity's project: "bringing up kids in decent conditions," Virginie Despentes, for example, decries, "is almost impossible. It is essential that women feel like failures. . . . We are held responsible for a failure that is in fact collective and cross-gender" (21). Mechanization promises to remove such fallibility by replacing it with a better version of itself.

In line with Atwood's contentious self-assessment that "I am not a writer of science fiction" (2004, 513), *The Heart Goes Last* acknowledges that technologies are already inside of reproduction, but reproduction's appearances in these global apparatuses look defamiliarized and disassociated, as slapstick, as contradiction and divergence. Since Consilience/Positron can manufacture objects for desire as well as desires themselves, for example, the characters eroticize blue-knitted stuffed animals mass-produced by prison labor. The humorous erotic encounters between the men or women with their teddy bears indicate a discomfort or disjuncture in mass manufacturing, the control of arousal, the intertwining of the body with the assembly line, and the disappearance of nature: something is not quite right. Stan's coprisoner Budge informs him that clients can choose add-ons to install in the robots' consciousness mechanism, but only if the flushing and sanitation mechanisms do not malfunction and the lube is appropriately applied. Budge lists standard add-ons: W, he says, is "for Welcoming. . . . But sort of neutral, like a flight attendant. T+H is Timid and Hesitant, L+S is for Lustful and Shameless. A+B is for Angry and Belligerent" (240), and so on. The contemporary body, as Atwood understands it in line with current feminist scholarship, is marked "cyborg"—it calculates pain and pleasure through its connectivity to technologies, plastics, pharmaceuticals, and information collected through constant surveillance and circulation, the body made as data. Yet the illusion of control and security that the apparatus insists on, where lust or shame are not natural instincts but rather codes that can be assembled to "scale up" and copied multiple times identically, is at the same time laughable, corrupt, and inefficient, as though the apparatus were being challenged by its own nature.

Sex-bots, Slut Machines, and the Global Engineering of Desiring Subjects

Atwood's success and failure to reconcile reproduction with commodity are worth taking seriously because she foregrounds a significant feature of our neoliberal moment. *The Heart Goes Last* describes the world engineered in

Consilience as technologizing reproduction in a vast bureaucracy, branded for ripe investment, and with no viable outside. Contradictions between reproduction and capital were already outlined by Rosa Luxemburg when she says: "The natural propagation of the workers and the requirements of accumulating capital are not correlative in respect of time or quantity. Marx himself has most brilliantly shown that natural propagation cannot keep up with the sudden expansive needs of capital" (341). Though, as Luxemburg remarks, reproduction was always a problem for capital by inserting delays in value-realization and accumulation, capital has always tried, as Marx demonstrated, to take control of an ever-increasing amount of time by capturing a larger percentage of the working day: shortening commutes, for example, making workers take their lunch at their workstations, or curtailing education in order to put children to work earlier. Neoliberalism changes the equation, making reproduction into a direct source of global profit. Rather than production depending on the controlled distributions of workers' natural birth and shortening of childhood in order to avoid instigating time delays in the productive cycle, as Luxemburg as well as Marx observed, consumption depends on reproduction's abilities to literalize commercializable social identities onto bodies. Instead of understanding the life of the laboring body required for accumulation as Luxemburg explained it, Atwood envisions world remaking through assembly reproductions of preprogrammed, duplicable human parts and sexual desires open to media saturation, excitement, surveillance, profit strategies, and control, as surplus in a world no longer constructed through labor but though consumption.

The Heart Goes Last depicts new institutions arising to contain and warehouse subjects in order to extract data from their experience, with the subject conditioned as data mine for the purpose of reduplication and sale. The prison Positron is connected to the town Consilience, an investment project with national and global pretensions in the business of producing and reproducing subjects. Victims of the economic and ecological collapse "choose" to self-incarcerate (five years before COVID-19 made world populations do just that). The volunteers come to live in what was once a disciplinary institution used to house criminals before it got gentrified. Before this, "prisoners were rented out as unpaid labour to international business interests" (47), but soon the planners find more reliable income in capitalizing on full employment, surveillance, and security systems, selling body parts, sentiment, and information, with a secret side project of selling customized sex robots called Possibilibots, free of regulation for global circulation, to meet whatever desire or fetish the world market could drum up. Possibilibots' assembly lines replicate not only bodies based on a type of realism, modeled on unaware voluntary prisoners, but also the full menu of subjective responses in experimental engineering departments specialized in Empathy and Expression for floor performances, celebrity, casinos, and shopping malls but also for the very particular sexual tastes of their elite clientele. The only way to escape from Positron is to impersonate one of the dolls, matching up their biometrics, don an Elvis outfit (for example), and ship out in a coffin. Atwood shows capital operating at the level of life, abstracting life into exchangeable units and turning the laboring body into a body made into a docile dead-like thing—or identity—in the interests of profitable extraction for sale and investment.

As would be expected, a good portion of the criticism on Atwood focuses on abortion and reproductive politics, particularly in how population collapse leads to an authoritarian takeover of reproduction.[9] Recent critics have read *The Handmaid's Tale* as celebrating "reproductive futurism," or the idea of a hegemonic future of unfettered growth secured in the image of the naturalized white child who promises the continuance of the gender binary system, its

---

[9] Heather Latimer, for example, understands *The Handmaid's Tale* as a critique of the "pro-choice" position that accepts the "pro-life" assumption that women's rights and fetal rights are opposed: "*The Handmaid's Tale* is a text which reveals how reproductive laws based on ideas of 'privacy', freedom', and 'choice' can become circular. That is, these terms can just as easily be used to strip women's rights as they can be used to grant them. ... [I]t also offers a critique of statutory abortion reforms themselves, such as *Roe v. Wade*, reminding us that they are compensatory at best" (214). Anne Balsamo is concerned with how, following the 1973 US Supreme Court decision *Roe v. Wade*, the development of new reproductive technologies increasingly pitted women's rights against fetal rights and has subjected women to surveillance and even criminalization. Balsamo's analysis sits on the cusp of a new availability of surrogacy and 1980s controversies about addiction during the "Crack crisis," and this perspective wants to rescue the biological woman from the scientific and political power exercised on her, focusing on the "technological isolation of the womb from the rest of the female body [that] promotes the rationalization of reproduction" and "the objectification and fragmentation of the female body" (91). More recent feminist perspectives like Lewis' and Sheldon's are less sanguine about presenting the female body as somehow outside or prior to technological, informational, commercial, and ideological interventions.

inequalities, and its genetically replicating lineages.[10] Sophie Lewis, for example, faults Atwood for re-naturalizing motherhood, where Atwood treats surrogacy as an authoritarian imposition, an alienating intervention into what otherwise would be—within this logic that Lewis criticizes—a natural, freely chosen relationship.[11] For Lewis, radical feminists or pronatalists who read *The Handmaid's Tale* as a warning against right-wing patriarchal ideologies of the Reagan era do not always see how the naturalized reproduction in the context of the biologized family that *The Handmaid's Tale* calls for itself reinforces the naturalization of conservative norms of race, ethnicity, gender, and alienated labor sustaining global inequality within an ideological privileging of infinite growth. Reproduction, she adds, was never outside the demands of the technologized workforce. "Your children are not your children" (153), Lewis reprises, because "[t]he regime of quasi-compulsory 'motherhood,' while vindicating itself in reference to an undifferentiated passing-on of 'life itself,' is heavily implicated in the structures that stratify human beings in terms of their biopolitical value in present societies" (21). For Lewis, Atwood's faith in a liberation from authoritarian control over production and reproduction in *The Handmaid's Tale*—what she calls liberalism or Canada—assumes that the remedy for Gilead's authoritarian overreach is in women's "natural" bounty.

---

[10] "Reproductive futurism" is adapted from Lee Edelman's contribution to queer theory *No Future*. In it, Edelman claims that politics is oriented around the figure of the child or "reproductive futurism," which he thinks of as "terms that impose an ideological limit on political discourse as such, preserving in the process the absolute privilege of heteronormativity by rendering unthinkable, but casting outside the political domain, the possibility of a queer resistance to this organizing principle of communal relation" (2). In response, Edelman advocates rejecting politics, rejecting the future, rejecting opposition, and rejecting any positive identity. Though I find some of Edelman's readings to be charming, I do not find the image of the Child to be as monolithic as Edelman seems to think by resorting to psychoanalytic models. For example, images of the Child that are mobilized in politics include appeals to sympathize with immigrants, to curtail gun violence, to end wars, to mobilize against police shootings, to fund public education, and to take action against climate change. I do not find these images always to be connected to heterosexual privilege. Also, Edelman does not consider the image of the Child that he objects to in relation to gender.

[11] "In Gilead, Atwood's fictional setting, human sexuation is neatly dimorphic and cisgendered—but that is apparently not what's meant to be dystopian about it. It's the 'surrogacy.'" With its vision of forced surrogacy, the *Tale* is many people's favorite sci-fi account of a totalitarian American regime, and by far the most popular analogy for the Trump regime among academics and op-eds alike. This is unsurprising: *The Handmaid's Tale* neatly reproduces a wishful scenario at least as old as feminism itself. Cisgender womanhood, united without regard to class, race, or colonialism, can blame all its woes on evil religious fundamentalists with guns" (10).

In contrast, *The Heart Goes Last* shows that the escape from authoritarianism into the liberal freedom of "Canada" has gone horribly wrong. Instead of the "naturalized" future child being endangered by politics, authoritarian or otherwise, desire is made to thrive, infinitely, as market culture. In Positron, for example, each job—like Stan's tending chickens—is really a useless "make-work job" (81) with the real goal of enhancing profitable desire, so that Stan's coop turns into a chicken rental market for horny men. The plot does not allow that an unadulterated "natural" child is rescuable from the interventions of scientific, political, or commercial management in a flight to a "liberalism" by the name of Canada. This theme of reproduction's place in all-things-marketable is even apparent in *The Handmaid's Tale* and the *Oryx and Crake* trilogy but only on the margins, as Rebecca Sheldon points out, where "other-than-human liveliness," "a reserve of vibrant potentiality," living energies, or, at the molecular level, "somatic capacities" can be patented and traded or turned into expensive remedies for secretly implanted diseases, disrupting the biological stability of the figure of the child by corrupting its parts. *The Heart Goes Last* goes even further in dismantling assumed oppositions between autonomous bodies and political technologies.

The novel envisions a centralized technological system organized to animate "choice" in order to extract value from it. This could constitute a feminist euphoria, with reproduction no longer residing in the birthing body in situations that feminists from Simone de Beauvoir to Shulamith Firestone identified as confining women to biological functions, domesticity, and inferiority. Yet, unlike in *The Handmaid's Tale*, Atwood here presents the line between the "inside" and "outside" of technology's authority as a technological trick. Whereas, in *The Handmaid's Tale*, Canada will set you free, in *The Heart Goes Last*, Charmaine and Stan, first on the outside, find that "[s]leeping in the car is cramped" (3) while they still feel "lucky" (3) to have a car at all before they send themselves to prison. Capital has drifted on (austerity), becoming increasingly autonomous from its former role in creating local conditions to assure reproduction. Yet the choice of joining the corporate community of Consilience does not offer reprieve as the corporate malfeasance and destruction of nature on the "outside" of Consilience blend into the destruction of human nature on the "inside" of its reproductive apparatus.

The Heart Goes Last shows an evolution in a lineage of the novel where women are associated with a historical transition in the culture of financialization because of their association with houses, domesticity, and their financialization. During the rise of mercantile imperialism, Charles Dickens situates his 1846–8 novel *Dombey and Son* during the railroad boom that underwrote Dombey's enterprise at the London docks, connecting it to an incipient shipping empire. Out of his fortune earned, Dombey builds a house, furnishes it with worldly and luxurious decorations, and lodges his wife there (almost as part of the furnishings), but when good luck turns to bad and the fortune is lost, Dombey's house shows the signs of the wreckage and waste of the financial downturn as his marriage dissolves: a "dull house" that is also "[m]ore somber and brown than ever," and within, a lady in the "dying light" (724). During the rise of neoliberalism, John Lanchester's 2012 novel, *Capital*, starts with a description of houses on a city street in 200 years of the ups and downs of urban investing, the "houses were now like people, and rich people at that, imperious, with needs of their own that they were not shy about having serviced" (14). Yet domesticity is interrupted by transformations in media, money, religion, and global terrorism, leading into the 2008 crisis as the houses lose their value.

Likewise, *The Heart Goes Last* locates a crisis in subjective reproduction within a climate of a 2008-styled real estate crash. Once in Consilience, clients are given a house for their one month in the town and share the house with another couple that lives there during the following month when the client is incarcerated. Eventually aware that the houses are built as part of the company's surveillance networks, these couples are exchangeable with each other, particularly in their replication of a desire to love and be loved by the company through its representatives. One day each month, Charmain rides her bike into an abandoned housing development—a relic from the town's agricultural past of Quaker sugar beet production, then its industrial past of auto production, and finally its financial foreclosures—now crumbling and also under renovation plans for infinite project expansion. There, under hidden cameras, she fucks Max, Stan's Alternate, who turns out to be a surveillance operative. Observing and manipulating Charmaine's "secret" meetings with Max, and then Stan's hooking up with Charmaine's Alternate Jocelyn, allow Consilience to collect information on and ultimately sell erotic tastes and desires. Consilience can, as the CEO Ed brags, "wipe out your previous love object and imprint you with a different one" (326) by a "little operation" that rewires your brain to agree to "whatever sexual use" (328) with the first object you see upon waking. Eventually, "like a superdildo, only with a body attached" (310), the desires can be engineered onto the skin or exoskeletons, the facial expressions and breathing patterns, the computer-chip memories, body heat, heartbeats, and goose bumps of "slut machines" (221) made from Chinese parts, customized, and exported to places like Holland, Vegas, or other sites replete with "cheap-bot shop[s]" (239). Consilience's practices—or malpractices—control subjective construction, as though subjects, like Elvis sex-bots, are part of a network of assembly of the most intimate and personal of experiences. "'I don't think they'll ever replace the living and breathing,'" one character remarks. Another character answers, "'They said that about e-books'" (222).

As Charmaine and Stan *choose* to enroll in Consilience's financial scheme of housing replacement and reproduction,[12] *The Heart Goes Last* makes us wonder in what sense reproductive "choice" can exist in relation to the total commodity that takes on an authoritarian character not unlike Gilead's. As the novel's prototype of "choice," Charmaine's prison job is to pull the switch to kill prisoners—at first "the worst criminals, the incorrigibles" (85), but eventually Charmaine is not so sure, though she still chooses to pull the switch, and quite happily, proud that she is doing her job well. It soon becomes clear that the purpose of the Positron Project is to collect "income from body parts ... [o]rgans, bones, DNA, whatever's in demand. . . . There's a big market for transplant market among aging millionaires, no?" (157), and Stan is on top of a list to become a source. Charmaine again chooses to pull the switch. The business of Consilience/Positron is to select the traits to reproduce humanity's future or, in Hannah Arendt's terms, to determine which *future* people with whom "to share the earth," "who should and who should not inhabit the world" (*Eichmann*, 279). "The next hot thing is going to

---

[12] "You're free to leave at any time," they are told, "if you don't like the ambience" (38).

be babies' blood," Charmaine is told. "There's no shortage" on getting babies. "People leave them lying around" (158). "Choice" here does not delineate an area of "liberal" or natural autonomy that the state contracts with the citizen but rather a principle of selection that is outside politics while bound to mechanization, automation, and commodified standardization.

Yet that is not all, because even death cannot escape Consilience's global pretensions. In fact, despite the reference to the natural state of death carried already in the title *The Heart Goes Last,* death is not necessarily death but rather an investment opportunity. Charmaine "chooses" to obey orders and kill Stan on Valentine's Day, but such killing does not affect a natural death but rather initiates a data transfer, and Stan reappears (after many Los Vegas antics with clowns). The questions raised in the title about the status of the natural-biological—is the heart already gone? Yet to go? On the verge? Does it ever really go? Was it ever really there?—are raised in the end as the paradox of "choice": Lodged pleasantly in her suburban home, Charmaine is asked by her alternate, the surveillance operative Jocelyn, if, in the face of the commodity's addictive seduction, "You want your decisions taken away from you so you won't be responsible for your own actions?" (379), and Charmaine stutters. "She might as well not have any head at all" (342). Does Charmaine "love" Stan, now an Empathy adjuster for Possibilibots? Does she or did she ever *have* a heart if the Positron implanted her desire in a data transfer, and what, then, is the status of the baby Winnie who is the product of a data breach? The happy suburban ending that Charmaine and Stan *choose* seems like a joke, coming as it does tacked onto a story about the manufactured survival of artificial subjectivity. Sophie Lewis remarks:

> If it is easier to imagine the end of the world than the end of capitalism, it is still perhaps easier to imagine the end of capitalism than the end of the family. (119)

Atwood imagines the end of imagining the family by imagining the family's unimaginability within the totally made world of the commodity. In an update of Luxemburg's observations, Atwood's novel underscores the total alienation of any naturalized social reproduction and yet our continual recourse to such emptied-out symbolic categories. The next section considers how, within world literature criticism, social reproduction, even as a world system on its own merit, continues to be out of sync with its appropriation in the worldly imaginaries of commodified global production.

Reproduction in World Literature Time

Atwood's idea of commodity reproduction is not exactly new. As Hortense Spillers famously pointed out, the commodification of reproduction for exchange can be traced to the slave trade: "[t]he captive female body locates precisely a moment of converging political and social vectors that mark the flesh as a prime commodity of exchange" (75), and Imani Perry agrees that "Black women's bodies became the economic engine of the slave economy in the United States" (37) and therefore underlie the development of the modern economy. The commodification of women's reproductive bodies for the purposes of controlling work and race can be noted contemporaneously as well, as Dorothy Roberts points out, in the new politics of fertility. Criticizing *The Handmaid's Tale* for presenting all women as "in it together" in the face of authoritarian policies on birthing, Roberts shows a trend where high-tech, capital-intensive reprogenetic technologies that were formerly marketed to white women are now also being marketed to women of color. Under neoliberal population policies with their shift to individual self-governance, the outcome, she observes, is that women of color are being asked to mitigate, through their private reproductive choices, social inequalities. "Population control policies that attribute social inequalities to the childbearing of poor minority women are a critical component of this punitive trend away from the state support for families and communities" (797). Even though genetic research has shown that race has no genetic correlation, she concludes, such technologies make women of color responsible for the "individual management of genetic risk" (798) by making decisions about the kind of life that will be possible for the future child without changing the social conditions into which that child will be born. The technologization of childbirth that is promoted as safe and secure, giving women control over the genetic makeup of their children, is resulting in the reinforcement of class and race divisions rather than critiques of power or of distributions of health care rights.

Alienation through the commodification of reproduction continues within different forms of mechanization and industrialization. Janelle Taylor, for example, explains, "Fetishism of the fetus consists in attributing to it value as 'life,' as if this were a property magically inhering in the fetus alone, in a manner that obscures the fact that the continued vitality of any actual fetus depends utterly and completely upon its continued sustenance by the woman who carries it" (189). Thus, as Sophie Lewis concludes, "the fetus becomes a commodity in people's minds regardless of whether the pregnancy is commercial" (116). Reproduction occurs within a circuit of exchange that divides the body into parts, treating parts of the body as zones of extraction and technological output. As Melinda Cooper demonstrates, "The biotech revolution . . . is the result of a whole series of legislative and regulatory measures designed to relocate economic production at the genetic, microbial, and cellular level so that life becomes, literally, annexed within capitalist processes of accumulation" (*Life as Surplus,* 19). Commodified, life itself is, Cooper elaborates, a composite of artificial intelligence, code sources, organ transplants, tissue development, and regeneration technologies, both financial and scientific, that, using chance applications, replicate in machines the processes involved in the making of life. "What regenerative medicine," she writes, "wants to elicit"—as well as market—"is the generative moment from which all possible forms can be regenerated—the moment of emergence, considered independently of its actualizations" (*Life as Surplus,* 127). This affects global trade rules as well as intellectual property laws relating to pharmaceuticals, agribusiness, and biotech to the point of upsetting ecological limits. A utopian project, the idea behind such technological investments is that the commodification of life redeems nature's deficiencies by converting nature into second nature.

For such techno-futurism, reproduction transitions from a social organization of domestic space to "scaled up" global distributions. Feminism has picked up on that potential. As Helen Hester has explained, social reproduction takes place on a "primarily local" (104) and largely autonomous plane that is restricted in scale (117). Feminism needs, says Hester, to "re-engineer the world" (9), specifically by understanding domestic labor-saving devices and other reproductive innovations like pharmaceuticals, information, digitality, and software as integrated in social systems that shape sociopolitical and material futures both inside and outside the limited spheres of the biological. Hester is mainly addressing new technologies of reproduction that might be appropriated and repurposed for political resistance against the conservative gender norms affirmed in medical practice. Yet Atwood's take on the commodification of reproduction interrogates the limits in submitting reproduction to the logic of the commodity that is "scaled up" and globalized. The "world" commodity has been historically if ideologically constructed in opposition to nature and reproduction. In this, Atwood contributes to a world literature critique that similarly envisions the commodifying pretentions of reproduction, life, nature, and subject formation in a precarious relation to a world "scaled up" in global commodity and systems terms. Nature is shown in resistance to commodification even as it is shown as its product.

In world literature criticism, a debate has taken shape over context, where the survival and reproduction of local cultures are precarious under the stronger "scaled up" imperialism that relegates the cultural locality to a subordinate and unequal status. It is the aim of these critics that this order of power now needs to be corrected. The cultural locality might be described as constituted through kinship or other types of intimate and naturalized social bonding, or through direct emotional responses considered natural and prior to the imperialist intervention. Are the terms for describing literary history adequate to the varieties of particularized cultures and identities that compose "world," or should "world" rather be thought as a group of identifiable themes and motifs that are abstracted for easier counting, comparison, translation, and exchange. Most famously, Franco Moretti talks about "the sheer enormity" (46) of world literature's task and controversially insists that new searchable, computational, and comparable categories and methods for literary history and analysis have to be developed that turn away from the particular cultural locality of a single closely read text in order to address grand systems of flow, circulation, and influence.[13] World literature criticism has sought to construct

---

[13] Moretti said this was "meant as a joke" (44).

a vocabulary for thinking about the relationship between the immediate, the intimate, and experiential reproductions of (indigenous) social relations ("the sensuous particularity of the text" (8) in Hitchcock's terms), on the one side, and the commodity that can be identified, under market globalization, through its abstractions, methods of quantification, trade value, calculabilities, and "scaling up," on the other.

Words like "world," "translation," and "planetary"[14] have been used to preserve the local as apart from the sheer enormity of the commodity's domination where, as in Atwood's big-picture, "life" and its link to nature are lost. "But he himself has been cut out of the photo" (240), laments Stan sadly as he observes a photo-model—taken at their honeymoon—of Charmaine's head being duplicated into a sex-bot. "Don't they—don't these women care about their earlier lives? Don't they resent—" (254). He later thinks, looking at himself dressed up as Elvis, "Is that all we are? . . . Unmistakable clothing, a hairstyle, a few exaggerated features, a gesture?" (269). As Hitchcock foregrounds, "the local comes sharply into view" (8) before the speeding up of world commodity circulation; yet in Atwood's speculative life-factory, something like an alienated nature comes into view in those moments of hesitation or ellipsis where the characters fleetingly remember a *something else* that *does not quite fit*: maybe nature and its time, a fleeting memory, delayed, possibly without reference. The world of world literature is thus caught in a similar balancing act between the world and the body that feminists like Atwood have noted in social reproduction.

---

[14] Chakrabarty, for example, notes, "life acts as a self-regulatory system and plays a role in maintaining planetary conditions conducive to the continuation of life" (167). "Planetariness" is even more central to Moraru and Elias' argument; they define it as a critique of globalization's homogenizing processes in favor of a *relationality*: "an ethicization of the ecumenic process of coming together or 'worlding'" (xii). As Moraru and Elias define it, "world" should be considered "a *multicentric and pluralizing, 'actually existing' worldly structure of relatedness critically keyed to non-totalist, non-homogenizing, and anti-hegemonic operations typically and polemically subtended by an eco-logic*" (xxiii). Other critics, as well, have pointed to breaks that "world" in its various forms introduces into the logic of commodity. Chantal Mouffe asks if "the production of new subjectivities and the elaboration of new worlds" (87) can "oppose the program of the total social mobilization of capitalism" (87) by undermining "the social imaginary necessary for capitalist reproduction" (88). Wai-Chee Dimock also does not think that capitalism is the only possibility for scaling up but mentions "[t]he morphology of language," some "categories of experience, such as beauty or death," and civil society (5).

As in Atwood, world literature criticism finds the subject precariously abandoned in relation to the world's scalability. This may follow from its philosophical underpinnings. For Kant, for example, the sublime, which he allegorizes as a hurricane, "cannot be contained in any sensible form" (129) being limitless and unrepresentable, "invisible forces that generate their own power" (87), a glimpse of "magnitude and might" (130), which makes anything compared with it small and our capacity to resist it "an insignificant trifle in comparison with their power" (144). "World," in the form of the sublime, is an imaginative projection beyond the immediately observable and bigger than the sensible, even threatening to it, and invites an inventive extension of the mind and its ability to represent and master outside of comparatively minuscule empirical or local experience, mortality, nature, and emotion: The subject made insecure by fear is then made secure by knowledge even as knowledge on that scale diminishes it.

Today, imagining "world" and the demands of scale "world" entails in terms of space, time, diversity, and responsibility is part of an ethical imperative to respond to global crises ranging from climate change to refugees, wars, pandemics, racisms, and inequality. In fact, if they cannot include an imaginary of "world" in the form of pandemics, environmental crises, resource depletion, economic polarization, or infinite growth (including imperialism and financialization), cultural theories will become increasingly unrecognizable and irrelevant. At the same time, while the subject in Kant overcomes his powerlessness by realizing his independence from and superiority over the challenge of magnitude to the categories of his reason, the contemporary subject, rather, understands "world" much more in line with Lukács' description of the totality of the modern commodity, where quantity and calculation appear as inhuman, impenetrable, mechanical, often hostile objects that crush, dispossess, and disappear the bounded sensible subject. For Lukács, even social relations (sensuousness, use value, the everyday) are crushed by the commodity character of the totally administered society, which, like the sublime, turns everything into quantity. The worker, says Lukács, recognizes himself as commodity because he no longer keeps "the cloak of the living thing" beneath "the quantifying crust" (169) of commodity relations. This describes how Charmaine gets lured into choosing Consilience:

During a downtime at the seedy café PixelDust where she works, having lost her job in geriatric care, Charmaine sees a man from Consilience/Positron on TV directly speaking to her and "reading her mind" (35): "Tired of living in your car?" the man on screen calls out. "Of course you are!. . . . You deserve better" (30), and Charmaine feels as though the man, looking directly into her eyes and inviting her into the ad, knows she exists. Here, in Lukácian fashion, the subject is reproduced by identifying as the commodity that offers to absorb her, to scale her up and lift her out of the demolition of the local. The reader may wonder here what Charmaine felt and experienced as subjectivity before the ad came to save her from the crash, if she was already conforming to the objectivity of the commodity so that she immediately recognized herself in the ad's address, or if there were *something else,* a contradiction.

Do the novel's failures, like the characters' stammers, allude obliquely to the commodity's breaking points, to something alienated in the commodity's world? As she describes the "scaled up" commodity of reproduction, Atwood's plotlines come up against an irreducibility, an interruption seeming like a memory or a *something else* in the ellipsis. This gap or delay may once have been called "domestic reproduction," "necessary labor," "nature" or sensibility, time or planetariness, sociality, or "woman"—an internal limit to the commodity's grasp.

The reproduction of subjects, according to world literature criticism and to feminist criticism alike, still, as time though not domestic time, contradicts the commodity from within it. World literature criticism understands time as a placeholder for this difference. Rob Nixon, for example, poses the imperative of much slower timeframes, "neither spectacular nor instantaneous but rather incremental and accretive" (2), to take account of the climate and other global problems like poverty. Likewise, Peter Hitchcock looks to literary seriality that "continues the work of decolonization by transnationalizing the time/space of its possibility" (43), or living on (26). Dipesh Chakrabarty also poses "natural reproductive life" (142), and not necessarily human life, as underlying the possibility of common responsibility that the "world" demands. In its temporalizations, Pheng Cheah maintains, "world literature points to something that will always exceed and disrupt capital" (11). "[I]mmanent sociality of human life"—including birth—," he adds, "is a power that makes worlds" (74). Similarly for Chakrabarty, "life" introduces into "world" an extension of time in the building of a multi-perspectival world dwelling. As a disturbance in the commodity world, reproduction, as a feminist like Atwood acknowledges, is also a metaphoric placeholder, perhaps an imagined future for a rich array of relationships and associations—relating, sharing, dwelling, recognizing, loving, and living—that take and expand time, time that the commodity, as Rosa Luxemberg once conveyed it, wants to reduce.

In taking up reproduction as a global issue, Atwood's novel intimates that the terms and narratives for imagining global power are irreconcilable with the sensible subject and its reproduction. Reproduction, once tied to domesticity and thus to women's oppressions elicited by the nuclear family, is now located in the commodity itself, with the commodity creating other types of inequalities and injustices through its logics of extraction through growth. The "scaling up" of "world" leaves subjects and their cultures precarious before the commodity's power and magnitude. The precarity of subjects before the commodity saturates contemporary politics, from the privatization of schooling, that turns schools into mechanisms for reproducing class society or extractable resources, to cuts in the social safety net, austerity policies, immigrant detention that breaks up families, and externalizations of the costs of corporate polluting. The politics of Atwood's narrative is not, then, so much in the ridiculous plotline, the comical scenes, or the shallow characters who are so easily duped but in the underside, the ellipses, where the unsaid pause motions toward a contradiction, inappropriable for "scaling up." As such, they break into the narrative with an allusion toward reproduction as something unrepairable within these mechanized cultures, calling for another politics.

4

Trans-commodity

I do not identify as transsexual, but I do identify as feminist, and transgender/transsexuality has become a vital issue for feminism, even a redefining one. In fact, in my understanding, feminism has to have an account of its relationship to trans, given (1) trans both affirms and undermines feminism's disordering of genders, bodies, and subjectivities as well as its critique of identity and the division of labor; and (2) trans draws a new frontier for gender and sexual politics and a new frontier for civil rights. Indeed, the overwhelming number of violent incidents and murders that have targeted trans people and particularly trans women of color, including police violence, as well as recent legislation that allows for the discrimination of trans people and trans children at the state level, demand the development of analytical principles and political involvement of feminism with trans people against all gender violence and gender-based unequal treatment.

Many feminists and trans people see each other as allies, but, still, trans theorists have noted frequently that the relationship and its history are vexed. In particular, not all feminism has seen eye to eye with trans-equal access issues like bathroom and sports access and has expressed its disagreement in terms that are discriminatory, hateful, or worse. In addition, trans theory often envisions gender as in active engagement with the social, breaking the barrier set by the "Third Wave" feminist bloggers in the first chapter where the social is an external alien force threatening the existence and security of the feminist subject. Though trans people certainly confront an often violently antagonistic sociality, they can pose a challenge to social realness and its durability, intimating that different—uncertain—social relations are already redistributing and reconditioning our practices, institutions, and priorities.

As trans theory often reads it, feminist theory has had, basically, two approaches to trans: one (the "radical feminist" or "gender critical"), mostly with a negative focus on male-to-female (MTF) transition, that suspects trans people of never becoming women but using transition to trick, violate women, and take their jobs; and second (the poststructuralist version) that treats trans as gender construction, and so not "really" a gender at all (according to its opponents). Against dismissive if not hateful premises of a "radical feminism" that polices the borders of gender as a fact of the body, I want to think about how feminism might align or realign with the radical potential of trans theory.

The reasons I turn to the commodity in order to discuss a potential of a trans-feminist alliance is that (1) as a historical narrative of alienation, the commodity poses a framework for analyzing current-day social precarity that both trans people and women face, that is, a disassociation from the terms of symbolic belonging and attachment; (2) the commodity explains the disconnections between something called "realness"—or the "empirical" terms of the body's recognition in an exchange society—and the ghostliness of this "realness"—the multiple unrecognizable and invisible passionate and historical traces that split through the surface of "realness." As Marx tells us, the commodity has an aesthetic/surface quality, its outward form that can be compared to or exchanged with others through an abstract standard, and also an inner life, the multiplicity of its contextual, intimate, embodied, situated, historical, and everyday uses: "Whoever directly satisfies his wants with the produce of his own labour," Marx explains the twofold structure of the commodity, "creates, indeed, use-values, but no commodities. In order to produce the latter, he must not only produce use-values, but use-values for others, social use-values" (307). Seen in light of the commodity, trans may be read as the place that makes visible both the exchange society mediated through "real" gender and the multiple buried, contradictory, and abstract histories of social relatedness resurfacing inside gender assignment.

I address the "radical feminist" fiasco later. First, I touch on the debate that trans theory has with poststructuralist feminism as the legacy of the essentialist/constructivist debates and suggest that gender's inescapable cavorting with artificiality (or construction) links it to the commodity as the embodiment of hidden social relations that Marx describes. Trans—like

"woman" as it has been defined in much feminist theory since the 1990s—
is an umbrella term for diverse situations, some but not all electing various
surgeries or hormonal treatments, some refusing to identify as gendered or
as one of the two binaries of the dominant gender system, some living only
part-time or even just dressing in alternative gender roles, some engaging in
same-sex partnerships and others with multiple partners of various genders
and races or no partners at all, some taking voice lessons and having cosmetic
surgeries and hair removal and some not, some "out" in all aspects of their
lives and others not. Yet, while Julia Serano says, "Each of us simply needs to
figure out what works best for us and what allows us to best express who we
feel we are" (29), gender expression is not just a personal choice or difference
but a constant and repeated engagement with social and historical markers,
expectations, institutions, habits, language, family structures, sensibilities,
medical knowledge, diagnosis, insurance, pharmacology, psychiatry, and
divisions of labor, framed in terms of already existing social practices and
forms of self-understanding—or "reality"—but not necessarily or precisely
restricted to repeating those.

Even as some trans people insist that "realness" or "passing" is a survival
strategy, gender "realness" can be seen as the body's literalization of the
division of labor or the society of exchange *against diversity*. I appreciate that
some trans people as well as some non-trans people feel their gender as real
both physically and psychologically, and I am mindful of any person's right to
identity, expression, and sexual freedom. Furthermore, I recognize that identity
constructivism does not necessarily offer a truer political or oppositional
strategy, as constructivist thought can as easily lend itself to market and state
appropriations as can essentialism (there are no guarantees). Nevertheless,
I still want to scrutinize the work that assertions of gender "realness" do in
a culture within which conventions of understanding gender as "real" have
confined people to consumerism and its inequalities. Trans people are not,
exclusively, the ones doing this. Both "radical feminist" essentialists and trans
"wrong body" essentialists promote a reading of gender as "realness," that is,
as the expression of an inner self that fits with the symbolic order on which
commercialism and the division of labor both depend. This perspective erases
the ghostly impact of sociality and culture on the alien body—or the body/

identity's "artificiality" as a result of its alienation from the social structure that gives it meaning.

By creating "positive images" or political affirmations of trans, women, or any identity in Hollywood or in advertising as in the popular 2020 Netflix documentary *Disclosure,* trans is adapted inside of a familiar narrative of liberal "progress" as market expansion. *Disclosure* is an uplifting celebration of celebrity trans identity as an aspirational hope for lonely and alienated people wanting to see versions of themselves on the screen. This makes trans seem as a new arena in which progressivism can boast of itself as incrementally inclusive. In practice, though, the current commercial mainstreaming of trans culture and politics as well as the increased embrace of trans identity might imply quite the opposite, where an acceptable image is popularized that excludes elements of that identity that would make it unacceptable. With the expanded claims of identities by commercial interests, gender is a word that may mark a social precarity or alienation. I am not sanguine, then, about the neoliberal marketing of everything that pretends to "fix" or compensate loneliness, trauma, or precarity by turning lonely or traumatized individuals into trans-commodities as *Disclosure* depicts. I am interested here, rather, in theory that has highlighted trans as an instance of the gender commodity's dysphoria.

Trans theory that recognizes the commodity's imbrication in gender can explain how the making of gender, as a historical project, is about the remaking of social relations and the division of labor. I here look to where two trans theorists—novelist and scholar of the long eighteenth century Jordy Rosenberg and YouTube performer Natalie Wynn, or *ContraPoints*—have considered the commodity as part of their trans critique. My purpose is not to suggest a singular intention behind transitioning or the many other modes of living askew of sex and gender norms, or to force trans to fulfill political needs that lie elsewhere. Rather, my purpose is to discuss instances when neoliberal politics is made visible *and unstable* through not only trans but gender in general, marking a political potential. Though I argue that gender as such and by definition is always, as a social and symbolic category, detached from the particular bodies it inhabits, I also argue that the popularization and mainstream acceptance of trans identities highlight this social detachment as particularly acute and generally normalized within neoliberalism. Since we recognize that we generally do not do gender the same ways as our parents or the same ways that it is done in other places, we might be able to agree that gender is historically contingent, embedded in constantly changing contexts and norms. Violence against trans people is a compelling reminder of the punishment inflicted on those who break the rules of doing gender right for the context where they do it; and yet, anybody who does not feel dysphoric—in some sense not recognizing themselves in terms of the meanings conferred by the gender assigned—might not be very reflective or historically conscious. If, under neoliberal hegemony, social identities are optimized in relation to their economic viability and the marketability of their traits, narratives, and features (as *Disclosure* suggests), then gender identity should feel distorted, wrong, or to varying degrees out of sync. Violence against trans people might in part be a response to a growing awareness that neoliberalism's economizing of gender and all identities makes people feel unbelonging, creating disassociations and disaffections with familiar means of social stability.

Trans history precedes the commodity capture of gender dysphoria and transition by medical discourse, treatment, and technologies that was popularized from the time of Christine Jorgensen's celebrity reassignment in the front pages of *The New York Daily News* in the early 1950s, as Julian Gill-Peterson has outlined.[1] Yet the twenty-first century's mainstreaming of medicalized transitioning cannot be thought outside the intersections of identity and commodity that twenty-first-century neoliberalism has ushered in. As Jack Halberstam, for example, stipulates, "young trans* people increasingly discover information about themselves online rather than through older trans* people" (64), while that information often prescribes "chemical scripts in which bodies can be energized or quieted, made fertile or infertile, awakened or numbed, made to feel more or to feel less" (29). A memoir like Juliet Jacques' *Trans* cites malls, movies, websites, and

---

[1] "In reality," Gill-Petersen maintains, "there was no revolutionary technological or medical shift in midcentury. Transsexuality is, rather, a medical discourse that distracts from forms of knowledge and being that are disqualified by its rationality and its timescale, minimizing a half-century of trans life and interaction with medicine that both precedes and informs it" (12).

music as guiding the trans character toward transition: "I entered Affleck's Palace, the five-floor 'alternative' shopping centre" (17), for example, or "I'd learned how to walk in them [heels] from a scene in *The Simpsons*" (48), or "I've become the media" (212). Both Wynn and Rosenberg likewise center gender commodification in their trans analysis. In these accounts gender's increasingly evident artificiality, its alienation, in the current climate may signal "the fear of a total collapse of social order" (41), as Rosenberg says of religious passion in his *Critical Enthusiasm*, the present transitioning to another social realness.

Butler, Performance Theory, and "Drag"

Majorly influential in opening new feminist pathways, Judith Butler's *Gender Trouble* (1990) offered the now commonly known description of gender as performance. Her evidence focuses on drag as the cutting edge of embodied gender construction that subverts the laws and norms of essentialism even while reenforcing them. "[D]rag," she notes, "fully subverts the distinction between inner and outer psychic space and effectively mocks both the expressive model of gender and the notion of a true gender identity" (186). Essentialism for Butler is a naturalization of social and symbolic norms on the body that assumes that the body's meanings precede the body's socialization; gender essentialism "hides" the production of gender the way the commodity "hides" the worker's input. Constructivism, meanwhile, assumes a body that does not transcend history but that can be "produced" through the actions of historical agents, though without guarantees of the political outcome. Though acknowledging that "we regularly punish those who fail to do their gender right" (190), Butler treated drag not only —or correlatively transgender, transsexualism, transvestism, gender-nonbinary—as an exclusive practice of a marginalized community but also as a paradigmatic instance that explains how gender categories stylize bodies at the most basic level of the gesture. In other words, we all do drag whether we are dressing in the clothes of an "opposite" gender or our assigned one, because any gender performance repeats the naturalization of gender with a difference, thereby revealing its constructedness and its changeability, its reconstructability and reiterability. In her introduction to the 2006 edition, Butler likens transsexualism to drag as exposing the unreality and artifice of gender's outer appearances, and specifically states that such identifications are *not* "*an example* of subversion" (xxiii) but rather an illustration of how naturalized categories of knowledge come into question, are legitimated and delegitimated.[2]

Butler's idea that gender is an action—even if restricted through the symbolic gender framework of its historical moment—rather than an ontology or a biological given was exciting for a feminism responding to a sexist culture presuming "women" were indelibly marked with attributes that socially and sexually subordinated them or confined them to exploited roles within the division of labor. Meanwhile, a reaction against Butler's legacy pervades trans writing, particularly for her denial of gender essentialism or for a misreading that says Butler makes gender into a free choice, as easy as getting dressed in the morning. For instance, in her now classic *Whipping Girl*, Julia Serano takes to task what she calls "deconstructive feminism"—a term for which she cites Butler as her only example (though she explicitly blames Butler's unnamed followers)—for its assumption that "femininity is artificial" because "[w]hile femininity is in many ways influenced, shaped, and enforced by society, to say that it is entirely 'artificial' or merely a 'performance' is patronizing toward those whom femininity simply *feels right*" (338). Butler, though, does not imply that gender is unreal because it is constructed but rather that gender does not transcend its historical situation and so is as real as its context. Yet

---

[2] Recently, it seems to me that Butler is pulling back on these premises, mostly in response to trans issues: "The problem, in fact," she notes, "was never biology as such, but only a certain account of biological sexual difference governed by natural teleology. The clear separation between the two was important for making the claim that no natural teleology governs the social development of a woman from a biological condition of being female. A social man could emerge from a biological female; a social woman could emerge from a biological female" ("Gender in Translation," 3). In this essay, Butler tries to come to terms with trans within the vocabulary that she developed to talk about gender. At the start, she seems critical about some people who "may want to say that sex is a fact—although the persistence of intersex and chromosomal variation rightly challenges our ideas of bodily dimorphism" (4). She calls this a "monolingual insistence" that does not take into account that all such claims are "haunted by migration" (10). Later on, however, she defends claims to body essentialism as "legitimate" as it "tells us about a group of people who are searching for livable lives within the language that they find or make or refuse. Indeed, one cannot be 'against' any of these positions, if each of them opens up a different trajectory of hope for living a livable life" (17).

some pro-trans perspectives beat back against the performativity thesis with an ethics of realism.

The "woman in a man's body" essentialist rationale for transsexualism sometimes appears in trans literature overlapping with the essentialisms of a "radical feminism" that believed we are born in an essential gender—one of two—that does not change throughout our lifetimes or histories. In a rare moment of conceding to the diagnostic model of gender dysphoria, Natalie Wynn of *ContraPoints* assures her viewers that every little girl (i.e., born girl even if assigned differently) wants to be a Disney Princess, and that would even be the case if there were Communism ("AMA Stream/June 2020"). She may be joking. Julia Serano, too, does insist on intrinsic "gender inclinations" (104), including some aesthetic preferences and emotional sensibilities, hardwired by an indelibly female subconscious self that is beyond social influence or conscious reach and that transcends both biology and socialization. By "subconscious sex," Serano means "an urge or desire to be female" (79), which started at the age of five or six, even though everyone treated her as a boy. This inner conviction consisted of, for example, winding herself in a curtain as though it were a dress when she had insomnia, or playing adventure games where she got turned into a girl and could not get back to boyness. She takes this to indicate that her subconscious brain always knew that she was meant to be female despite her assignment. She does not explain what gives her assurances that these symbolic behaviors—like wearing a dress—necessarily, always, and everywhere qualify biologically or subconsciously as given girl behaviors.

As well, Serano believes that mainstream acceptance of transsexuals will follow from a greater understanding and a greater understanding will follow from solidifying the meanings in the vocabulary used to describe transsexualism. Presenting a blueprint to avoid misinterpretations, Serano provides a transsexual glossary, a reclaiming of self-representation, autobiographies, bodies, sexualities, and perspectives with "words that accurately describe their gendered experiences in both past and present" (30). In this, Serano has little in common with anything poststructuralist. Such attaching of words to meanings as though they belong together essentially or ontologically—a restricted use of language as non-signifying and non-contextual—underlies, as well, the enforcement of gender norms by science and other means to restrict women's access to economic, educational, and political involvement and to keep them bound in institutional norms set by the family, the social institutionalization of sex roles whose most restrictive manifestations feminism has abhorred. Ironically, perhaps, the attachment between words and "real" meanings of experience parallels some of the essentialism that "radical feminist" Janice Raymond (discussed later) assumes when she says that one is only ever "really" the sex they are assigned at birth. Both "radical feminism," which thinks trans cannot achieve "true womanhood" because they do not have the experience of a feminine body from birth, and trans theory, which insists trans is the experience of real femininity even if they have been mis-assigned a false gender at birth, have similarities in their joint espousal of an essential truth in gender and a historically stagnant language use.

The politics of realism that Serano espouses, I argue, replicates the commodity's version of reality that denies its own social production. "The fantasized body can never be understood in relation to the body as real," writes Butler. "The limits to the "real" are produced within the naturalized heterosexualization of bodies" (96). Trans theory has recognized its imbrications with commodity theory. Starting his history in the 1950s with the rise of Hugh Heffner's mainstream pornography empire, the beginning of cross-sex surgery in the United States in Henry Benjamin's clinic, and the test trials for the birth control Pill in Puerto Rico, Paul Preciado, for example, reads sex and gender as a technique for intensifying bodily sensation with an eye to the selling of pills, excitation machines, and pornography. "What if," he asks, "in reality, the insatiable bodies of the multitude—their cocks, clitorises, anuses, hormones, and neurosexual synapses—what if desire, excitement, sexuality, seduction, and the pleasure of the multitude were all the mainsprings of the creation of value added to the contemporary economy?" (*Testo Junkie*, 37).[3] While Susan Stryker asserts that "[f]or most people, there

---

[3] In response to Preciado, Gill-Peterson notes that the plasticity of the body (that Preciado attributes to its commodification) is transferred onto the trans child even before the mid-twentieth century when medical diagnoses and medical products claimed control over that body. The idea that the trans child's identity is available to morphology and alteration feeds a developmental logic of whiteness (recapitulation) at the heart of clinicalized trans identities, says Gill-Petersen, where children pass through primitive stages and then change as they move through evolutionary categories. This

is a sense of congruence between the category one has been assigned to at birth and socialized into and what one considers oneself to be" (27), and Julia Serano agrees that "everyone else around me seems to feel entitled to their gender to the point where they take it for granted" (182), the sense that "everyone else" *may* have of their gender, even if unacknowledged, is that they are out of sync with it and alienated, having to maintain it through constant workouts, dieting, dressing, medicating, surgeries, therapies, eating disorders, sex, media, role playing, makeup, trips to the salon, and the like, and never feeling quite right in their role expectations nor exactly the same as the gender of their parents—this is what is called "History." The essentializing of gender in certain articulations of trans or feminist thinking turns gender into an extractive object whose social content is buried, so that the relation between identity and the social appears precarious and punitive.

Butler acknowledges disagreements with Marx. Even though Butler occasionally concedes to Marx in her discussions of how "woman" and "man" acquire fixed and reified meanings, for Butler the theory of commodity developed by Marx and then Lukács "presupposes a potential adequation between the 'I' that confronts its world, including language, as an object, and the 'I' that finds itself as an object in that world" (196). In other words, the theory that the workers put his life into the commodity and then stand separate from it, lost and alienated, implies that there is an essential reality that is not attached to the commodity's movement, its resignification through exchange that produces reality. For Butler, we can never be adequate to our gender (the Symbolic); we are always failing to do it right under the punitive mandate that we must. So, language, the Symbolic, and gender for Butler— using psychoanalytic models—do not confront the subject from the outside in an objectified form, as does the product of labor, but as an interiority.[4]

---

mainstreaming affirmation of bodily malleability as developmental leaves aside the punitive model that applies most often to children of color for non-normative self-presentations including trans (122–3).

[4] She also criticizes Monique Wittig's Marxism and Lukács' for espousing the notion of "reification," and in Wittig's case interpreting the "mark of sex" as an imposition, an external institutional form unmoved by particular practices and with history ending as dimorphous gender does (*Gender Trouble*, 35).

Even so, Butler can still be seen as overlapping with Marx in parts of her thinking. As with the commodity, the Symbolic for Butler has the appearance of reality even as it has been separated from its referential interiority and its origin, projecting back from its future an origin as phantasm. The Symbolic enters desire's circuits of exchange, even though it is inadequate and forecloses on its enabling conditions. In parallel, the made object, Marx elucidates in the *Economic and Philosophic Manuscripts of 1844*, is composed of the workers' lives and subjectivities that they put into the object (or that the object sucks out of them, like a vampire) even as the object, like the Symbolic for Butler, is separated and assumes an outside existence:

> Just as in religion, the spontaneous activity of the human imagination, of the human brain and the human heart, operates independently of the individual—that is, operates on him as an alien, divine or diabolical activity—in the same way the worker's activity is not his spontaneous activity. It belongs to another; it is the loss of his self. (74)

Even though for Butler, in contrast, the origin of the Symbolic is but a projection of the Symbolic onto a "before," the constitution of our identities in history, gender, is, similar to the commodity object, the objectification of social relations that confronts us as an unrecognizable, illegible, alien, external, even punitive (like God, the devil, or the market) version of ourselves. "*What will they think when they see the male name on your headstone?*" (*Trans*, 146). Trans makes visible the gender dysphoria that pervades gendered being as such.

Gender dis-identifications, just like gender identifications, must be understood as part of the condition of modern commercial life that confronts us from the outside with advertising and celebrity telling its audiences to run to the gym or buy a luxury car in order to achieve mental health, security, and social viability that are not achievable. Jack Halberstam acknowledges, "there is no accounting here [in "gender dysphoria" diagnosis] that a person's distress over their gender identity may be the result of social exclusion, family violence, or reduced employment opportunities rather than a struggle with gender identification" (47). In this view, trans is the name for an identity that, understanding its precarity in relation to the social, seeks to enact the social world it envisions itself part of. *"[W]hat if we're not trapped in the wrong body but trapped in the wrong society?"* (*Trans*, 305). As Natalie Wynn says in her contentious show on "Opulence," citing Shon Faye from Jenny Livingston's 1990 popular cult film *Paris Is Burning*, realness is "not just a sassy word for a convincing costume but a tragicomic disguise of the chasm between what is being emulated and what is absent (namely racial justice, class equality, and safety)." The reason, then, that trans is mainstreaming now could be that within a neoliberal culture of the commodity, social precarity is mainstream, making workers obsolete and political systems unrepresentative. Trans projects a desire for a sociality that does not yet exist.

TERF

The word TERF is a pejorative for a person who dressed up transphobia with radical feminism.

—Natalie Wynn, "Gender Critical"

As a feminist writing on trans issues, I cannot ignore the conflict that frames the conversation between trans theory and what trans critics call "trans-exclusionary radical feminism" (TERF). The "radical feminist" interpretation of trans alleges that trans is reinforcing gender norms by claiming as intrinsic or natural certain attributes and behaviors that specifically fall under social gender codes (e.g., Caitlin Jenner's desire to paint her nails is in the repertoire of the reasons she gave for transitioning) or that trans are just men trying to trick their way into women's-only spaces (this would include the recent spate of legislation against trans people in sports).

The TERF pokes its head up in unlikely places. *The New York Times* reported that J. K. Rowling on Twitter has mocked the term "women who menstruate" in an article about menstrual hygiene during COVID-19 lockdown (Gross) and defended Maya Forstater, a tax expert at the Center for Global Development who wrote a series of tweets opposing the UK's Gender Recognition Act that would allow people to choose their own gender designation on official state documents. In a follow-up article on her own website, Rowling doubled down: Here, she confessed her long-held secret of being the victim of domestic abuse and how she suspected some trans people who rejected surgery as wanting to gain entry into women's bathrooms for the purpose of assault and violation: "When you throw open the doors of bathrooms and changing rooms to any man who believes or feels he's a woman—and, as I've said, gender confirmation certificates may now be granted without any need for surgery or hormones—then you open the door to any and all men who wish to come inside. That is the simple truth." Rowling claimed that the bathroom legislation "triggered" her earlier trauma: "I couldn't shut out these memories and I was finding it hard to contain my anger and disappointment about the way I believe my government is playing fast and loose with womens [*sic*] and girls' safety." I am sympathetic to Rowling as a victim of assault, though I am less sympathetic that Rowling seems to be using the bathroom to present the dangers to women that lurk around any social space where gender is produced and reproduced or where gender confirmation as a pre-scripted social ritual is practiced.

Rowling is not very original. She clings at the coattails of a line of women calling themselves feminist who, in the name of feminism and women's safety, have disparaged trans people as fake women and therefore lurking predators. The most frequently cited example, Janice Raymond, writes, in the 1994 introduction to *The Transsexual Empire*,

My view is that . . . the male-to-female transsexual is . . . the incarnation of a male fantasy of feeling like a woman trapped in a man's body, the fantasy rendered flesh by a further male medical fantasy of surgically fashioning a male body into a female one. These fantasies are based in the male imagination, not in any female reality. (xx)

This allegation becomes the basis for Raymond's blaming of transsexuals for the exploitation of women in cosmetic surgeries, for example, for the exploitation of sex workers, for men taking women's jobs, for putting women at risk by asserting their male privilege to enter their women's-only and lesbian separate "safe spaces," and for reinforcing sexual stereotypes that have been harmful to women. Indeed, transsexualism is even responsible, in this reading, for the failures of the healthcare system as it elevates technical solutions to moral and ethical problems in order to consolidate its expertise, control, and profits. "All transsexuals," Raymond appallingly concludes, "rape women's bodies by reducing the real female form to an artifact, appropriating this body for themselves" (104). Though Raymond is not alone (as exhibited by J. K. Rowling's nearly exact adoption of these premises), and she is certainly not representative of feminism's main current attitudes toward trans, Raymond's anti-trans "radical feminism" may seem dominant as her voice was often showcased, being particularly, and spectacularly, obnoxious.

Raymond definitely had collaborators. Sheila Jeffreys, for example, wrote of "Transfemininity" that "Femininity is sexually exciting to the men who seek it because it represents subordinated status and thus satisfies masochistic sexual interest" (46). Jeffreys uses the word "autogynephilia" (50) to describe transitioning, a clinical word that means a form of narcissism where men get excited by their own image as women (often linked to masochism and internalized hatred). Mary Daly, who dedicated her *Gyn/Ecology* (1978) to Janice Raymond, writes in the 1985 introduction to *Beyond God the Father* (1973) that "a 'transsexed' male is still male. . . . A transsexed patriarchal god is still patriarchal and will function . . . to serve the interest of the fathers, for such a symbol is external to the experienced reality of women and nature" (xviii), mixing up a symbol representing patriarchal power with a historical person having, most likely, many psychological and experiential relationships with symbols of patriarchal power. As well, in *Gyn/Ecology* Daly likens transsexuals to robots who erase women from culture and replace them with technology. Identifying on the side of such feminism, Michael Schwalbe, more recently, takes transsexualism to task for not satisfying feminist political desire: "Pass successfully and reinforce the gender binary? . . . It is this individualist, apolitical, unsociological stance on transsexualism that bothers radical feminists. Rightly so" (141). Such vituperation treats transsexualism as a malignant twin of patriarchy, even as Schwalbe leaves out any direct engagement with trans people's own accounts. This view leaves non-transsexual ("cis") and feminist women blameless for reinforcing gender norms when *they* pass successfully even though most gender norming is theirs.

In trans writing, the two events most often referenced to exhibit the cultural effects of such trans exclusionary rhetoric are the Michigan Womyn's Music Festival, a women's-only event that occurred from 1976 to 2015 (most recently remembered in the TV series *Transparent*) that admitted only "womyn-born womyn" and excluded transsexuals, and the British record label Olivia Records with the transsexual Sandy Stone at its direction (who allegedly did not reveal her trans identity when taking the job). Sandy Stone did write back in answer to Raymond and her crew. First presented in 1987 and published subsequently in journals, collections, and online, "The *Empire* Strikes Back: A Posttranssexual Manifesto" presents a version of transsexual history that turns Raymond on her head by exposing her view's complicity with that of the patriarchal medical and technological logic she claims to oppose in opposing transsexualism: "we find the epistemologies of white male medical practice, the rage of radical feminist theories and the chaos of lived gendered experience meeting on the battlefield of the transsexual body" (13). Reviewing first the early accounts of transition that were written by those undergoing surgery, Stone finds that the sex change medical bureaucracy demanded the confession of "wrong body" for a diagnosis, so its specialists invented the gender reification that Raymond, for example, attributed to the transsexual as such. Often, those seeking transition would have read surgeon Harry Benjamin's pathbreaking 1966 book *The Transsexual Phenomenon*, which includes the "wrong body" as a tell-tale symptom requiring surgical treatment. "As clinicians and transsexuals continue to face off across the diagnostic battleground," she deduces, "the transsexuals for whom gender identity is something different from *and perhaps irrelevant to* physical genitalia are occulted by those for whom the power of the medical/psychological establishments, and their ability to act as gatekeepers for cultural norms, is the final authority for what counts as a culturally intelligible body" (15). From there, Stone develops a theory of reading that—demoting science and technology—likens trans to interpretation (rather than transparency, "realness," or authenticity), likens trans people to embodied texts (genres), and likens transsexualism not only to intertextualism but also to mixed genre.

Privileging language and narrative over science and medicine, Stone's account keys into not only a poststructuralism of the gendered body that posits gender fluidity against powerful institutions and protocols that want to fix and conventionalize its "realness" and meaning. Also, Stone's emphasis on interpretation as lived gender likens trans to critique and characterizes anti-trans scholarship as though participating in anti-theory trends in critical theory. Stone says that transsexual "passing"—when an individual succeeds in not being identified as trans—occurs when the intertextual possibilities get subordinated and the body's identity can appear to align transparently with its socially assigned meaning, which, Stone observes, "*is itself a medically constituted textual violence*" (14). This description of "passing" dovetails with Rita Felski's description of an anti-critical standpoint where readers have a direct experience of the text as surface. Criticizing the skeptical "mood" of theoretical reading, Felski hopes to save literary studies from its "crisis" by reverting to spontaneous encounters with texts' surfaces that scholarly or "critical" approaches have belittled: She brackets out discussions of power and ideology, ignoring the layerdness of linguistic meaning and disregarding skepticism: "scholar-critics learn to look down on empirical knowledge, to disparage the staleness of the everyday life-world, to call into question the natural and self-evident" (25), Felski laments. Stone's account of transsexualism exposes the bankruptcy of Felski's polemic: Accepting what we see on the empirical surface of social/textual beings is to erase the "*intertexual possibilities of the . . . body*" (14), or the "troubling and productive multiple permeabilities of boundary and subject" (14); historical, cultural, and social struggles over the production of symbolic meanings are repressed under the naturalized appearance. In Marx's sense, while the transsexual—like the worker—puts his work, language, experience, and unconsciousness into the gendered object, the object no longer belongs to him—it belongs instead to the symbolic apparatus of social recognition and its commercial and medical establishments.

The conception of the body as multi-textual and multi-generic challenges the "wrong body" diagnosis in all its guises and even the idea of "realness" that bolsters up the division of labor and its culture of the commodity. It implies that we *read* bodies, meaning that our encounters with bodies are mediated through layers of textual meanings, historical inferences, and theoretical influences. Our subconscious is not stuck in place at birth, like an object.

Freud's concept of a human Unconscious in dreams and play did not stultify phantasy and did not attribute subjectivity to a singular event like dancing in the curtains or to a recognition of type (or genre) based on observing an empirical surface but saw it developing through substitutions and distortions in unfolding encounters with historical contexts, texts, language, and internal energies: "We have already learnt that a single symptom corresponds quite regularly to several meanings *in succession*. In the course of years a symptom can change its meaning or its chief meaning, or the leading rôle can pass from one meaning to another" (46). Freud uses words like "reading," "interpretation," and "translation" to illustrate how images in phantasy and dreams are not self-evident but layered, detaching and reattaching to narratives of experience in different forms and positions. The Unconscious is resistance against assigned social place; so, as Sylvia Federici has written, "the struggle to destabilize our assigned identities cannot be separated from the struggle to change the social/ historical conditions of our lives and above all undermine social hierarchies and inequalities" (2019: 31). The TERF insistence that a man will be nothing but a man runs parallel to a "wrong body" diagnosis where the brain is hardwired for an unchanging genre of experience, an unchanging canon. Trans, as Juliet Jacques reflects, is being trapped not in the wrong body but rather "by a society that didn't want me to modify it" (76).

ContraPoints

"I like stuff. I like shiny things," YouTube star Natalie Wynn declares in "Opulence." Wynn ended her career as a doctoral student in philosophy at Northwestern University in 2015 when she decided that what she judged as the political irrelevancy of some philosophical projects was just making her miserable. Instead, she would more directly counter what she saw as authoritarian trends in online culture but not just online. "Why does Donald Trump's apartment look like Liberace married a Turkmenistani dictator and moved into a Cheesecake Factory?" ("Opulence"). "Why don't we fight the pageantry of fascism," she responds, "with pageantry of our own?" ("The Aesthetic"). Wynn started engaging in YouTube as a New Atheist, but even after she grew disillusioned with this movement, YouTube algorithms were still directing her toward other alt-right content. Wynn's YouTube program is part of a conversation with right-wing online activists and content-makers: Using Socratic methods and techniques of persuasion and taking seriously even the most outrageous slurs of a hate culture out of control, she sets up dialogues with her adversaries where she theatrically plays all the characters in the conversation, often staging these conversations through drag-like performances, spectacular costuming, elaborate sets, occasional slapstick, dramatic lighting, tons of makeup, long claw-like multicolored sparkly nails, and narratives (e.g., in her show on "Jordan Peterson" she takes a bath with a cardboard cut-out of Peterson and pours white liquid soap on his face while the camera cringes in and out of focus). It is "possible to express yourself by becoming someone else," she explains the dialogical theatrics in a lecture at *XOXO Festival 2018*. The conversational mode of point-counter-point allows her to give personality, character, drama, and credibility to the opposition, even when the opposition is hateful, at a time when the United States and the world too have been steeped in so much political polarization that many find it nearly impossible to understand, identify with, or politically engage the other half.

The topics on her channel range from online phenomena like canceling, shaming, incel, alt-right, "traps," and cringe to philosophical concepts like aesthetics, the West, degeneracy, apocalypse, and capitalism, and contentious concepts for cultural debate over gender like gender critical, autogynephilia, men, and transtrenders, and points of political contention like the Left, violence, and racism, often citing cultural critics like Badiou, Deleuze, Butler, Benjamin, Hume, Kant, Hegel, Marx, Spinoza, Wittgenstein, Plato, Aristotle, Herodotus, and John Berger, and explaining in accessible terms how they can be applied against rising fascism even as she rejects the history of philosophy for its lack of relevancy. Sometimes, Wynn's show feels like therapy or confessional as she airs her despair, her loneliness, her self-deprecation, or her dysphoria-related emotional distress, which she calls "The Darkness" and treats in an over-the-top horror-movie aesthetic with skulls and lightening. Sometimes, parodying philosophers, aristocrats, or filmic tropes, she responds to comments on her site as well as to memes, social media, and other YouTubers with channels, who are mostly conservative, presenting herself in extravagant colors and sets (filmed in her own small apartment and crowdsourced), making popular culture inside of ongoing discussions about popular culture.

"Sometimes a cigar," Wynn says, citing Sigmund Freud in her show on "Are Traps Gay?", "is just a beautiful woman's penis." ("Are Traps Gay?" takes on the transphobic excuse for assault that alleges trans people are tricking or "trapping" straight men into gay sex.) In 2017, Wynn started her transition. Addressing how her transition related to her internet-based video production, Wynn says it seemed to her that an "old version of myself was always hanging around next to me and I can never escape it" (*XOXO Festival*), with that old version popping up in screen images carrying her deadname that she could not erase. Her transition thus transpires on YouTube over the course not only of the enrichment of the production value of her program but also of her becoming increasingly a media celebrity and political commentator: She was interviewed on the popular podcast *Chapo Trap House* and cited in *The New York Times* and *New York Magazine* on trans issues, for example, and called by *Vice* "the Oscar Wilde of *YouTube*." Wynn told me in a May 2020 livestream video chat with her over half million patrons (clocking at nearly five hours) that her critique of commodity and fascism was unrelated to her transition. In her June 2020 livestream, she was even more explicit. Emphatically, she said that gender transition was "definitely not an invented desire of the consumer society"; in fact, it was "quite the opposite." "When was the last time," she asked, "you saw an advertisement for transitioning?" Though she acknowledged that the ideal of womanhood is based in consumption, she only has seen media representations of trans people as "dangerous, perverted, and tragic victims." Even if films like *Disclosure* were not exuding commodity shine around trans celebrity, this response assumes that all advertisement is positive affirmation (rather than, as in horror movies, selling you fear and inadequacy, or lack); it assumes a separation between the type of desire a gender transition puts into play and the increasing prevalence in media of gender experiments since David Bowie, Calvin Klein underwear ads, and the 1980s. Dating such gender excitation from the 1950s when Hugh Heffner wires up his bed with media for work and play, trans theorist Paul Preciado elaborates, "Pharmacopornographic biocapitalism"—the production, circulation, and sale of chemical- and media-induced gender biocodes— "does not produce things. It produces movable ideas, living organs, symbols, desires, chemical reactions, and affects. In the fields of biotechnology and pornocommunication, there are no objects to produce; it's a matter of inventing a subject and producing it on a global scale" (*Testo Junkie*, 54). As a result, she goes on, "It's not at all difficult to go to a bodybuilder's website to order ten doses of 250-milligram testosterone for seventy-five dollars, postage included. This is the paradox inherent in the strict legal controls that govern the pharmacopornographic regime: gender is for sale" (*Testo Junkie*, 233). A case in point, *ContraPoints* overlays the making of a woman with the creation of a shiny YouTube phenomenon.

"I like stuff and I want more stuff . . . I'm a dumb dumb and I like shiny things," Natalie Wynn says again, this time to a floating bust of Socrates at the beginning of "What's Wrong with Capitalism Part II." In the "What's Wrong with Capitalism?" duology, Wynn does battle with two giant reptilic creatures— she calls them not capitalists but capital itself—dressed up and playing cards in a black-and-white penthouse with gauche paisley wallpaper and doom-and-gloom horror-flick music resounding in the background and with a picture window overlooking a generic skyscraper-littered urban landscape far below. Here Wynn develops what she calls in an interview with Liza Featherstone of *The Nation* "aesthetic intervention" (22), where the argument is made through aesthetic play and pleasure is found in the argument itself. As capital's pre-evolutionary, pre-modern unconscious, these luxuriant underwater creatures rise to outmoded overlord status. Not only is the dialogical set-up the stage-setting of the *ContraPoints* format, but the dialogical inhabits the ironic style, as well, composed of layered meanings, intertexts, and visual contradictions. The reptiles, for example, are granted spectacular metaphysical power even while appearing pathetic in their awkward gestures and their inability to know what to do when the phone rings. In this episode, Wynn analyzes a *Buzzfeed* show called "Is it Worth It?" where two men compare a $2 pizza with a $1,000 pizza made of shiny gold only to find that the $1,000 made them feel empty and guilty as they consume its tastelessness under the glow of New York's financial district.

Most everything, in Wynn's telling, seems to have an outer face, aesthetic, or appearance, on the one side, mostly tied to its position within consumerist aesthetics and desire and shiny like gold, doubled by a deeper sense, hidden from appearances, that intimates not only its social value but also social relations that are artificial within the current organization of realness. Jordana Rosenberg reads the commodities in Marx similarly. Commodities, he notes, have "a double character" (shared with labor); their value in exchange, or their outer appearance, suppresses the use within the social relations and cultures that made them: "sameness and difference are dialectically concatenated in the commodity . . . ; the *same* labor . . . is determined as different and opposed to itself" (*Critical Enthusiasm*, 174). Likewise, beauty for Wynn is about the outer display of pure pleasure that "uses artifice," as she says about drag ball culture in "Opulence," "to create the illusion of a lifestyle that has been kept beyond your reach." Underneath such a display is a "subtext of injustice." Whatever constitutes the surface appearance is made pleasurable because it is illusory, a shiny aesthetic of abundance where you can dream of owning everything, inverting and suppressing a "vague feeling that everything is wrong" ("What's Wrong with Capitalism Part I") and a deep feeling of inequality, precarity, and dysphoria where happiness is denied. As Wynn presents herself as an object of opulence, gender itself implicitly enters the conversation as a surface appearance offering pleasure while keeping happiness beyond reach, inferring that everything is wrong. As for myself, I cannot understand Wynn's critique of capital outside of her analysis of gender, despite her denials.

One might read in Wynn's formulation of commodity fetishism and its engagement with aesthetics a splintering of the body from a soul (the splintering of exchange value from use value) similar to the "wrong body" thesis (which Wynn does not always uphold). Like the deadname floating around on the internet, the soul, with its doubling and subtextualization, is the worker's sense of himself as not fitting into the world of social exchange to which his physical body has been put. Like the spirit in the commodity, the soul in Wynn's telling is the secular residue of an immanent passion— similar to a religious passion—that is detached from social use and seemingly untimely. The illusion of the grandeur of exchange, or "glamour," she says in "Opulence," is a kind of magic or enchantment associated with witchcraft, paganism, and sexual deviance. Glamour therefore covers up that it offers "not the promise of social transformation"—the unreachable—"but of individual transformation"—the false promise that you could dress that well too—where you could become the master of people like you. From this critique of glamour, Wynn immediately turns to a read on trans: Trans women are "fed up with realness"; they are "fed up with having to serve the world a fantasy all the time." Here, transgender, like the commodity, is, then, an impossible-to-realize shiny abundance layered over despair and a deep dissatisfaction with the way things are. "You don't know what it's like," she taunts us in "Gender Critical," "to have a body that is so non-normative that you've been shut out of whole areas of society," or "a lifestyle so foreign," she says in "Opulence," "that it could only be the result of divination." In its alienation from the norms of the "real" world of exchange, transgender signals a set of ghostly social relations that appear artificial and cannot yet be realized because they are not yet. At the same time, though, these social relations, like the deadname, still exist somewhere, popping up even when unwanted and signaling the difference that "realness" cannot submerge.

For Wynn, world history follows the temporal patterns of the commodity and therefore of transgender. The unspoken of gender rises out of the ruins of a social system as the dead souls (deadnames) of the commodity, its ghostly untimeliness. "We live in an age of opulence and inequality" where "social unrest is on the rise," Wynn says in "Opulence," and this social unrest is the sign of a "growing irritation with abusive men in power." Wynn ends "Opulence" by describing the comeback of nineteenth-century vampire gothic in a series of videos, by YouTuber Dan Bell, about a high-end mall near Baltimore that commerce had abandoned because it was the site of a murder of a woman who worked there as a cleaner. As Wynn lies in a red-lined coffin sporting fangs and heavy lipstick to match, she cuts in images of the mall's wreckage as "the decaying opulence that is the carcass of twentieth-century consumerism," where you can sense the lingering ghosts of workers and shoppers. In a sense, transgender is the commodity's interiority, this ghostliness, a dysphoria from the world animated by unsymbolizable socialities just below the surface.

We learn from a certain reading of Hegel, Wynn says in her video "Men," that society is based on certain principles (like the mall) that, as they unfold in history, come upon the contradictions within those principles, and history is forced to make itself anew. This means that underneath social appearances of realness is the alienated object in the form of the dead woman worker, the historical transition seemingly artificial or mystical because it is not yet socially realized. Better than Hegel, Wynn prefers Hume, she says in her "Jordan Peterson" episode, because Hume "argued that from a strictly empirical perspective you can't really know much about important things like morality, causation, and the self because those aren't the kinds of things you can observe." The mystical, non-communicable, unexplainable, or unobservable quality of gender—its soul—is a fold in history, the irrational, the outside, the pleasurable, the spectacular, or even the decay of reason's appearances that mark the site of a new unalienated embodiment. As she explains in relation to her transition in "Canceling," "I no longer believe there can be any rational justification of gender identity. Some things in life just can't be rationally explained." Like the mall, gender is the ruins of an old aesthetic that promises happiness and gives, instead, a dysphoric division of labor and death: "[g]ender as we know it just isn't working anymore," she says in "Men." The rational social principles that compose what we know of as gender, in the face of the contradictions inside those very principles—the ghostliness or inexpressibility of unrest—may, she says, lead to a rupture which is already present. Trans, here, names that rupture.

Confessions of a Fox

For Natalie Wynn, the twenty-first century is on the edge of the implosion of the commodity, its obsolescence and decay, just as it is on the edge of the implosion of gender that organized social relations during the commodity's reign. Wynn is not the only trans theorist to make a connection between the obsolescence of the commodity and the obsolescence of the gendered division of labor that has kept in place its "realness." Like Wynn, Jordy Rosenberg locates a trans transition narrative as intersecting with a narrative of historical transition in modes of capital accumulation. Rosenberg finds in the commodity's ghostliness a subjectivity that is in transition between pre-industrialism and a new post-mercantilism demanding a different ordering of bodies, subjectivities, and social relations. Suppressed history is remade into a ghost of religious passion now displaced, linking the neoliberal transition away from commodification currently to the transition to commodification in the eighteenth century. Enthusiastic passion splits the commodity between its outer appearance and its inner, self-determining immediacy. Such passion speaks the interiority but can only be heard at times when subjectivities are undergoing historical transition.

Jordy Rosenberg's 2018 novel *Confessions of a Fox* is about the legendary English eighteenth-century folk hero Jack Sheppard. Jack Sheppard was famous for stealing and then escaping from prison on multiple occasions at a time when much new legislation redefined the rules of accumulation and property ownership in order to further separate working people from their means of livelihood. These new laws would propel them into urban industry. Peter Linebaugh's classic history of the eighteenth century's making of the working class—*The London Hanged*—begins with a chapter on Jack Sheppard. "At a time when economists have been hard put to explain how laboring people could actually live given the wage rates that prevailed," Linebaugh explains, "Sheppard's life can raise the question of the relationship between thievery and survival" (8). The first chapter of *The London Hanged* shows how Jack Sheppard's legendary fame as an escapee results from his defiance of changes in laws governing property, changes that diminished worker autonomy as well as collective holdings, rights, and guilds. This makes Jack a transitional figure, bridging two stages where his body was being forced into social relations from which his intimate sense of himself was in flight. Linebaugh explores the workhouse where Sheppard was brought as a child and the loom that mechanized weaving and took control of production away from the workers, a transition in the traditions of labor that inspired an insurrection until the army had to be called in to put it down. Idleness was coming under increased repression with new laws that restricted movement, congregating, assembling, and forming unions between workers. In this moment of historical transition, Jack Sheppard was able to escape authority, making himself invisible by dressing up in various apparel (37) to take on multiple identities. This defiance seemed "miraculous" (25), "mythical" (37), and "magic" (23), inspiring centuries of oral storytelling as well as dramatic and literary embellishments that made him into a folk hero, starting during Sheppard's lifetime with *A Narrative of all the Robberies, Escapes etc. of John Sheppard*, a 1724 autobiography ghostwritten by Daniel Defoe (who was said to be at the Sheppard's hanging), Macheath in John Gay's 1728 *The Beggar's Opera*, and up through Mac the Knife in Bertolt Brecht's 1928 *Three Penny Opera*.

Even with this iconic attention, the histories, Linebaugh says, "were not especially concerned with his early years" (8–9). This is where Rosenberg intervenes. This transition in property law and its rules of accumulation, for Rosenberg, enlists gender identities to establish their realities. Not only would Sheppard be apprehended for stealing garbage, flowers, and watches, but also, at a time when the authorities were controlling the population by secretly importing testosterone from the colonies, Sheppard gets caught breaking into the shipments. Sheppard's body was small enough to slip out of shackles and between bars, up hidden stairways and through grates—"a specter evaporating back into the City" (69)—leading Rosenberg to imagine him assigned female at birth with a deadname that cannot be mentioned. What remains in place of the deadname is what Jack calls his "Luxuriance," spirit or soul: "Something loosen'd inside him, spiraling down from his heart to his torso's nether root. It was a Feeling he had always known—it flashed up. . . . When his eyes caught hers . . . [h]is heart was *thamping* against his chest" (34). Jack experienced "Luxuriance" as a passionate attachment to his lover Bess, a sex worker.[5] Undefined and indeterminable but corporeal, this "Luxuriance" was "something still unwoken, something lying close-packed like a bomb at his core, poised to shiver into a coruscated, glinting shower of—of—of what, he knew not. But there was *Something* beyond" (33). As "Luxuriant," Jack and Bess' relationship was unassimilable to a money relation, linguistically indeterminate, and undisciplinable by the police, even though they tried.

---

[5] Bess' subsequent appearances in historical accounts as white "occludes the possibility of history itself" (31) by occluding racial relations from their role in accumulation's expansion.

We learn in *Confessions* that this Sheppard story is different than all known prior iterations of the history: "Jack was assigned female at birth? This is a significant departure" (12). The unique manuscript is discovered on sale at a university library "Welcome Back to School/Fuck You event" (x) when—a familiar story!—the university is being neoliberalized and the library turned into administrative offices for the Department of Human Resources (HR). The Sheppard story is thus doubled by a set of footnotes and autobiographical narratives on the bottom of the pages written in the character of a trans professor, an expert in eighteenth-century literature. The professor loses his job because he is unwilling to surrender the rights to the footnotes to a large publishing conglomerate ("a much reviled churner-outer of educational testing materials" (83)) in league with his dean. He becomes the target of corporate surveillance and intimidation as the publishing company along with the university administration joins forces to steal the rights over his scholarly notes that prove "the earliest authentic confessional transgender memoirs in Western history" (122). The neoliberal struggle over the ownership of ideas, histories, identities, origins, and transitions for market use is thus a moment in the unfolding transhistorical rationality of the commodity that passes through stages like footnotes below the text.

The formatting of the novel envisions transition as part of the material look of the page. The eighteenth-century "found" narrative inhabits the top, while the present time that tells of its discovery at the library appears under a thick line, with stars, hashtags, and crosses connecting it to the text above, as commentary but not just commentary: also the professor's own first-person account of his experience providing commentary while keeping the rights to the manuscript, having nothing to do with the story content of the found manuscript. The line on the page thus marks a difference between a past starring trans Jack Sheppard as laying claim to property rights at one historical transition, on the one hand, and the trans narrator in a struggle to do the same in some version of now, on the other, both moments of transition in the laws and methods of accumulation.

The temporal split in the narrative layout is familiar: In 1993, Jacques Derrida published a book entitled *Jacques Derrida* with his former student Geoffrey Bennington writing the top part of the page explaining Derrida's deconstructive thinking, split by a line from the bottom part where Derrida recounted his autobiography in relation to his circumcision, an exercise he called "circumfession." Bennington talks, for example, about Derrida's ideas on sexual difference and feminism, where feminism's affirmation of "woman" is a "complication of the empirical and transcendent" (206), while Derrida from the other side of the line describes his mother's body as she dies and her death's ghostly influence on his writing. The autobiographical cut between the philosopher's thought on the top part of the page and his empirical, corporeal, though haunted, life underneath the line is analogized in the story of his circumcision, the surgical cut to the foreskin of the penis through which Derrida's body assumes its assigned identity as philosopher and as Jew. The line on the page does not cut out the other text, but, rather, the other autobiographical text multiplies the meanings in the more academic writing on the top, cutting through it. Deconstruction teaches us that the cut or the interruption releases yet defers the many meanings in identity that identity like the commodity is always closing down and essentializing, assigning a "true" and singular origin. This references as well Marx's tale of the commodity's cut of production away from the worker's body, an alienation of the worker's life spirit.

Rosenberg makes clear the connection he sees between Derrida, surgery, primitive accumulation, and the commodity in an article he writes on dissection in the eighteenth century: "[t]he dissection of the commodity," he notes, "is . . . the dissection of a body that both is and is not there—a body that recurs in different ghostly semblances throughout the text" (2015, 197). Dissection, he goes on to say, is a "theory of mediation" (2015, 199) as it conjures up "the labors that are congealed within this form" (2015, 199), releasing the irrational subtext, multiple indeterminant meanings, the "radical contingency" (2015, 201), and "utopian potential" (2015, 201) of the working body. In *Confessions*, the scene of top surgery is true to this description. Jack solicits the aid of a surgeon Evans, whom he finds in another room of the "establishment" where his lover Bess lives and works. Evans has a reputation for writing "a lengthy Disquisition on Sexual Chimeras" (137), supernatural monsters, a "category of creature . . . that does not strictly speaking, exist" (137) and is afflicted with "Macroclitoradeus," "a human of both sexes, although often with one part more luxuriant than the other" (138). Through the "scientific Management of the body" (138), Evans could "*accelerate, emphasize*—certain of those intensities" (138). During the surgery, however, Evans faints, leaving Jack cut open and bleeding and the surgery incomplete. Bess takes over, continuing the operation by consulting a textbook (like the one the narrator-professor is preparing?), just before the police burst into the "establishment" to arrest immigrant labor and sex workers of color—a demographic that includes Bess[6]—because of a new ordinance that the authorities put in place the night before in order to better guard the mercantile influx of valuable imports (testosterone).

The surgery scene demonstrates that the body is not amenable to the restrictions and controls that policing and scientific authorities are placing on it in the transition from mercantilism to commodity capitalism, "*[g]ettin' us used to centinels breathing down our necks*" (150). The body overflows; like the text, it bleeds out from the cut. What Jack experiences as an unburdening of the gender event on his body—a hollow chasm "between Jack's insides and his skin" (151), his "*Somethingness*" (145)—resembles a supernatural, self-regulating release, something that breaks the quarantine and the city rules and re-instructs science, a "new thrumming" (151) that is undefined, unassigned, utopic, euphoric, naked, and wild. Under Bess' knife, Jack's body expands as a depository of linguistic reference: he becomes "spider-shanked" (150), "buff-beefed" (150), and "rather huggy" (151), defying, in multi-textualization, the consolidation of essential meaning on the body proper through the assigned name. From below in the footnotes of our present-day future, the publishing corporation insists on acquiring the rights to this singular piece of evidence

---

[6] According to the professor-narrator, this is the only Jack Sheppard account to acknowledge Bess' subcontinental origin as a *lascar*: "Here is another detail of the manuscript that bears further mention. Bess identifies as 'lascar': a term that had broadened from its original usage denoting a South Asian sailor in service to the East India Company (from *lashkar*, or *khalasi*, orig. Persian: 'an army'; through the Portuguese, 'lasquarin,' 'lascari'; amd then the British, 'lascar': cf. K. N. Chauduri, *The English East India Company* (Routledge, reprint 2000). Not a single Sheppard text describes Bess as South Asian. Not one. So then, between this characterization and that of Jack's assigned sex, what we have here is either the most or the least authentic Sheppard document in existence" (27). Similarly to Jack's body, whose surgery releases inner luxuriance and an explosion of meaning suggesting alternative social systems, migrations, associations, and structures of belonging, Bess' identity is in translation through these multiple terms where the specific associations of the context are open to movement.

for an early modern gender transition and giving it an owner/author, a continuation of the practices of ownership by dispossession, by assigning a name. Instead of the dark line dividing the eighteenth-century text above from the twenty-first century's below, these temporalities overflow into each other like Jack's liquids escaping. The surgery operates—so to speak—as a central philosophical flag calling attention to the identity of the text itself as full of cuts, chasms, and overflows with its futures remixing the past that may or may not have been found in that library.[7]

Rosenberg's fiction of an eighteenth-century found text, separated on the page above autobiographical notes from the future, borrows much of its content as well from his prior scholarship on eighteenth-century philosophical and literary contributions to British capitalism's transition from mercantilism to commodity production, *Critical Enthusiasm: Capital Accumulation and the Transformation of Religious Passion*. In this study (which never mentions either gender or sex), Max Weber marks the transition to modernity—a line on the historical page—as where religion is overthrown by reason, but Rosenberg contests Max Weber's thesis that modernity comes about through a transition to secularization and disenchantment, cutting off religious influence. Instead, Rosenberg finds that the religious passion of enthusiasm— an immediate, self-regulated experience of God, spirit, knowledge, and the body—overflows within eighteenth-century thinking on market autonomy, aesthetic experience, periodization, and commodification, like a *Luxuriance*. The eighteenth-century witnesses a "rise of historicist thought and the drive

---

[7] For Derrida, translation exposes that the "inner kernel" of meaning in signification is never there but always desired, so that translation is, for Derrida, a tale of absent origin always in a chain of recontextualizations just like Bess' original home is inaccessible and Jack Sheppard also has no known origin, letting him pass unseen between contexts. Translation for Derrida is the failure of translation, the inability to locate the original full language—the failure to find the "inner kernel" of meaning that can move between language systems unscathed: "[T]he thesis of philosophy is translatability in this common sense, that is, as the transfer of a meaning or truth from one language to another without any essential harm being done" (*Ear of the Other*, 120). Derrida thinks there is always harm or at least always something lost in the cut, just as there is with the translation of gender or nation-of-origin onto bodies. This cut from an origin—an origin that is never there in the first place—is how words in translation acquire meaning—and all words like all genders are always already in translation: always already cut and looking for an origin that was never there. Surgery, gender, and translation are the same.

to periodization" (48): Political economists (e.g., Shaftesbury) attributed accumulation to what they imagined as past enthusiastic religions (e.g., Islam, particularly in Egypt) where tyrannical religious theocracies allowed leaders to amass wealth. (In contrast, for Marx, primitive accumulation is not attributable to a theological power but rather is the ongoing, modern dispossession of laboring bodies cut from the means of producing and reproducing themselves, a theft like the mercantilist theft of testosterone from the colonies in *Confessions*.) Secular modernity's identity is defined through its fictional but incomplete cut from that past.

Though not directly referring to gender transition, *Critical Enthusiasm* presents a theory of transition to secularization that can be likened to gender transition in *Confessions*, where trans is the direct expression of historical transition in the body as the passions are repressed by the new regulatory laws. While acknowledging that the historical scope and contextual meanings of enthusiasm are overdetermined,[8] Rosenberg in *Critical Enthusiasm* analyzes how enthusiasm became, in eighteenth-century thought on modernity, the expression of self-regulation, akin to the theory of self-regulating markets in political economy. Enthusiasm is here the embodiment of immediate subjective activity of some duration that gives an "unmediated communion with God" (6), an "impestuous fervor" that, as Rosenberg explains, "expressed . . . a theory of history itself" (6), like *Luxuriance*. Yet, the multiplicity of uses acquired by "enthusiasm," as it was applied to an expansive range of situations (e.g., legal, political, artistic) that pushed out from the barriers of religious discourse,[9] meant that while religion or the burgeoning commodity economy could not capture or contain all of its implications and uses, neither could

---

[8] According to Rosenberg, enthusiasm had many historical applications and appearances, from Plato where enthusiasm described "an individual convoked to a state of excitement by the perception of something much larger than himself" (9); through to the sixteenth century when it applied to a spiritual acceleration, an experience of immediacy, or a mania of understanding; to during the English Civil War, when it came to refer to a spiritualism outside of monarchical authority; and then to the eighteenth century when enthusiasm was bound up with the question of the subject's relation to the social order.

[9] "I wish to argue, not so much that enchantment persists, but that the discursive force of enchantment has been a defining framework for Western historicist thought since the early Enlightenment. . . . [M]odernity is much more complexly enchanted than previous accounts have posited" (*Critical Enthusiasm*, 13).

the meaning of enthusiasm detach itself completely from all its past allusions. Enthusiasm was still, in its many guises (Rosenberg focuses on Locke and Shaftsbury, among others), a non-empiricist reading of understanding, the body, and the subject, and it was this that made it problematic for eighteenth-century philosophers. As trans, Jack Sheppard in *Confessions* is doubtlessly an enthusiast: The first time Bess utters his name in a bar, "[h]e became loosed from his Body, floating up to the splintered-beam ceiling of the pub" (43), and then he, with a pleasure he has never before experienced, utters his own name for the first time: "becoming Jack Sheppard," he was "entering History" (44). By unleashing such passion, gender expression is neither empirical nor corporeal, neither true nor false, but rather the presence of a spirit that is both of its reality and outside of it. In Rosenberg's terms, its traditions "furnish a critical mode of thinking through the complex graftings of subject and world" (*Critical Enthusiasm*, 23).

In both of his books, Rosenberg relates how the commodity becomes the secular form of the spiritualized subjectivities of enthusiastic prophets. In *Critical Enthusiasm*, the bodies of the prophets stricken with enthusiasm, like the commodity, double the empirical surface with an interior spiritual dynamic that experiences a direct communication with God, an interior landscape with a voice.[10] "For Marx," writes Rosenberg in *Critical Enthusiasm*, "the ghostliness of a culture populated by objects that appear to interact of their own inanimate accord, is an index of the advancement of capital accumulation. . . . Under capitalism, an object is attributed a supernatural aura" (23), just as for the enthusiast. For Jack, commodity-objects shared this religious passion of enthusiasm, for the toys he was robbing "were speaking to him, she [Bess] said, like a Lover, or a Priest. . . . *They were asking for your help. . . .* And each one was asking for the same thing. *Liberate us*" (112).[11] Rosenberg traces changes

---

[10] Rosenberg says that the commodity is "*the form of appearance* of the capitalist mode of production. It is so . . . because, as the product of capitalism, the commodity's phantom-like objectivity obscures the real social relations upon which production is based" (22).

[11] From *Confessions'* "footnotes": "Karl Marx famously posed a counterfactual. 'If commodities could speak, they would say this: our use-value may interest men, but it does not belong to us as objects. . . .' Surely . . . , the commodity does speak. To say that it doesn't is to blot out an entire bloody history [of slavery]. . . . There is *nobody* who is unmarked by this bloody history" (296).

that set the stage for the age of the commodity mostly through implementing numerous new laws that targeted objects previously lying around unused, like the toys, and silencing their passions. Jack and his associates are prohibited from traditional means of acquisition and possession by a wide range of new laws generalizing the laws used to repress religious passion. Jack's penultimate arrest happens when he admires and then picks a primrose[12] from the riverbank and gets immediately apprehended by a sentinel for breaking the "Anti-Foraging Act" with which Jack was not even familiar because it was so new (271).[13]

Jack's theft of the primrose was not the only situation in *Confessions* that marked a transition to the commodity. In parallel, Bess' parents lived in a spiritual community in the colonies which grew the plant that made testosterone until Speculators stomped into the forest to retrieve it and transport it to the European ports, inspiring Jack's many attempted thefts. Hiding in the berm, she watched her parents die defending her home and its harvest. As the new laws that usher in the commodity age make the voices of objects inaccessible and unsolicitous, they also restrict ownership of the testosterone that allows the bodies' passions to speak. From her hiding place, Bess notices that a "girl stood above me. . . . She look'd *like* me. I did not know if she was an Emanation or a sprite" (196). The girl vanishes after the fight. Commodification—even and especially gender commodification—creates insecurity by reducing the potential adequations between the passionate "I" that confronts its world and the "I" that is a social object within it. Just as the commodities' passions, their multiplicity of meanings, and their voices are silenced by the authorities enforcing new property laws, the multiplicities of meanings in subjective identities are also suppressed in the transition to the commodity age. For Jack,

---

[12] Native to North America and introduced into Europe in the seventeenth century, the evening primrose is known as a hermaphroditic plant that contains both stamens and carpels.

[13] The "footnote" in *Confessions* also mentions the Cabbage Act and the Vagrant Act which *Critical Enthusiasm* foregrounds as well. *The London Hanged* adds the Riot Act, the Transportation Act, the Combination Act, the Workhouse Act, and the Black Act from the beginning of the eighteenth century. "The years between 1717, when Sheppard started his apprenticeship industriously, and 1723, when he ended it idly," Linebaugh concludes, "saw another transition, that of the consolidation of a new dynasty" (16). The elements constitutive of this "transition" to a "new dynasty" are "repression, finance capitalism and the weavers' struggle" (16).

Bess, and the professor-narrator, the new laws of ownership mean restrictions on their access to testosterone and therefore the loss of their ghosted doubles, as with the commodities' loss of passion. Having been apprehended in his attempt to blow up the ship carrying the imported testosterone stolen from the subcontinent, Jack's first body dies in fifteen minutes of hanging on a tree, while the second body is rescued from the scaffold by the mob, buried, unburied by his friends, and revived by a "chirugeon" for 50p (306). Upon dying, his phantom-self cries out in wild enthusiasm, like the toys on the shelves, for liberation.

In the text's final chapters, the professor-narrator, like Sheppard, escapes to a library in an undisclosed location and an undisclosed time in the undetermined future. From there he learns, in reviewing the archives, that Sheppard's manuscript is littered with anachronistic additions, quotes, and terminologies added by its multiple ghostly authors: pirates, graduate students and hackers over the course of the prior centuries. The publishing corporation is asserting its claims over the found text by trying to attribute it to a single author in a single time with a single meaning and a single line of ownership, a transnational act of dispossession through a copyright that erases the social relations included in the various inputs and influences from its various social and historical contexts. The commodity needs enforcement by the police, the military, and the corporate university authorities, suppressing its diversities of meanings, voices, and associations composing the social relations that made it. The publishing company and its surveillance representative now chase down the professor, and he flees. Likening Jack's escape acts to these ghostly texts, the narrator calls what Jack did—filing through iron cuffs, scaling through windows, stealing apparel for disguise, and the rest of it—"epistemic disobedience" (84, 134, 294) following the critic Walter Mignolo,[14] Derrida's work on the archives,[15] and Saidiya Hartman's readings of slave-ship

---

[14] "[D]ecolonial thinking and doing focus on the enunciation, engaging in epistemic disobedience and delinking from the colonial matrix in order to open up decolonial options—a vision of life and society that requires decolonial subjects, decolonial knowledges, and decolonial institutions" (9).

[15] In *Archive Fever*, Derrida begins, "In an archive, there should not be any absolute dissociation, any heterogeneity or *secret* which could separate, or partition, in an absolute manner" (3). This process of naming an archive—or of memory—(Derrida calls this *consignation*) assigns the archive

commercial logs where the voices of the slave/commodities become audible in the textual intervals. As Saidiya Hartman elaborates:

> By throwing into crisis 'what happened when' and by exploiting the 'transparency of sources' as fictions of history, I want to make visible the production of disposable lives (in the Atlantic slave trade and, as well, in the discipline of history), to describe the 'resistance of the object' if only by first imagining it, and to listen for the mutters and oaths and cries of the commodity. By flattening the levels of narrative discourse and confusing narrator and speakers, I hoped to illuminate the contested character of history, narrative, event, and fact, to topple the hierarchy of discourse, and to engulf authorized speech in the clash of voices. (11–2)

For Hartman as for Rosenberg, commodification reduces the histories that speak through the body and its texts without license. These histories, says Rosenberg's professor, "we wear like dreams—fragments of a life untethered from this world, messages from a future reflected to us like light off broken shards" (315). Within this logic, trans is the archive, "the contested character of history, narrative, event, and fact" living in the body as its past and future: trans is the multi-authored narrative of repressed social alternatives that history embeds in the body as gender, crying for liberation.

Conclusion

When feminist or trans theory insists on "realness" or on an essential core, gender, then, too appears immutable like property, often conforming to

---

a singular place and law (just as copywrite does for Rosenberg or "gender assignment" does at birth), but Derrida thinks it is time to "interrogate or contest, directly or indirectly, this archontic principle, its authority, its titles, and its genealogy, the right that it commands, the legality or the legitimacy that depends on it" (3–4). The archive, in that sense, is always in transition. As he says later, "Have we ever been assured of the homogeneity, of the consistency, of the univocal relationship of any concept to a term or to such a word as 'archive'?" (33). This could also apply to gender or sex. He concludes: "Thus it is for every concept: always dislocating itself because it is never one with itself" (84). So, the archive is the impression of *secret* multiplicity within a legal space belonging to a single name. Derrida does compare this metaphysics of the archive to castration (also, circumcision), as a cut that establishes the unity and also breaks it apart (46).

a neutral, empirical surface description or a fact of nature within a social system that appears also as an immediate fact of nature when it is, rather, a hegemonic mechanism for spatial and geopolitical control *that has won*. Submerged beneath its commodification, traces of gender's history and *its future* mutter oaths and cries that may not be recognizable within its current "real" appearances. Multi-textual, multi-authored, multi-periodic, and multi-generic, gender is the multiplicity lost inside the commodity's embodiment. Some feminist theory shares with some trans theory this understanding of gender's doubling where gender as the surface appearance of the body's "realness" also has within it a multitextualism: many layers of history's defiance against the dispossession and alienation of an alternative "realness."

Rosenberg and Wynn locate the increasing mainstream attention to trans within a phase of capital's neoliberal transition. The "post-Fordist" phase of capitalism that neoliberalism represents has turned increasingly away from social belonging, supports, and care, in practices ranging from cuts to social services, health care, and education to the "Uber-ization" of work, cuts in benefits, cuts in development, and de-unionization, leading to increased social precarity worldwide: There are ever new laws against each primrose we touch. In an age of financialization when capital can reproduce itself without reproducing subjects, genders are made visible that were buried by the binary of sexual difference no longer serving its old purpose of controlling distributions and divisions of laboring bodies. Gender is becoming, under neoliberalism, obsolete as a means of control. In the ruins of accumulation's rationalization of social relations, gender escapes. What this critical trans perspective advances, and what feminist theory must adopt, is thinking that can tease out from the decaying carcass of sexual difference the ghostly potential of a modified society screaming for Liberation.

Conclusion

In 2018, celebrated feminist Canadian author Margaret Atwood was canceled. For those of you in the future who have not heard of canceling, canceling is an internet phenomenon where crowds of users decide that someone has expressed an unacceptable idea and that person's public speech should not be permitted, sometimes leading to big embarrassment campaigns and job dismissals. Cancellation is not about argument or debate, where evidence and logic would be presented and fallacies in other opposing positions may be exposed and refuted. Rather, the ideas are determined to be too distasteful to be heard or thought at all on a moral basis, and the person who has espoused them now personifies those ideas and should be debased, shamed, muted, and pushed out of the public square through public declarations and "unfollowing." Often, the infractions that prompt cancellation are deemed racist, sexist, homophobic, or transphobic, words that encompass a wide spectrum of speech-content and action, from assault and outright hate-slurs to being friends or associates with someone who once held beliefs that are currently unsavory or making someone feel uncomfortable; the words "racism," "sexism," "homophobia," and "transphobia" then come to stand in for an array of equated though wildly different acts and utterances, as though the words themselves transparently and with certainty refer to simple, identifiable, and irrefutable objects or thought-objects without history rather than to mutable descriptions and abstract judgments. In such circumstances, discontent and disagreement have risen to the level of a moral spectacle rather than a debatable position or an agenda for improvement with reasons. I do not espouse a right-wing position on canceling that would equate it to McCarthyism and deem it an infraction of First Amendment rights to free speech. Canceling can easily be differentiated from government control of the press, of assembly, or of dissent by jailing people or other like forms of state-sponsored repression. Nevertheless, I do see canceling as the spectacular escalation of anti-intellectualism to the point of scapegoating, a religious-like, self-righteous mob behavior that eclipses theory, interpretation, democratic deliberation, politics, and ideas; it is the application of right-wing vigilante tactics to left-of-center social movements' purification rituals.

So, what did the author of *The Handmaid's Tale* and other feminist classics, feminist icon Margaret Atwood, do to incite this impassioned response? In November 2016, she signed an open letter called "UBC Accountable" written by Canadian writers and faculty members who criticized the University of British Columbia for its mishandling of the case involving the chair of the Creative Writing Program and award-winning novelist, Associate Professor Steven Galloway. (Since the case is ongoing, documents have not been released to the public, and so the specific nature of the allegations is publicly, for the most part, unknown.) Following rumors and reports that he was in a long-term relationship with a graduate student, Galloway was accused of bullying and sexual harassment—what the university called "a record of misconduct that resulted in an irreparable breach of trust," according to university president Phillip Steenkamp—and fired in a public online announcement after a former Supreme Court judge, Mary Ellen Boyd, hired by the university to do an independent investigation, dismissed all but one of the charges against him as unsubstantiated. (There were no police reports filed. Galloway is currently suing the university, some of the faculty, and the complainant for defamation.)[1] The open letter that Atwood signed called for privacy, due process, and fair treatment for all. When the letter was denounced for not expressing enough sympathy for traumatized victims of sexual abuse, some signatories withdrew their signatures, but not Atwood. Instead, she wrote an article in 2018 in the *Globe and Mail*, first noting the lack of public information or evidence yet from which to judge the case and then stating unequivocally her "radical" belief that "in order to have civil and human rights for women there have to be civil and human rights, period, including the right to fundamental justice,

---

[1]   The incident may have been caught up in the media fervor that surrounded similar allegations at the time against Canadian Public Radio's host Jian Ghomeshi, whose sexual aggressions (unlike Galloway's) had been rumored for years.

just as for women to have the vote, there has to be a vote."[2] This article reached the attention of a US readership, and hence the cancellation. The media outcry continued until the Hulu series of *The Handmaid's Tale* began airing and the sequel to *The Handmaid's Tale*, *The Testaments*, was published and won the Man Booker Prize in 2019, at which point the spirit of public denunciation was diverted elsewhere, and Atwood was again adored.

The incident does not stand alone. Women and sexual minorities are indeed made vulnerable and harmed in a culture that sells sex aggressively in the many ways that our culture does. Yet, at the same time, women and sexual minorities are made vulnerable by a historical transition where capital captures surplus increasingly by seizing the means of reproduction as it cuts access to while vilifying social supports. Besides registering an understandable and strong anger at continued occurences of sex crimes, such spectacles as the one directed at Atwood paint public spaces as inaccessible and in fact dangerous to vulnerable people and social belonging as a quaint remnant of a naive past's damning trust in the social. This, of course, is not the fault of the victims but rather the appropriation of their fear and pain into broader public, hegemonic discourses of individual resilience and public sector inefficiency. From "#MeToo" to Title IX clampdowns on college campuses and a pro-gun lobby that advocates expanding gun rights to give women a weapon to fend off rapists, cultural movements were keying into a fantasy of perilous sex, painting social life as composed of threats lurking at every corner waiting to pounce on unwary female victims. "We've seen young women commit suicide after being slut-shamed and bullied online and off," Jessica Valenti begins her best-selling rallying cry for the "Third Wave," *Full Frontal Feminism*. During the same period, however, as Judith Levine and Erica Meiners point out, "contrary to what most Americans believe, sexual assaults of both children and adults have steadily declined over the past quarter century, along with the

---

[2] Sophie Lewis cites the same article in *The Globe and Mail*, calling Atwood's position a "contrarian involvement in the defense of Steven Galloway, a professor of literature accused of rape at the University of Columbia, over the course of which she routinely conflated left-wing and right-wing politics as equally distasteful" (174). I hardly think that not taking a position until the evidence was presented and advocating for due process can be considered very contrarian, and the allegation that Atwood is defending Galloway against rape charges seems also off the mark.

whole of what the state identifies as 'violent crime,' which fell by 75 percent from 1993 to 2017" (2). Levine and Meiners attribute this fear of the social to a growing public sensitivity to everyday interactions and "ordinary occurrences" (3): "harassment at work and on the street, 'rapey' behavior on dates, assault by acquaintances and strangers, and sexual exploitation in schools, sports, and religious institutions" (3). As well, allegations of sexual aggression in this declarative form historically have served as an alibi for violence against or incarceration of Black men and for the gun lobby's stronghold on US legislatures at the state and federal levels.

Addressing the recent tidal wave of Title IX enforcement as a new mode of "extending the reach of campus bureaucracy into everyone's lives" (17), Laura Kipnis has also detailed the perception of a pervasive culture of sexual harassment and violence on campus, especially against women, a fearful reaction to the type of ordinary and everyday interactions that Levine and Meiners also observe.[3] This, according to Kipnis, has made anything associated with sex seem not just uncomfortable but dangerous for women and beyond their control as well, demanding police and other legal interventions, but not only with regard to sex. Also, by inference, ideas that might be unpleasant or unnerving as well as relationships that are unfamiliar or distressing are made suspect if not criminal, as women see themselves as powerless to handle such a treacherous social environment and left on their own to experience trauma resiliently. As Wendy Brown describes it, "The weak cannot act, only react; this is what their moralizing critique is, and because it is all they have, they will pursue it doggedly until it triumphs" (174–5). Even as there is no doubt that sexual assault is persistent and needs to be routed out, and Kipnis like me is sympathetic to its victims, the overblown picture of social menace and sex maniacs lurking everywhere in

---

[3] Susan Watkins understands the Title IX investigation fury on US college campuses as a conscious move on the part of the Obama administration to counter falling popularity ratings in the polls. "In 2011, with negative personal-approval ratings and 15 million unemployed, Obama needed low-cost gestures towards 'home and change' to galvanize supporters for his second-term election. Three issues were selected, after careful focus-group testing: gay marriage, immigrants' children and sexual assault on campus" (69). This took attention away from a spat of police killings of Black men that "were becoming an embarrassment for Obama" (69).

the dark is easily confused with the less ominous quality of most of what is called "sexual misconduct" (which has no legal definition outside of its use in specific locations or clear nonlegal referent). A perception of such hidden but pervasive social terrors gives the impression of powerlessness, even to the point, as Kipnis warns, that women might feel unable to respond at all to *any* of the social problems that face them or any sexual advance that they just do not want. As Susan Watkins summarizes, "Ideas of personal trauma replaced structural notions of male dominance and female subordination; the subject was no longer 'women as a class' but 'me'" (71). Women have identified new feminist politics against this horror movie of social life where "femininity," as victim, is the name given to the failures of social and political institutions (including feminism's legacy, in which Atwood played a part) to provide safety and well-being, and a "new generation of feminism" is the name given to the call for spontaneous, free, individual, autonomous actors to preserve moral order by expressing themselves.

Gender Commodity has identified a cultural trend where gender is a commodity. According to this logic, gender identity or feminist identity—as commodity—promises stability against a social world made unstable by the same forces of commodification that make social life seem horrible. Canceling Margaret Atwood follows this course. Such scenes as Margaret Atwood's cancellation are now familiar. Less familiar, perhaps, is this story of women's endangerment detected in other settings and contexts that does not objectify women for sex alone but rather objectifies them as consumers, as subjects. Also, the narrative of women's endangerment by social monsters and sexual aggressors is appropriated into other narratives about women's endangerment by social institutions in local cultures, particularly in other places. For example, the idea that the social institutions that have traditionally been the avenues for regulating excessive exploitative practices or protecting rights are now jeopardizing women's well-being is popping up in justifications for international policies, and not only military ones. Financial interest in women's initiative, empowerment, self-reliance, access to jobs, or entrepreneurship also depends on an image of the bloodsucking overreach of the developmental state as treacherous to defenseless women, as I discuss in Chapter 2, where a self-regulating feminism steps in as a durable, heroic lifeline—akin to markets—in place of the defunct and outmoded public sector. As well, as I discuss in Chapter 2 and again in Chapter 3, the precarity of social reproduction is given as the cause and justification for technological fixes, surveillance, and corporate management to infiltrate ever more deeply into bodies, relationships, and intimate spaces, offering security while, in actuality, undermining security.

In Chapter 4, I consider some strains of trans theory where commodification and gender determinism go hand in hand. Those social forces with an interest in commodification have used gender identities as ideological forces to hold in place a division of labor between productive spheres (where objects are made) and reproductive spheres (where subjects are made). Some trans theory and some essentializing feminisms have turned defensive against theories that politicize a historical separation between bodies and genders that the logic of commodity ushers in and have grown protective of conventions for understanding gender as "is." This division of labor, however, is reaching a breaking point where it is no longer needed to organize social space or accumulation. Reproduction is no longer treated as a natural origin of care, unreachable by the violence of capital, but is implicated as a field of capital intensification. The trans theory I analyze understands affirmative gender identities as having come upon a historical limit. This limit is coterminous with a decline in interests of productive sectors in the surpluses gained in ideologically separating subject- and family-production from capital's technologization as they find ways of taking over the reproductive sectors for profit potentials. This is a source of social instability and vulnerability. Some of this trans theory demonstrates how the social world is made scary, inadequate, alienating, and precarious for subjects by the very processes through which the same social world is made adequate for commodity objects, including gender identity commodities.

Along these lines, the gender commodity, by promising a security it cannot deliver, covers over the vulnerabilities that are part of our condition of social being and belonging. Such vulnerabilities are assumed to be caused by the social institutions, democratic cultures, social connections, and public forms of support that, in the logic of the commodity, come at us with fangs bared. As

Judith Butler has frequently pointed out, we are "constituted by our relations but also dispossessed by them" (*Precarious Life*, 24). She goes on:

> [t]here are . . . losses that afflict us, from illness and from global conflict; and there is the fact as well that women and minorities, including sexual minorities, are, as a community, subjected to violence, exposed to its possibility, if not its realization. This means that each of us is constituted politically in part by virtue of the social vulnerability of our bodies. . . . Loss and vulnerability seem to follow from our being socially constituted bodies, attached to others, at risk of losing those attachments, exposed to others, at risk of violence by virtue of that exposure. (20)

An effect of the social organization, our vulnerability is, at the same time, what connects us to others and makes us responsible to them. In the wake of the 2008 financial crisis, its continuation in global austerity policies, drone warfare that mechanizes warfare outside of politics and human decision, increasing economic polarization, corporate and financial rule, "scaled up" and accelerating economies driven by technological intensifications, ecological damage devoid of the political will to confront it, pandemic, and the shrinking of the "soft arm" redistribution and reproductive functions of the state (e.g., pensions, healthcare, education, and the like), an ideological vision has prevailed of the individual as self-sustaining *and* bound to failure, with markets as the only security. This is what makes the social seem full of demons, destruction, disaffection, and terrifying uncertainty when it is actually responsible for the conditions of our futurity.

Acknowledgments

I start by thanking all feminists—past, present, and future. They make everything possible.

The support and encouragement from the people at Bloomsbury have been invaluable. I'd like especially to thank Haaris Naqvi for his professionalism, encouragement, kindness, and enthusiasm throughout the process.

As well, I am grateful for the continued support of Florida State University, particularly to the Office of Research for The Committee on Faculty Research Support (COFRS) program summer grant and the Sabbaticals committee.

Many have given help along the way with advice, suggestions, or editorial attention. Kenneth J. Saltman has helped think through the entire project and commented on multiple iterations of it. Jeffrey Di Leo has been a source of ongoing inspiration. In gratitude, I'd also like to mention Christian Haines, Aaron Jaffe, Chris Michaels, Christian Moraru, and Irene Padavic.

Works Cited

Abu-Lughod, Lila. "Do Muslim Women Really Need Saving? Anthropological Reflections on Cultural Relativism and Its Others." *American Anthropologist* 104, 3 (2002): 783–90.

Arendt, Hannah. *Crises of the Republic*. San Diego, New York, London: Harcourt Brace & Company, 1972.

Arendt, Hannah. *Eichmann in Jerusalem: A Report on the Banality of Evil*. New York: Penguin Books, 1963, 1964.

Arendt, Hannah. *On Revolution*. New York: Penguin Books, 1965.

Arruzza, Cinzia and Tithi Bhattacharya, and Nancy Fraser. *Feminism for the 99%: A Manifesto*. London and New York: Verso, 2019.

Atwood, Margaret. "Am I a Bad Feminist?" *The Globe and Mail* (January 13, 2018 and July 9, 2020): https://www.theglobeandmail.com/opinion/am-i-a-bad-feminist/article37591823/ (accessed July 20, 2020).

Atwood, Margaret. "*The Handmaid's Tale* and *Oryx and Crake* in Context." *PMLA* 119, 3 (2004): 513–17.

Atwood, Margaret. *The Heart Goes Last*. New York: Anchor Books, 2015.

Balsamo, Anne. *Technologies of the Gendered Body: Reading Cyborg Women*. Durham, NC and London: Duke University Press, 1996.

Bataille, Georges. *The Accursed Share: An Essay on General Economy; Volume I: Consumption*. Trans. Robert Hurley. New York: Zone Books, 1988.

Baudrillard, Jean. *Forget Foucault*. Trans. Nicole Dufresne. Los Angeles, CA: Semiotext(e), 2007.

Baudrillard, Jean. *Seduction*. Trans. Brian Singer. Montréal: New World Perspectives, 1990.

Baudrillard, Jean. *Symbolic Exchange and Death. Revised Edition. Theory, Culture & Society*. Trans. Iain Hamilton Grant. Los Angeles, CA: Sage, 1993.

Baudrillard, Jean. *The Consumer Society: Myths & Structures*. London: Sage, 1998.

Bauman, Zygmunt. *Consuming Life*. Cambridge, UK and Malden, MA: Polity, 2007.

Beauvoir, Simone de. *A Very Easy Death*. Trans. Patrick O'Brian. New York: Pantheon Books, 1965.

Beauvoir, Simone de. *Memoirs of a Dutiful Daughter*. Trans. James Kirkup. New York: HarperCollins, 1959.

Beauvoir, Simone de. *The Second Sex*. Trans. H. M. Parshley. New York: Vintage Books, 1952, 1980.

Benjamin, Walter. *Illuminations: Essays and Reflections*. Ed. Hannah Arendt. Trans. Harry Zohn. New York: Schocken Books, 1968.

Benjamin, Walter. *Selected Writings, Volume 2, Part 1, 1927-1930*. Ed. Michael W. Jennings, Howard Eiland, Gary Smith. Trans. Rodney Livingstone et al. Cambridge, MA and London: Harvard University Press, 1999.

Bennington, Geoffrey, and Derrida, Jacques. *Jacques Derrida*. Trans. Geoffrey Bennington. London and Chicago: Chicago University Press, 1993.

Braidotti, Rosi. *The Posthuman*. Cambridge, UK and Malden, MA: Polity, 2013.

Brooks, Kim. "Feminism Has Failed Women." *The New York Times* (December 23, 2020): https://www.nytimes.com/2020/12/23/opinion/coronavirus-women -feminism.html?action=click&module=Opinion&pgtype=Homepage (accessed December 23, 2020).

Brown, Wendy. *In the Ruins of Neoliberalism: The Rise of Antidemocratic Politics in the West*. New York: Columbia University Press, 2019.

Butler, Judith. "Gender in Translation: Beyond Monolingualism." *philoSOPHIA* 9, 1 (Winter 2019): 1–25.

Butler, Judith. *Gender Trouble: Feminism and the Subversion of Identity*. New York and London: Routledge, 1990, 1999, 2006.

Butler, Judith. *Precarious Life: The Powers of Mourning and Violence*. London and New York: Verso, 2004.

Butler, Judith. *The Force of Non-Violence*. London and New York: Verso, 2020.

Chakrabarty, Dipesh. "The Human Condition in the Anthropocene." *The Tanner Lectures in Human Values* (February 2015). https://tannerlectures.utah.edu/Cha krabarty%20manuscript.pdf (accessed November 23, 2019).

Chamayou, Grégoire. *A Theory of the Drone*. Trans. Janet Lloyd. New York and London: The New Press, 2015.

Cheah, Pheng. *What is a World? On Postcolonial Literature as World Literature*. Durham, NC and London: Duke University Press, 2016.

Chitty, Christopher. *Sexual Hegemony: Statecraft, Sodomy, and Capital in the Rise of the World System*. Durham, NC and London: Duke University Press, 2020.

Chu, Andrea Long. *Females*. London and New York: Verso, 2019.

Cixous, Hélène and Clément, Catherine. "The Untenable." In *Dora's Case: Freud – Hysteria – Feminism. Second Edition*. Eds. Charles Bernheimer and Claire Kahane. New York: Columbia University Press, 1985, 1990, pp. 276–93.

Cooper, Melinda. *Family Values: Between Neoliberalism and the New Social Conservatism*. Brooklyn, NY: Zone Books, 2017.

Cooper, Melinda. *Life as Surplus: Biotechnology and Capitalism in the Neoliberal Era*. Seattle: University of Washington Press, 2008.

Crenshaw, Kimberle. "Demarginalizing the Intersection of Race and Sex: A Black Feminist Critique of Antidiscrimination Doctrine, Feminist Theory and Antiracist Politics." *University of Chicago Legal Forum* 1989 (1989): 139–68. HeinOnline.

Crenshaw, Kimberle. "Mapping the Margins: Intersectionality, Identity Politics, and Violence against Women of Color." *Stanford Law Review* 43, 6 (July 1991): 1241–99.

Daly, Mary. *Beyond God the Father: Toward a Philosophy of Women's Liberation*. Boston: Beacon Press, 1973, 1985.

Derrida, Jacques. *Archive Fever: A Freudian Impression*. Trans. Eric Prenowitz. Chicago, IL and London: The University of Chicago Press, 1995.

Derrida, Jacques. *The Ear of the Other: Otobioraphy, Transference, Translation. Texts and Discussions with Jacques Derrida*. Ed. Christie V. McDonald. Trans. Peggy Kamuf. New York: Schocken Books, 1985.

Despentes, Virginie. *King Kong Theory*. New York: The Feminist Press at the City University of New York, 2009.

Deutscher, Penelope. *Foucault's Futures: A Critique of Reproductive Reason*. New York: Columbia University Press, 2017.

Dickens, Charles. *Dombey and Son*. Oxford, UK and New York: Oxford University Press, 1974, 1982.

Dimock, Wai-chee. *Through Other Continents: American Literature Across Deep Time*. Princeton, NJ: Princeton University Press, 2008.

Dockterman, Eliana. "A Doll for Everyone." *Time. Special Edition. The Science of Gender* (2020): 88–93.

Duggan, Lisa. *The Twilight of Equality: Neoliberalism, Cultural Politics, and the Attack on Democracy*. Boston: Beacon Press, 2003.

Edelman, Lee. *No Future: Queer Theory and the Death Drive*. Durham, NC and London: Duke University Press, 2004.

Engels, Friedrich. *Origin of the Family, Private Property, and the State*. Trans. Alick West. *Marx/Engels Internet Archive* (*Marxists.org*), 1993, 1999, 2000. https://www.marxists.org/archive/marx/works/download/pdf/origin_family.pdf (accessed June 27, 2021).

Fanon, Frantz. "Algeria Unveiled." *A Dying Colonialism*. Trans Haaken Chevalier. New York: Grove, 1965, pp. 35–67.

Featherstone, Liz. "The Lavish Pleasures of Natalie Wynn." *The Nation* (March 8–15, 2021): 20–3, 30–1.

Federici, Silvia. *Beyond the Periphery of the Skin: Rethinking, Remaking, and Reclaiming the Body in Contemporary Capitalism*. Oakland, CA: PM Press, 2020.

Federici, Silvia. *Re-enchanting the World: Feminism and the Politics of the Commons.* Oakland, CA: PM Press, 2019.

Felski, Rita. *The Limits of Critique.* Chicago and London: University of Chicago Press, 2015.

Ferguson, Michaele. "Neoliberal Feminism as Political Ideology: Revitalizing the Study of Feminist Political Ideologies." *Journal of Political Ideologies* 22, 3 (2017): 221–35.

Fisher, Mark. *Capitalist Realism: Is There No Alternative?* Brooklyn, NY: Zone Books, 2009.

Ford, Clementine. *Fight Like a Girl.* London: Oneworld, 2016, 2018.

Fortunati, Leopoldina. *The Arcane of Reproduction: Housework, Prostitution, Labor and Capital.* Ed. Jim Fleming. Trans. Hilary Creek. Brooklyn, NY: Autonomedia, 1995.

Fraser, Nancy. "Feminism, Capitalism and the Cunning of History." *New Left Review* 56 (March/April 2009): 97–117.

Fraser, Nancy. *The Old Is Dying and the New Cannot Be Born: From Progressive Neoliberalism to Trump and Beyond.* London and New York: Verso, 2019.

Freud, Sigmund. *Civilization and Its Discontents.* Ed. and Trans. James Strachey. New York: W. W. Norton & Company, 1961.

Freud, Sigmund. *Dora: An Analysis of a Case of Hysteria.* Ed. Philip Rieff. Trans. James Strachey. New York: Collier Books Macmillan, 1963.

Fromm, Erich H. *Escape from Freedom.* New York: Henry Holt and Company, 1941, 1969.

Gallop, Jane. "French Theory and the Seduction of Feminism." In *Men in Feminism.* Eds. Alice Jardine and Paul Smith. New York and London: Routledge, 1987, pp. 111–15.

Galloway, Alexander. "Are Some Things Unrepresentable?" *Theory, Culture & Society* 28, 7–8 (2011): 85–102.

Gill-Peterson, Julian. *Histories of the Transgender Child.* Minneapolis, MN and London: University of Minnesota Press, 2018.

Gill, Rosalind and Elias, Ana Sofia. "'Awaken your Incredible': Love Your Body Discourses and Postfeminist Contradictions." *International Journal of Media & Cultural Politics* 10, 2 (2014): 179–88.

Gill, Rosalind and Orgad, Shani. "Confidence Culture and the Remaking of Feminism." *New Formations* (2017): 16–34. DOI: 10.398/NEWF:91.01.2017.

Gonnermann, Annika. "The Concept of Post-Pessimism in 21st Century Dystopian Fiction." *The Comparatist* 43 (October 2019): 26–40.

Goodman, Robin Truth. "Interview with Carrie Lynn Evans." *New Books Network* (May 10, 2019): https://newbooksnetwork.com/robin-truth-goodman-the-blo omsbury-handbook-of-21st-century-feminist-theory-bloomsbury-2019/.

Goodman, Robin Truth. "Introduction." In *The Bloomsbury Handbook of 21ˢᵗ-Century Feminist Theory*. Ed. Robin Truth Goodman. New York and London: Bloomsbury, 2019, pp. 1–18.

Grace, Victoria. *Baudrillard's Challenge: A Feminist Reading*. New York and London: Routledge, 2000.

Greer, Germaine. "Reality Bites." *The Guardian* (July 24, 2006): https://www.theguardian.com/film/2006/jul/24/culture.books (accessed March 22, 2020).

Greer, Germaine. *The Female Eunuch*. New York and London: Harperperennial, 1970.

Greer, Germaine. *The Whole Woman*. New York: Anchor Books, 2009.

Gross, Jenny. "J.K. Rowling Under Fire by L.G.B.T.Q, Groups Over Tweets." *Nytimes.com* (June 7, 2020): https://www.nytimes.com/2020/06/07/arts/Jk-Rowling-controversy.html?action=click&module=Latest&pgtype=Homepage (accessed June 8, 2020).

Halberstam, Jack. Trans*: *A Quick and Quirky Account of Gender Variability*. Oakland, CA: University of California Press, 2018.

Hall, Stuart. "Introduction: Who Needs 'Identity'?" *Questions of Cultural Identity*. Reprint Edition. Thousand Oaks, CA: Sage, 1996.

Haraway, Donna. *Modest_Witness@Second Millenium.FemaleMan©_Meets_OncoMouse™: Feminism and Technoscience*. New York and London: Routledge, 1997.

Haraway, Donna. *Staying with the Trouble: Making Kin in the Chthulucene*. Durham, NC and London: Duke University Press, 2016.

Hartman, Saidiya. "Venus in Two Acts." *Small Axe, Number 26*, 12, 2 (June 2008): 1–14.

Harvey, David. *A Brief History of Neoliberalism*. Oxford, UK and New York: Oxford University Press, 2005.

Hekman, Susan. *The Feminine Subject*. Cambridge, UK and Malden, MA: Polity, 2014.

Hemmings, Clare. *Why Stories Matter: The Political Grammar of Feminist Theory*. Durham, NC and London: Duke University Press, 2011.

Hester, Helen. *Xenofeminism*. Cambridge, UK: Polity, 2018.

Hewitt, Nancy A. "Introduction." In *No Permanent Waves: Recasting Histories of U.S. Feminism*. Ed. Nancy A. Hewitt. New Brunswick, NJ and London: Rutgers University Press, 2010, pp. 1–12.

Hitchcock, Peter. *The Long Space: Transnationalism and Postcolonial Form*. Stanford, CA: Stanford University Press, 2010.

Horkheimer, Max and Adorno, Theodor W. *Dialectic of Enlightenment: Philosophical Fragments*. Ed. Gunzelin Schmid Noerr. Trans. Edmund Jephcott. Stanford, CA: Stanford University Press, 2002.

Irigaray, Luce. "Produire de la Séductión?: 'La femme n'est rien et c'est là sa puissance." *Histoires d'elles* 21 (March 1980): 4.

Jacques, Juliet. *Trans: A Memoir.* London and New York: Verso, 2015, 2016.

Jardine, Alice A. *Gynesis: Configurations of Woman and Modernity.* Ithaca and London: Cornell University Press, 1985.

Jeffreys, Sheila. *Beauty and Misogyny: Harmful Cultural Practices in the West.* London and New York: Routledge, 2005.

Johanson, Mary Ann. "A Girl Walks Home Alone at Night Movie Review: Blood Pressure." *Flick Filosopher* (March 31, 2015): https://www.flickfilosopher.com /2015/03/a-girl-walks-home-alone-at-night-movie-review-blood-pressure.html (accessed October 13, 2018).

Kant, Immanuel. *Critique of the Power of Judgment.* Ed. Paul Guyer. Trans. Paul Guyer and Eric Matthews. Cambridge, UK: Cambridge University Press, 2000.

Kipnis, Laura. *Unwanted Advances: Sexual Paranoia Comes to Campus.* New York: Harper Collins, 2017.

Kirkpatrick, Kate. *Becoming Beauvoir: A Life.* London and New York: Bloomsbury, 2019.

Kluger, Jeffrey. "Raising Daughters." *Time. Special Edition. The Science of Gender* (2020): 34–37.

Lanchester, John. *Capital: A Novel.* New York and London: W. W. Norton & Co., 2012.

Latimer, Heather. "Popular Culture and Reproductive Politics: *Juno, Knocked Up* and the Enduring Legacy of *The Handmaid's Tale.*" *Feminist Theory* 10, 2 (2009): 211–26.

Lauretis, Teresa de. *The Practice of Love: Lesbian Sexuality and Perverse Desire.* Bloomington and Indianapolis: Indiana University Press, 1994.

Leigh, Danny. "Interview: The Skateboarding Iranian Vampire Diaries." *The Guaridan* (May 7, 2015): https://www.theguardian.com/film/2015/may/07/skateboarding-i ranian-vampire-ana-lily-amirpour-feminism-porn-girl-walks-home-alone-at-nig ht (accessed October 14, 2018).

Levine, Judith and Meiners, Erica R. *The Feminist and the Sex Offender: Confronting Harm, Ending State Violence.* London and New York: Verso, 2020.

Lewis, Sophie. *Full Surrogacy Now: Feminism Against the Family.* London and New York: Verso, 2019.

Linebaugh, Peter. *The London Hanged: Crime and Civil Society in the Eighteenth Century.* Second Edition. London and New York: Verso, 2003.

Lontringer, Sylvère. "Exterminating Angel: Introduction to *Forget Foucault.*" In *Forget Foucault.* Ed. Jean Baudrillard. Trans. Nicole Dufresne. Los Angeles, CA: Semiotext(e), 2007, pp. 7–25.

Lukács, Georg. *History and Class Consciousness: Studies in Marxist Dialectics.* Trans. Rodney Livingstone. Cambridge, MA: The MIT Press, 1971.

Luxemburg, Rosa. *The Accumulation of Capital.* Trans. Agnes Schwarzchild. London and New York: Routledge, 2003.

Marx, Karl and Engels, Fredric. *The Marx-Engels Reader. Second Edition.* Ed. Robert C. Tucker. New York and London: W. W. Norton & Company, 1978, 1972.

Mayer, So. "Film of the Week: A Girl Walks Home Alone at Night." *Sight & Sound* 25, 6 (June 2015): https://www.bfi.org.uk/news-opinion/sight-sound-magazine /reviews-recommendations/film-week-girl-walks-home-alone-night (accessed October 14, 2018).

Mcmahon, Alle. "Germain Greer Defends Views on Transgender Issues Amid Calls for Cancellation of Feminism Lecture." *ABC* (October 25, 2015): https://www.abc .net.au/news/2015-10-25/germaine-greer-defends-views-on-transgender-issues/ 6883132 (accessed March 22, 2020).

McRobbie, Angela. "Feminism, the Family and the New 'Mediated' Maternalism." *New Formations* 80/81 (July 2013):119–37.

McRobbie, Angela. "Top Girls?" *Cultural Studies* 21, 4–5 (2007): 718–37.

McRobbie, Angela. *The Aftermath of Feminism: Gender, Culture and Social Change.* Los Angeles: Sage, 2009.

Mifsud, Courtney. "Lessons From Animals." *Time. Special Edition. The Science of Gender* (2020): 26–31.

Mignolo, Walter D. *The Darker Side of Western Modernity: Global Futures, Decolonial Options.* Durham, NC and London: Duke University Press, 2011.

Mitchell, Juliet. *Psychoanalysis and Feminism: A Radical Reassessment of Freudian Psychoanalysis.* New York: Basic Books, 1974, 2000.

Moraru, Christian and Elias, Amy. "Introduction: The Planetary Condition." In *The Planetary Turn: Relationality and Geoaesthetics in the Twenty-First Century.* Eds. Amy J. Elias and Christian Moraru. Evanston, IL: Northwestern University Press, 2015, xi–xxxvii.

Moraru, Christian. "'World', 'Globe', 'Planet'" Comparative Literature, Planetary Studies, and Cultural Debt after the Global Turn." *State of the Discipline Report: The 2014-2015 Report on the State of the Discipline of Comparative Literature* (December 3, 2014). https://stateofthediscipline.acla.org/entry/%E2%80%9Cworld%E2%80%9D-%E2%80%9Cglobe%E2%80%9D-%E2%80%9Cplanet%E2%80%9D-comparative-l iterature-planetary-studies-and-cultural-debt-after (accessed December 4, 2019).

Moretti, Franco. *Distant Reading.* London and New York: Verso, 2013.

Mottahedeh, Negar. *Displaced Allegories: Post-Revolutionary Iranian Cinema.* Durham, NC and London: Duke University Press, 2008.

Mouffe, Chantal. *Thinking the World Politically*. London and New York: Verso, 2013.

Nixon, Rob. *Slow Violence and the Environmentalism of the Poor*. Cambridge, MA and London: Harvard University Press, 2011.

O'Malley, Sheila. "A Girl Walks Home Alone at Night (2014). *Rogerebert.com* (November 21, 2014). https://www.rogerebert.com/reviews/a-girl-walks-home-alo ne-at-night-2014 (accessed October 13, 2018).

Ong, Aihwa. "A Bio-Cartography: Maids, Neo-Slavery, and NGOs." In *Migrations and Mobilities: Citizenship, Borders, and Gender*. Eds. Seyla Benhabib and Judith Resnick. New York and London: New York University Press, 2009, pp. 157–84.

Ong, Aihwa. *Fungible Life: Experiment in the Asian City of Life*. Durham and London: Duke University Press, 2016.

Penny, Laurie. *Bitch Doctrine: Essays for Dissenting Adults*. London: Bloomsbury, 2017, 2018.

Penny, Laurie. *Meat Market: Female Flesh Under Capitalism*. Winchester, UK: Zero Books, 2010, 2011.

Perry, Imani. *Vexy Thing: On Gender and Liberation*. Durham, NC and London: Duke University Press, 2018.

Phipps, Alison. *The Politics of the Body: Gender in a Neoliberal and Neoconservative Age*. Cambridge, UK and Malden, MA: Polity, 2014.

Plant, Sadie. "Baudrillard's Woman: The Eve of Seduction." In *Forget Baudrillard?* Eds. Chris Rojek and Bryan S. Turner. London and New York: Routledge, 1993, pp. 88–106.

Powers, Nina. *One Dimensional Woman*. Winchester, UK: O Books, 2009.

Preciado, Paul (Beatriz). *Testo Junkie: Sex, Drugs, and Biopolitics in the Pharmacopornographic Era*. Trans. Bruce Benderson. New York: The Feminist Press, 2013.

Preciado, Paul B. *An Apartment on Uranus: Chronicles of the Crossing*. Trans. Charlotte Mandell. South Pasadena, CA: Semiotext(e), 2020.

Preciado, Paul B. *Counter-sexual Manifesto*. Trans. Kevin Gerry Dunn. New York: Columbia University Press, 2018.

Puar, Jasbir K. *Terrorist Assemblages: Homonationalism in Queer Times*. Durham, NC and London: Duke University Press, 2007.

Puar, Jasbir K. *The Right to Maim: Debility/Capacity/Disability*. Durham, NC and London: Duke University Press, 2017.

Raymond, Janice G. *The Transsexual Empire: The Making of the She-Male. Reissued with a New Introduction on Transgender*. New York and London: Teachers College Press, 1994.

Rich, Adrienne. *Of Woman Born: Motherhood as Experience and Institution*. New York and London: W. W. Norton & Company, 1986, 1995.

Roberts, Dorothy E. "Race, Gender, and Genetic Technologies: A New Reproductive Dystopia?" *Signs: Journal of Women in Culture and Society* 34, 4 (2009): 783–804.

Rose, Jacqueline. *Mothers: An Essay on Love and Cruelty*. New York: Farrar, Straus and Giroux, 2018.

Rosenberg, Jordan/a. "Monstrously Unpositable: Primitive Accumulation and the Aesthetic Arc of Capital." *J19: The Journal of Nineteenth-Century Americanists* 3, 1 (Spring 2015): 197–204.

Rosenberg, Jordana. *Critical Enthusiasm: Capital Accumulation and the Transformation of Religious Passion*. Oxford, UK and New York: Oxford University Press, 2011.

Rosenberg, Jordy. *Confessions of the Fox*. New York: One World, 2018.

Rotman, Jackie. "Vaginas Deserve Giant Ads, Too." *The New York Times* (June 25, 2019): https://www.nytimes.com/2019/06/25/opinion/women-sex-toys-adverti sements.html?action=click&module=Opinion&pgtype=Homepage (accessed June 25, 2019).

Rottenberg, Catherine. *The Rise of Neoliberal Feminism*. New York: Oxford University Press, 2018.

Rowling, J. K. "J.K. Rowling Writes about Her Reasons for Speaking out on Sex and Gender Issues." *The Ickabog* (June 10, 2020). https://www.jkrowling.com/opinions/ j-k-rowling-writes-about-her-reasons-for-speaking-out-on-sex-and-gender-iss ues/ (accessed June 19, 2020).

Rushdie, Salmon. Letter. "Brickbats Fly Over Brick Lane." *The Guardian* (July 29, 2006). https://www.theguardian.com/books/2006/jul/29/comment.letters (accessed July 22, 2006).

Ruti, Mari. *The Age of Scientific Sexism: How Evolutionary Psychology Promotes Gender Profiling and Fans the Battle of the Sexes*. New York and London: Bloomsbury, 2015.

Schwalbe, Michael. *Manhood Acts: Gender and the Practices of Domination*. Boulder, CO and London: Paradigm Publishers, 2014.

Scott, Joan Wallach. *The Fantasy of Feminist History*. Durham, NC and London: Duke University Press, 2011.

Scott, Joan Wallach. *The Politics of the Veil*. Princeton, NJ and Oxford, UK: Princeton University Press, 2007.

Serano, Julia. *Whipping Girl: A Transsexual Woman on Sexism and the Scapegoating of Femininity*. Berkeley, CA: Seal Press, 2007, 2016.

Sheldon, Rebekah. "Somatic Capitalism: Reproduction, Futurity, and Feminist Science Fiction." *Ada: A Journal of Gender New Media & Technology* 3 (November 2013): https://adanewmedia.org/issues/ (accessed December 26, 2019).

Spillers, Hortense J. "Mama's Baby, Papa's Maybe: An American Grammar Book." *Diacritics* 17, 2 (Summer 1987): 64–81.

Steinmetz, Katy. "Exploring the Gender Divide in the Toy Aisle." *Time. Special Edition. The Science of Gender* (2020): 94.

Stone, Sandy. "The Empire Strikes Back: A Posttranssexual Manifest" (1992). https://sandystone.com/empire-strikes-back.pdf.

Stryker, Susan. *Transgender History: The Roots of Today's Revolution. Second Edition.* New York: Seal Press, 2008, 2017.

Taylor, Janelle S. "A Fetish Is Born: Sonographers and the Making of the Public Fetus." In *Consuming Motherhood.* Eds. Janelle S. Taylor, Linda L. Layne, Danielle F. Wazniak. New Brunswick, NJ and London: Rutgers University Press. 2004, pp. 187–210.

Valenti, Jessica. *Full Frontal Feminism: A Young Woman's Guide to Why Feminism Matters, Second Edition.* Berkeley, CA: Seal Press, 2007, 2014.

Valenti, Jessica. *Sex Object: A Memoir.* New York: Harper Collins, 2016.

Varma, Rashmi. "Anti-Imperialism." In *The Bloomsbury Handbook of 21st- Century Feminist Theory.* Ed. Robin Truth Goodman. London and New York: Bloomsbury, 2019, pp. 463–80.

Varsity (author byline removed). "Germaine Greer: Transgender Women Don't Know What It's Like to 'Have a Big Hairy Smelly Vagina.'" *Varsity* (January 27, 2015). https://www.varsity.co.uk/news/8105 (accessed March 17, 2020).

Vice News. "Contrapoints Is De-Radicalizing Young, Right-Wing Men (HBO)." *YouTube* (March 14, 2019). https://www.youtube.com/watch?v=2Nrz4-FZx6k.

Vogel, Lise. *Marxism and the Oppression of Women: Toward a Unitary Theory.* Leiden and Boston: Brill, 2013.

Watkins, Susan. "Which Feminisms?" *New Left Review* 109 (January/February 2018): 5–76.

Weeks, Kathi. *Constituting Feminist Subjects.* London and New York: Verso, 1998, 2018.

Wiegman, Robyn. *Object Lessons.* Durham, NC and London: Duke University Press, 2012.

Wynn, Natalie. "Are Traps Gay?" *ContraPoints, YouTube* (January 16, 2019). https://www.YouTube.com/watch?v=PbBzhqJK3bg.

Wynn, Natalie. "Canceling." *ContraPoints. YouTube* (January 2, 2020). https://www.YouTube.com/watch?v=OjMPJVmXxV8.

Wynn, Natalie. "ContraPoints Patron AMA Stream/June 2020." *YouTube* (June 28, 2020), https://www.youtube.com/watch?v=AGZfCa-C-aY&feature=youtu.be.

Wynn, Natalie. "ContraPoints Patron AMA Stream/May 2020." *YouTube* (May 28, 2020), https://www.YouTube.com/watch?v=2R51yqDjxUM&feature=youtu.be.

Wynn, Natalie. "ContraPoints XOXO Festival (2018). *YouTube* (November 9, 2018), https://www.youtube.com/watch?v=0Ix9jxid2YU.

Wynn, Natalie. "Jordan Peterson." *ContraPoints, YouTube* (May 2, 2018), https://www.youtube.com/watch?v=4LqZdkkBDas.

Wynn, Natalie. "Men." *ContraPoints. YouTube* (August 23, 2019). https://www.YouTube.com/watch?v=S1xxcKCGljY.

Wynn, Natalie. "Opulence." *ContraPoints. YouTube* (October 12, 2019), https://www.YouTube.com/watch?v=jD-PbF3ywGo.

Wynn, Natalie. "The Aesthetic." *ContraPoints, YouTube* (September 29, 2018), https://www.youtube.com/watch?v=z1afqR5QkDM.

Wynn, Natalie. "What's Wrong with Capitalism (Part 2)." *ContraPoints. YouTube* (March 31, 2018). https://www.YouTube.com/watch?v=AR7ryg1w:IQ.

Wynn, Natalie. "What's Wrong with Capitalism (Part I)." *ContraPoints. YouTube* (December 30, 2017). https://www.YouTube.com/watch?v=gJW4-cOZt8A.

Wynn, Natalie., "Gender Critical." *ContraPoints, YouTube* (March 30, 2019), https://www.youtube.com/watch?v=1pTPuoGjQsI.

Yee, Vivian. "Saudi Law Granted Women New Freedoms. Their Families Don't Always Agree." *The New York Times* (March 14, 2020): https://www.nytimes.com/2020/03/14/world/middleeast/saudi-women-rights.html?action=click&module=News&pgtype=Homepage (accessed March 14, 2020).

Index

www.ingramcontent.com/pod-product-compliance
Lightning Source LLC
Chambersburg PA
CBHW050445280326
41932CB00013BA/2247